The Inner Journey
Views from Native Traditions

Series Editor: Ravi Ravindra
Associate Series Editor: Priscilla Murray

Titles in *The Inner Journey* series:
Views from the Buddhist Tradition
Views from the Christian Tradition
Views from the Gurdjieff Work
Views from the Hindu Tradition
Views from the Islamic Tradition
Views from the Jewish Tradition
Myth, Psyche & Spirit
Views from Native Traditions

The Inner Journey
Views from Native Traditions

Edited by Linda Hogan

PARABOLA Anthology Series

MORNING LIGHT PRESS

Published by Morning Light Press 2009

Editor: Linda Hogan
Series Editor: Ravi Ravindra
Associate Series Editor: Priscilla Murray

Morning Light Press
10881 North Boyer Rd.
Sandpoint, ID 83864
morninglightpress.com

Printed on acid-free paper in Canada.

Philosophy
SAN: 255-3252

Library of Congress Cataloging-in-Publication Data

Hogan, Linda.
  The Inner Journey : Views from Native Traditions / edited by Linda Hogan.
    p. cm. -- (Parabola anthology series)
  Summary: "A compilation of articles and interviews originally published in Parabola Magazine written by various Native American spiritual seekers, representing spiritual traditions from tribes in both North and South America"--Provided by publisher.
  ISBN 978-1-59675-026-5 (978-1-59675-026-5 : alk. paper)
  1. Indians--Religion. 2. Indian philosophy. 3. Spiritual life. I. Title.
  E59.R38H65 2009
  299.7--dc22
                          2008041181

To those of this beloved earth, our ancestors,
and to our wisdom-keepers

General Introduction to
The Inner Journey: A Parabola Anthology Series

When *Parabola: Myth, Tradition, and the Search for Meaning* was launched in 1976, the founder, D. M. Dooling, wrote in her first editorial:

> *Parabola* has a conviction: that human existence is significant, that life essentially makes sense in spite of our confusions, that man is not here on earth by accident but for a purpose, and that whatever that purpose may be it demands from him the discovery of his own meaning, his own totality and identity. A human being is born to set out on this quest. ... Every true teaching, every genuine tradition, has sought to train its disciples to act this part, to become in fact followers of the great quest for one's self.

For over thirty years, *Parabola* has honored the great wisdom traditions of every culture, turning to their past and present masters and practitioners for guidance in this quest. Recognizing that the aim of each tradition is the transformation of human life through practice supported by knowledge and understanding, *Parabola* on behalf of its readers has turned again and again to Buddhist and Christian monks, Sufi and Jewish teachers, Hindu scholars, and Native American and other indigenous peoples, evoking from each of them illumination and insight.

Over the years *Parabola*, in each of its issues, devoted to a central theme of the human condition as it is and as it might be, has gathered remarkable material. "The Call," "Awakening," "Food," "Initiation," "Dreams and Seeing," "Liberation," "The Mask," "Attention": in these and in scores of other issues, a facet of the essential search is explored, always with the aim of casting light on the way.

The purpose of the *Parabola Anthology Series* is to gather the material published in *Parabola* during its first thirty years in order to focus this light and to reflect the inner dimensions of each of these traditions. While every religious tradition has both external and inner aspects, the aim of each is the transformation of the whole being. The insights and understandings that ring true and carry the vibration of an inner meaning can provide guidance and support for our quest, but a mere mechanical repetition of forms which were once charged with great energy can take us away from the heart of the teaching. Every tradition must change and evolve; it has to be reinterpreted and re-understood by successive generations in order to maintain its relevance and application.

Search carries a connotation of journey; we set out with the hope for new insight and experience. The aim of the spiritual or inner journey is transformation, to become more responsible and more compassionate as understanding and being grow. This demands an active undertaking, and insights from those who have traveled the path can provide a call, bring inspiration, and serve as a reminder of the need to search.

For this series, selections have been made from the material published in *Parabola* relating to each of the major traditions and teachings. Subtle truths are expressed in myths, poetry, stories, parables, and above all in the lives, actions, and expressions of those people who have been immersed in the teaching, have wrestled with it and have been informed and transformed by it. Some of these insights have been elicited through interviews with current practitioners of various teachings. Each of the great traditions is very large, and within each tradition there are distinct schools of thought, as well as many practices, rituals, and ceremonies. None of the volumes in the present series claims to be exhaustive of the whole tradition or to give a complete account of it.

In addition to the material that has been selected from the library of *Parabola* issues, the editor of each volume in the series provides an introduction to the teaching, a reminder of the heart of the tradition in the section, "The Call of the Tradition," as well as a list of books suggested for further study and reflection. It is the hope of the publishers and editors that this new series will surprise, challenge, and support those new to *Parabola* as well as its many readers.

—Ravi Ravindra

Contents

The Call of the Tradition

The whole universe is endowed with the same breath—rocks, trees,
grass, earth, all animals, and men.

—Hopi saying, as recorded by Alexander Stephen

Moved. The great sea stirs me. The great sea sets me adrift,
It sways me like the weed on a river-stone.
The sky's height stirs me. The strong wind blows through my mind.
It carries me with it, so I shake with joy.

—Uvuvnuk, Iglulik Eskimo woman

I am blind and do not see the things of this world; but when the
light comes from above, it enlightens my heart and I can see, for the eye
of my heart sees everything; and through this vision I can help my
people. The heart is a sanctuary at the center of which there is a little space,
wherein the Great Spirit dwells, and this is the Eye. This is the Eye
of the Great Spirit by which He sees all things, and through which we
see Him. If the heart is not pure, the Great Spirit cannot be seen.

—Black Elk

My brother the star, my mother the earth, My father the sun, my sister the
moon, to my life give beauty, to my body give strength, to my corn give
goodness, to my house give peace, to my spirit give truth, to my elders give
wisdom. We must pray for strength. We must pray to come
together, Pray to the weeping earth pray to the trembling
waters and to the wandering rain. We must pray to the whispering moon,
pray to the tip-toeing stars and to the hollering sun.

—Taos Pueblo

Conscience is a little three-cornered thing in the heart that stands
still when we are good, but when we are bad it turns around a lot. If we
keep on going wrong, soon the corners wear off
and it does not hurt any more.

—Arizona Indian saying

The Inner Journey: Introduction

The plateaus, great basin, the upwellings of this continent, the mountains, rivers and coasts of this world are all the histories of Native American traditions still growing and living. The traditions and mythologies come from the body of this earth. The land itself contains the stories. Each place has its original name, and these traditions are yet embedded in the bodies of people whose life ways survived a sweeping history of death, forced assimilation, and tragedy. For some people, the sacred boundaries of their world are the four great mountains. For another tribe it is the edge of the forest or the watery beginning of land, the place where whales washed up to provide for the people. It is the desert with its spring rains and hot sands, the tall grasses where buffalo feed. A part of the inner journey is knowing the cave we emerged from or the stalk upon which people climbed into this world. It is the Blue Lake of the Taos Pueblo, which is their history, mythology, and place of emergence.

An old world lives in new people who carry the cells of the ancestors who lived before them. The relationship between the human and the land is a great part of the inner journey. Our words contain a remembered knowledge of the currents of water, stories of the sky people. This relationship which comes from knowledge of place is a spiritual tradition. Though each tribe's spiritual history is different than that of the others, we are still singing or dancing up the corn, singing turtles to the sea, repeating the ceremony of a deer coming, enchanted, out of the forest.

The work contained in this collection shows a continuing line of the human apprenticeship with earth, a relationship that still exists and grows. Broken at times in the past, but renewed, or in the process of being renewed, we have to ask how, after years of attempts at assimilation, massacres, and the many political policies against Native nations, how do these traditions, knowledge systems, and mythologies continue to survive? The answer, often vividly revealed in these essays, speaks to the strength of our lives and our hold to survival here on this land. They continue through story, song, and ceremony. The European worldview never took hold over these, nor over the Native sovereign nations that dwell in their own known place. These essays, poems, and stories explain, in beautiful detail, why this ongoing connection to the cosmogony of the people remains true. The Great Mysterious dwells in and about this world, the universe.

The Yaqui Deer Dance has continued each spring, as have the Corn Dances of the Pueblos throughout the harvest season. Ceremonies, such as the Navajo Chantways, are remembered in intricate detail along with the stories, songs, prayers, and sand paintings that accompany them. And all end in a return of balance and harmony, so important to our people. *Hozho*. Balance.

There is also the Navajo first laugh ceremony, blessing an infant. Or a Stomp Dance begins at midnight around a central fire in the Southeast, where women wear turtle shells on their legs and dance without fatigue, moving in the glide of design reminiscent of the curved shapes on old pots. Or in a small enclosure, with others inside earth, prayers are made around a fire, or a pipe is passed and people speak. Elsewhere, in isolation, on a hill, a human being still seeks a vision. The inner journey is also the outer journey.

We are the "place-worlds" we inhabit. Even if we have been removed from our homelands and learned new ones, we return to our original homelands and feel them. They remember us. The spiritual consciousness of the world and of creation recalls our beauty to us.

The world also gives us knowledge and wisdom. For traditional-thinking Indigenous peoples, the spiritual world contains both its daily science, a knowledge of the environment, which is now called ecology, a reality figuring into the mythologies, oral traditions, and spiritual life from an understanding of place that might be inhabited for up to 20,000 or more years of observation and deep knowledge of nature, because whatever the place, whoever the people, wisdom comes from the earth. It is a spiritual ecology, an ecological spirituality in a world sentient and aware.

It is a way of seeing. There are laws, known and obeyed, that are natural laws, not ones made by humans. Some of these, as in Dreamtime, came from the First Ones. They are sacred experiences. These exist within the potency of the natural world itself, known and understood by people in their long-inhabited homelands with holy sites and storied places.

On a continent made up of a multitude of tribes with just as many traditions and complex mythologies, there are many differences. Yet the similarities are even more numerous: The emphasis on the earth, the nature of a world sentient, aware, and forever in flux, the ongoing creation of human and world together.

As countries within a larger one, we know the larger America around us, yet still have our own astronomies. Rattlesnake constellation. Turtle. Badger. Each nation has its own narrative, as well as its own sky and earth gods and goddesses. At times these are systems too complex for the European mind to understand, as Father Beard Haile said in his introduction to *The Upward Moving Way of the Navajo*, and the fact that the "pre-human realms and events can be talked about by Navajo professionals," is significant to the validity of the traditions. (See Karl Luckert, ed. *American Tribal Religions* Vol. 7, Lincoln: University of Nebraska Press, 1980.)

Even the languages are more complex than English, and they contain embedded knowledge, words with their own long histories and associated meanings. We can say that in many, the idea of God is a verb and not a noun. As for the creators and gods, it is sometimes a world of fallible gods, those who live on earth, come from the water, fall from the sky, and help the animals make land for the humans. There are imperfect creators. In myth, sometimes spiritual intervention comes from the gods or tricksters, sometimes with wisdom, just as often with humor and love.

No other people on this continent have been viewed and misunderstood as indigenous peoples. Primitive. Lacking in intelligence. But no other peoples are still as unknown. Europeans once described us as dogheaded men and men with eyes in our chests. Columbus, in his journals, according to the essay "Native Earth" by Peter Matthiessen, wrote about the people as *indios*, not because he imagined them to be inhabitants of India but because they were "*una gente in Dios*," a "People in God." He loved the land and yet destroyed it. He admired the people and yet killed them in unimaginable ways. This view continued with each new group of Europeans arriving here, unaware of the complexity and intelligence of the cultures. In his book, *The Surrounded*, Flathead writer D'Arcy McNickle knew that, even in the thirties, the surrounding people still did not understand "The Indian." Nor do they now. Romanticized, stereotyped, those last to be massacred are those most emulated by the others.

It wasn't until 1978 that the Native American Religious Freedoms Act was passed. Until then, it was illegal for Native Americans to practice their traditional religious ceremonies in a country where freedom of religion was considered to be a basic right. Since then, many amendments have been made to the act. Working groups continue to work out the fine details on that legislation. And the Indigenous Peoples Human Rights Act was only passed by the United Nations this year.

In thinking of these essays, I must say that some materials about Natives have become generic. The word "Shaman," for example, is loosely used in these articles and essays. It has become an overused word, even though its original meaning comes from the Siberian and Northern Eskimo. Non-Indian observers and scholars still come from another way of thinking and learning. Their educations have given them the overused word to apply to anyone who has been recognized as having a certain wisdom, a healer, a helper of the people. It has come to have a new meaning for scholars and students of Native materials.

Even though this word, as well as the use of the past tense, appears often in the volume, so does the indigenous perspective of the world. We know each other. We have our own histories. We know our place. Our center is here and the cosmos we know is not from the transplanted world but the original. We seek the continuing return of our first knowledge and intelligence.

Yet from outside our tribes, there is often a closeness of spirit and care for the living world. There are many who now think of the words "to seek" as meaning that everything has a spirit and we want to understand them, who know the songs and stories remain alive in the world. We seek to understand the plants, animals, and waters, to care for them. It means to develop a compassionate heart. It is to learn, through humor at times, the loss of ego. It is to know that there is not a Biblical-like end of the world. We live in a circular, sacred cosmos. Human participation is part of the constant process of the unfolding of this world. Traditions and ceremony are part of this unfolding. It is still an unfinished world in constant genesis.

Across the centuries it is still here. The spirit of aboriginal life continues. Like all people, we desire a great open view of both humanity and its life on earth, or earth's life in the human. There are few stories of the end. We live in a circular cosmos. The world we are only walking a small journey, planting a garden, going to work for our hours, yet with origins, some unremembered, but all sacred. We humble ourselves beside a tree and this is a holy communion. We are partaking in a bond with all creation. Our work, our search, is to make beauty and harmony and, even participating in ceremony, it begins within ourselves and the world. This is the search for wholeness and it is one with the land, searching out the source, the long-held traditions that are more than tradition, that are the sacred center.

CHAPTER ONE

Resistance as Survival

Politics make lies sound truthful and murder reasonable.

—T. Black Feather

This first essay is significant to all the other articles, stories, and essays that follow. Political resistance has been essential to the survival of American Indian spirituality and the survival of the people who were not meant to survive. The connections with tribal spirituality, community, and the land allowed this seventh generation to live. The late Vine Deloria, Jr., from South Dakota, was one of our beloved native scholars and thinkers on spirituality, law, and political history.

Parabola
Volume: 10.2
Exile

Out of Chaos

Vine Deloria, Jr.

When we talk about exile today we are more than likely to have a political situation in mind; but the original use of the word is considerably more enlightening. The roots of the idea of exile are most prominently displayed in a religious or mythic context. Moses and Oedipus immediately come to mind—as well as a host of other historical and mythological figures—all experiencing exile or suffering the sense of alienation which such a status entails. The religious aspect of exile, in contrast to its political meaning, involves many intangible factors which help us change and enhance our knowledge of the world.

The mythic and traditional idea of exile entails the expulsion of the chosen one from his comfortable and often exalted position in society. He is then thrust into a barren place where he has to abandon his former knowledge of this world. He learns humility and faith, comprehends the transcendent nature of ultimate reality, and is initiated into the mysteries and secrets of the other, higher world. Then the exile returns to his society armed with his superior knowledge and creates fundamental and lasting reforms, so that society marks its distinctive identity from the time he received his exilic commission.

Considering all the modern racial and ethnic groups to whom the idea of exile might be applied, none appears more deserving or representative of this status than North

American Indians. In the half-millennium since the discovery of the western hemisphere, almost all Indian tribes have been forcibly removed from all their ancestral homelands and subjected to cultural and religious indignities comparable in many ways to the manner in which the old culture heroes were stripped of their beliefs and presuppositions. At least this view is the popular explanation of the condition of Indians in modern American society. But there is considerably more to the story.

We immediately remember the removal of Indians from the Ohio Valley and deep South as the most prominent historical instance of Indian exile. The bitter picture of thousands of Cherokees, Creeks, and Choctaws, their heads bowed in sorrow, walking west in the driving rain of a cold winter is deeply etched on our consciousness. Federal policy to clear the country east of the Mississippi of Indians was carried out with almost scientific precision, even gathering small bands of Winnebagos in Wisconsin and moving them a few hundred miles to Nebraska. Removal was understood as a sensible solution to the Indian problem until the 1890s; plans were even suggested to gather all the tribes in western Oklahoma, ring the area with forts, and maintain a massive concentration camp until such time as the Indians had either acculturated or vanished.

When we look at a map of the United States, however, we find that there were tribes that escaped this fate. Beyond the Mississippi-Missouri border, tribes were generally settled on reservations within their aboriginal homelands; and if we note that many groups are still living within their original occupancy areas, we might argue that exile is not an appropriate description of the condition of western Indians. But we would be mistaking the possession of the title to lands for the right to live on them freely, and substituting our own political concepts for the rich feeling toward lands that has always characterized Indian society.

Within the western context we are always inclined to see land as a commodity and think first of its ownership; in contrast, the traditional Indian understanding of land focuses on its use and the duties people assume when they come to occupy it. When an Indian thinks about traditional lands, he always talks about what the people did there, the animals who lived there and how the people related to them, the seasons of the year and how people responded to their changes, the manner in which the tribe acquired possession of the area, and the ceremonial functions it was required to perform to remain worthy of living there.

The idea of lands, therefore, tells us the difference between Indian and non-Indian views so we can determine whether or not an exile has occurred. Whites acquire land through purchase and sale, and land is a quantifiable, measurable entity; their primary responsibility as land-owners is simply to prevent a loss of value; hence any responsibility the landowner may have is only to himself. Indian tribes acquire land as a gift from higher powers, and in turn they assume certain ceremonial duties which must be performed as long as they live on and use the land. Removing an Indian tribe from its aboriginal territory, therefore, results in the destruction of ceremonial life and much of the cultural structure which has made ceremony and ritual significant. So the western tribes, although not completely removed from their lands in a geographical sense, experienced exile in much the same way as did their brothers from the east. Restrictions in the manner in which people use lands are as much a deprivation of land as actual loss of title.

Indian exile, because of its impact on ceremonial responsibilities, includes a religious dimension which modern political exile lacks. If we understand ceremony and ritual, performed as a condition of living in certain places, as the critical element which distinguishes each Indian group, then the cultural life of the people, its continuance or destruc-tion, is the important fact in considering whether an exile has occurred. So while the Sioux, Apache, Blackfeet, and Crow, for example, all live within their original lands, persistent efforts to change their culture and exclusion from sacred places has produced a profound sense of exile.

A good example of this intangible, cultural/religious exile can be seen in the struggle of Taos Pueblo during this century to regain the Blue Lake area. Deprived of exclusive use of the lake, located near the Pueblo and central to its ceremonial life, when a national forest was established at the turn of the century, the Pueblo was given a "use permit" that only enabled it to visit the lake and conduct ceremonies but did not give it exclusive use. When the Pueblo filed its claims in the Indian Claims Commission, it carefully segregated the claim for the Blue Lake area and asked for restoration of the land to the Pueblo instead of a financial payment for its loss. After an intensive struggle in Congress the Pueblo finally succeeded in getting a bill passed in which the United States recognized in the Pueblo the title to the lake area.

It might appear to the casual observer that title was the primary concern of the Pueblo during this argument and that the Pueblo was only acting in the same manner as any other land owner faced with similar circumstances. Such was not the case. Rather, from the Pueblo point of view, its religious responsibilities to the lake and surrounding lands were paramount and could only be carried out in their totality by the complete exclusion of all other activities from the area.

Obligations demanded by the lands upon which people lived were part of their understanding of the world; indeed, their view of life was grounded in the knowledge of these responsibilities. Tribal ritual life was intimately related to the seasons of the year. Other species shared the land and also responded to the annual rhythms of nature. Thus the people perceived that a social contract existed between men and the other animals. The human ceremonial life confirmed the existence of this equality and gave it sustenance. One could, perhaps, list the tribes according to the complexity of their ceremonial year and project their approximate longevity. We need not distinguish sedentary agricultural tribes from migratory hunting and fishing tribes. Indians had an intimate and precise knowledge of the habits and personality of both plant and animal life, and therefore successful relationships with fish and game were no less indicative of the responsibility to land than were successful agricultural activities.

Migratory tribes suffered a considerably greater exile than did agricultural tribes when the Indians were restricted to the reservations. Some of the most important ceremonies needed to be conducted at certain sacred places at specific times of the year. While tribes could hold ceremonies at the proper time, they could not always hold these rituals at the proper place. Sometimes the sacred materials essential to the ceremony could only be obtained at these sacred places, and so different materials had to be substituted. These conditions changed ceremonial life considerably, introducing a process of erosion which has since eaten away the substance of rituals and responsibilities. One might even say that the ceremonial year of the migratory tribes was highly dependent upon sacred places, whereas the sacred calendar of sedentary tribes had long since become dominant over special places for enactment. On this basis, perhaps, we can determine both the longevity of a tribe and the degree of trauma which confinement produced.

Not only did their geographic confinement work to destroy the sacred calendars of tribes, but the effort to perpetuate a traditional life within the confines of the reservation was vulnerable to overtures by the federal government, seeking to make the people abandon old ways and adopt new practices which were carefully orchestrated by a new sense of time—a measured time which had little to do with cosmic realities. It is debatable which factor was most important in the destruction of tribal ceremonial life: the prohibition of performances of traditional rituals by government, or the introduction of the white man's system of keeping time. The answer to this question can be found in an analysis of the impact of each factor on individual tribes.

Many of the old people among the Sioux felt that the government prohibition of the ceremony of the "keeping of the soul," an important condolence ceremony which linked generations of the tribe together in a more comprehensive cosmic reality, brought about the real destruction of ceremonial life in that tribe. On the other hand, in the Pacific Northwest the government tried to impose an agricultural system, and the farming calendar conflicted directly with fishing activities, producing the same erosion of ceremonial life. Prohibition of the potlatch was not nearly as important as the government's insistence that the Indians become farmers and the orientation of all programs to achieve that end.

Certainly the combination of these factors must be present in the immediate past of every tribe. We can safely suggest that the new sense of time introduced into Indian life produced a sense of alienation which made Indians strangers in a land that was becoming increasingly strange—as whites changed it to suit themselves—and that the old ceremonies might have provided an emotional bulwark against this alienation, but their prohibition only increased the feeling of exile among the people of the tribe.

Unless time is understood as sacred, experienced in all its fullness, and so dominant a consideration in the life of a people that all other functions are subservient to it, it is impossible to have a complete and meaningful ceremonial life. Rituals lose their efficacy because they are performed within a secular time which does not always make room for them or give them the status they deserve. They soon take on the aspect of mechanical adjustments made to solve problems which occur within that kind of time. Forced adaptation to secular, mathematically measured time has produced a fundamental sense of alienation.

Although the loss of land must be seen as a political and economic disaster of the first magnitude, the real exile of the tribes occurred with the destruction of ceremonial life and the failure or inability of white society to offer a sensible and cohesive alternative to the traditions which Indians remembered. People became disoriented with respect to the world in which they lived. They could not practice their old ways, and the new ways which they were expected to learn were in a constant state of change because they were not a cohesive view of the world but simply adjustments which whites were making to the technology they had invented.

Had whites been able to maintain a sense of stability in their own society, which Indians had been admonished to imitate, the tribes might have been able to observe the integrity of the new way of life and make a successful transition to it. But the only alternative that white society had to offer was a chaotic and extreme individualism, prevented from irrational excesses only by occasional government intervention. The experiences of Indians since the 1880s have been uniform in the sense that they have been confined within the boundaries of white individualism and whenever and wherever they have attempted to recapture the old sense of community, technology and domestic American politics have combined to beat back their efforts.

There is no question that American Indians have been mired in a century-long exile. Almost anything that has happened to Indians in the decades since the establishment of the reservations can and must be seen in this light. Individual incidents are but minor episodes indicating the extent of the pattern that has encompassed tribal life. We find little of the ebb and flow of sentiment and understanding which keeps a community healthy and growing, only apparent movement back and forth between the poles of political independence and dependence. In Indian cultural and religious life we have seen a unilateral shedding of old forms coupled with a paralyzing inability to create new customs and traditions which have a relationship with the past. While Indians have copied many ways of white society, on the whole they have done so badly and sporadically. Tribal governments, for example, do not behave like the old tribal councils, nor, unfortunately, do they perform like modern municipal governments. Their activities suggest some strange hybrid institution which has no knowledge of its constituents or responsibilities.

What, if anything, can Indians do to escape or overcome this condition? Originally, as we have seen, exile had a specific religious direction which suggested that exilic alienation was necessary to prepare an individual for a significant mission. The Old Testament, if we can accept some of its prophetic ideas, saw the exile of the Jews as the means of preparing them to move forward from a parochial, tribal religion and become advocates of a more universal interpretation of the meaning of human social life. Their exile did not produce a new religious understanding so much as it enabled the people to see themselves as representatives of a tradition which had within itself the potential to become an exemplary society, at peace with its neighbors and its environment. We may not be able to apply this model completely to the situation in which American Indians find themselves, but it is certainly important to our discussion of exile to try to do so.

We might, therefore, expect American Indians to discern, out of the chaos of their shattered lives, the same kind of message and mission that inspired the Hebrew prophets. Indians would, in this situation, begin to develop a new interpretation of their religious tradition with a universal application. They would further begin to seek out areas in which they could communicate with sympathetic people in the larger society, and put their own house in order. A process of intense commitment to certain social goals might then emerge in which the traditional values of pre-contact days would be seen as religious principles having a universal application. Most important, Indians would begin to probe deeper into their own past and view their remembered history as a primordial covenant.

It would be important and significant if we could report, in the activities of Indians today, the emergence of such behavior and beliefs. Unfortunately, the nature of modern society precludes, or at least substantially inhibits, the development of new religious realities and statements. The vast majority of people, including Indians, believes that the world is primarily a physical thing, and the existence or importance of spiritual realities is given but token acknowledgement. Indians are the popular

American minority group, and the white majority deeply believes that Indians *already* have the secret mysteries which will produce a wise and happy life. Therefore Indians are plagued with a multitude of well-wishers and spectators hoping to discern, from within the Indian communities in which they visit, some indication of the substance of religious experience. This inundation of pilgrims makes it impossible for Indians to experience the solitude and abandonment which exile requires in order to teach its lessons.

Finally, modern American life is comparable to a large and bountiful Christmas tree. It promises only joy and fun, and never suggests a period of doubt when ultimate realities are experienced and understood. Indians are wandering in this plush fantasy desert in the same way as sensitive non-Indians. It will require considerably more thought and significantly less recreation and entertainment before Indians will be able to discern in their own traditions the substance and energy which lies dormant.

The exile of today is filled with frustration because it is being experienced in the midst of many other intensely competitive factors, all of which require energy and attention and none of which provide any lasting sustenance. It may be that technology has so insulated human society that the religious context of exile is now a thing of the past, incapable of realization in a wholly artificial world. If so, we have lost an important key to unlocking the potential which human social existence suggests. It may be that American Indians contain the last best hope for spiritual renewal in a world dominated by material considerations. The multitude of non-Indians arriving at reservation doors seeking answers would seem to indicate an intuition in many hearts that Indians do give us the last hope for resurrection. Perhaps out of the confusion of modern Indian society will come a statement about the world that we have come to expect when exiles return.

CHAPTER TWO

THE WORLD BEFORE: BRAVE OLD WORLD

Prophecies and stories of change preceded the conquest of the Americas and the sometimes permanent transformations of religious traditions. Here are stories of before and after. They may be similar to the stories found in later sections because the web of connections is wide and far-reaching. These speak to tradition and radical change, recall initiations that were once for the good of the people. Some tell, through memory passed on by the oral tradition, how earth was made and how things used to be before enforced changes in religion, education, and a world thrown out of balance. Yet, even in this section, we can see the way to a return, and it is happening now. Tribes are making a return to knowledge from the brave old world.

Parabola
Volume: 23.1
Millennium

REMAKING THE WORLD

Brulé Sioux

There was a world before this world, but the people in it did not know how to behave themselves or how to act human. The Creating Power was not pleased with that earlier world. He said to himself: "I will make a new world." He had the pipe bag and the chief pipe, which he put on the pipe rack that he had made in the sacred manner. He took four dry buffalo chips, placed three of them under the three sticks, and saved the fourth one to light the pipe.

The Creating Power said to himself: "I will sing three songs, which will bring a heavy rain. Then I'll sing a fourth song and stamp four times on the earth, and the earth will crack wide open. Water will come out of the cracks and cover the land." When he sang the first song, it started to rain. When he sang the second, it poured. When he sang the third, the rain-swollen rivers over-flowed their beds. But when he sang the fourth song and stamped on the earth, it split open in many places like a shattered gourd, and water flowed from the cracks until it covered everything.

The Creating Power floated on the sacred pipe and on his huge pipe bag. He let himself be carried by waves and wind this way and that, drifting for a long time. At last the rain stopped, and by then all the people and animals had drowned. Only Kangi, the crow, survived, though it had no place to rest and was very tired. Flying above the pipe, "Tunkashila, Grandfather, I must soon rest": and three times the crow asked him to make a place for it to light.

The Creating Power thought: "It's time to unwrap the pipe and open the pipe bag." The wrapping and the bag contained all manner of animals and birds, from which he selected four animals known for their ability to stay under water for a long time. First he sang a song and took the loon out of the bag. He commanded the loon to dive and bring up a lump of mud. The loon did dive, but it brought up nothing. "I dived and dived but couldn't reach the bottom," the loon said. "I almost died. The water is too deep."

The Creating Power sang a second song and took the otter out of the bag. He ordered the otter to dive and bring up some mud. The sleek otter at once dived into the water, using its strong webbed feet to go down, down, down. It was submerged for a long time, but when it finally came to the surface, it brought nothing.

Taking the beaver out of the pipe's wrapping, the Creating Power sang a third song. He commanded the beaver to go down deep below the water and bring some mud. The beaver thrust itself into the water, using its great flat tail to propel itself downward. It stayed under water longer than the others, but when it finally came up again, it too brought nothing.

At last the Creating Power sang the fourth song and took the turtle out of the bag. The turtle is very strong. Among our people it stands for long life and endurance and the power to survive. A turtle heart is great medicine, for it keeps beating a long time after the turtle is dead. "You must bring the mud," the Creating Power told the turtle. It dove into the water and stayed below so long that the other three animals shouted: "The turtle is dead; it will never come up again!"

All the time, the crow was flying around and begging for a place to light.

After what seemed to be eons, the turtle broke the surface of the water and paddled back to the Creating Power. "I got to the bottom!" the turtle cried. "I brought some earth!" And sure enough, its feet and claws—even the space in the cracks on its sides between its upper and lower shell—were filled with mud.

Scooping mud from the turtle's feet and sides, the Creating Power began to sing. He sang all the while that he shaped the mud in his hands and spread it on the water to make a spot of dry land for himself. When he had sung the fourth song, there was enough land for the Creating Power and for the crow.

"Come down and rest," said the Creating Power to the crow, and the bird was glad to.

Then the Creating Power took from his bag two long wing feathers of the eagle. He waved them over his plot of ground and commanded it to spread until it covered everything. Soon all the water was replaced by earth. "Water without earth is not good," thought the Creating Power, "but land without water is not good either." Feeling pity for the land, he wept for the earth and the creatures he would put upon it, and his tears became oceans, streams, and lakes. "That's better," he thought. Out of his pipe bag the Creating Power took all kinds of animals, birds, plants, and scattered them over the land. When he stamped on the earth, they all came alive.

From the earth the Creating Power formed the shapes of men and women. He used red earth and white earth, black earth and yellow earth, and made as many as he thought would do for a start. He stamped on the earth and the shapes came alive, each taking the color of the earth out of which it was made. The Creating Power gave all of them understanding and speech and told them what tribes they belonged to.

The Creating Power said to them: "The first world I made was bad; the creatures on it were bad. So I burned it up. The second world I made was bad too, so I drowned it. This is the third world I have made. Look: I have created a rainbow for you as a sign that there will be no more Great Flood. Whenever you see a rainbow, you will know that it has stopped raining."

The Creating Power continued: "Now, if you have learned how to behave like human beings and how to live in peace with each other and with the other living things—the two-legged, the four-legged, the man-legged, the fliers, the no-legs, the green plants of this universe— then all will be well. But if you make this world bad and ugly, then I will destroy this world too. It's up to you."

The Creating Power gave the people the pipe. "Live by it," he said. He named this land the Turtle Continent because it was there that the turtle came up with the mud out of which the third world was made.

"Someday there might be a fourth world," the Creating Power thought. Then he rested.

Told by Leonard Crow Dog, recorded by Richard Erdoes. "Remaking the World (Brulé Sioux)" from *American Indian Myths and Legends*, edited by Richard Erdoes and Alfonso Ortiz (New York: Pantheon Books, 1984). Copyright © 1984 by Richard Erdoes and Alfonso Ortiz. Reprinted by permission of Pantheon Books, a division of Random House.

Parabola
Volume: 20.1
Earth, Air, Fire, Water

The Earth Is Set Up

White Mountain Apache

Four people started to work on the earth. When they set it up, the wind blew it off again. It was weak like an old woman. They talked together about the earth among themselves. "What shall we do about this earth, my friends? We don't know what to do about it." Then one person said, "Pull it from four different sides." They did this, and the piece they pulled out on each side they made like a foot. After they did this the earth stood all right. Then on the east side of the earth they put big black cane, covered with black metal thorns. On the south side of the earth they put big blue cane covered with blue metal thorns. Then on the west side of the earth they put big yellow cane covered with yellow metal thorns. Then on the north side of the earth they put big white cane covered with white metal thorns.

After they did this the earth was almost steady, but it was still soft and mixed with water. It moved back and forth. After they had worked on the earth this way, Black Wind Old Man came to this place. He threw himself against the earth. The earth was strong now and it did not move. Then Black Water Old Man threw himself against the earth. When he threw himself against the earth, thunder started in the four directions. Now the earth was steady, and it was as if born already.

But the earth was shivering. They talked about it: "My friends, what's the matter with this earth? It is cold and freezing. We better give it some hair." Then they started to make hair on the earth. They made all these grasses and bushes and trees to grow on the earth. This is its hair.

But the earth was still too weak. They started to talk about it: "My friends, let's make bones for the earth." This way they made rocky mountains and rocks sticking out of the earth. These are the earth's bones.

Then they talked about the earth again: "How will it breathe, this earth?" Then came Black Thunder to that place, and he gave the earth veins. He whipped the earth with lightning and made water start to come out. For this reason all the water runs to the west. This way the earth's head lies to the east, and its water goes to the west.

Retold by Palmer Valor in Grenville Goodwin, *Myths and Tales of the White Mountain Apache* (Tucson: University of Arizona Press, 1994), p. 1. Copyright © 1994 The Arizona Board of Regents. Reprinted by permission of University of Arizona Press.

Parabola
Volume: 23.1
Millennium

The Story of Noanase

Kaggaba-Wiwa

Among the children of The Mother there was one whose name was Noanase. The Mother herself granted him a great power at the break of dawn. Noanase learned many things: he had the power to heal people, and to concentrate. But he wanted more, always more. He saw that through his powers he could take advantage of his elder brother Mulkiasi, and he started to work evil upon him, to steal his strength. Mother told him: "You are going to ruin that power … you have already ruined it! I am going to take it away from you and I will send it far away."

The Mother took the magic power and sent it to a faraway village that is called Jamaica. Noanase said to himself, "Today they give me their advice and take power away from me, but by the end of the world I will be chief." When Mother heard this, she grabbed him and sent him to prison on a mountain. While there, Noanase started remembering the power he used to steal strength from his elder brothers.

At the beginning, he made little noise. He couldn't feed himself well and went hungry because the people complied with the law. But today there are many murderers, and now Noanase is growing great. He has grown up. Today, we hear noises up that mountain; we hear many noises! Unless we feel remorse soon, Noanase is going to break loose, and then much violence will come about because he lives on blood and suffering. When somebody kills, he is fed. The gun, the weapon, the accident, falling sticks that kill: all feed Noanase. When we think evil, when we think about robberies or assaults, when we covet another man's woman, Noanase rejoices and bursts out laughing.

Today he says, "I am everybody's chief because everyone is looking for me." History says, "When massacres, robberies, and murders start happening, it will be the time for Noanase to rejoice at the sight of so much evil." Many people are already following Noanase's way. He did not have vassals before, but today many people follow him, and he wants more. We no longer look at Serankua's path, the path of the soul; we don't follow the ideas of Siukuki and Luviko, but instead we go along the path of Noanase.

It may be that the moment for Noanase to break loose is coming close. When this happens, there will be violence and illnesses. There will be warring, melancholy, pain, and suffering. Thus the end of the world is coming close.

That is why history says, "We have to feel remorse soon. It is still a time for living." It is time for us to learn history—it is time for the younger as well as for the elder brother to listen to the history of the ancient ones, and to be concerned that Serankua should give us her support.

Will there come a time when younger brother will open his eyes, when he will wake up? When is he going to open up his ears? When will he discover the path of truth?

Told by Ramon Gil Barros, January 1988. The text was compiled by Sylvia Botero and Juan Ospina.

Parabola
Volume: 23.1
Millennium

MESSAGE TO THE YOUNGER BROTHER
Wisdom Teachings of the Kaggaba-Wiwa People

Ramon Gil Barros

Ramon Gil Barros—Kangemna, in his native tongue— is a native Kaggaba-Wiwa who belongs to two of the four indigenous peoples which for centuries have inhabited the Sierra Nevada de Santa Marta in Colombia. His father was a Wiwa or Arsario, and his mother a Kaggaba or Kogi. The Sierra Nevada de Santa Marta, a cluster of mountains with high snowy peaks, rises on the Colombian shore of the Caribbean sea. The inhabitants are deeply traditional and have kept alive to this day a culture that spans many centuries. Their knowledge about life, nature, human beings, and the spiritual realm has been transmitted orally through the generations, from their earliest ancestors up to the present.

Ramon is a spiritual and political leader, as well as a guide for his native people when they come in cultural contact with contemporary regional or national societies and governments. He has deepened and transmitted the wisdom of the Kaggaba and the Wiwa, wisdom which he received from his father and his uncle (both Mamas, or wise men), and from other important Mamas such as Juan Mamatacan and Valencia Sarabata.

Representing Parabola *at this meeting was Gladys Jimeno Santoyo, Director General of Indigenous Affairs for the Ministry of the Interior in Columbia, and founding director of* Ojodea-gua *magazine. Their encounter took place in September 1997, in the city of Santa Marta.*

Gladys Jimeno: *Ramon, now that the end of the century is approaching, we have been asked to speak to you by* Parabola, *which would like to present some diverse reflections about that theme. These times offer an opportunity to look into the past and to reflect about human-kind, the world, and where we stand in regards to life, other human beings, and the earth. As a Kaggaba-Wiwa who has lived, experienced, received, and filtered a knowledge both traditional and living, how do you see our contemporary world and its past?*

Ramon Gil Barros: Our Mamas, as we call the old wise men who are also chiefs and guides for the Kaggabas and for the Wiwas—and also the Mamas from the two other peoples in the Sierra Nevada, the Ikus or Arhuacos, and the Kankuamos—told us a long time ago that changes are coming: ends of cycles, and another end of the world. As a child, I used to ask the Mamas what they were talking about. They would tell me: "The sea will come, and it will climb up the slopes of the sierra, covering the lands until it reaches the tundras; and it will stop climbing only when it reaches the snowy peaks. ..." Then I would ask, "But if the sea will cover the sierra all the way up to the tundra, then where are we going to live? What will happen to us?" "We are not talking of the sea of water," they would answer, "but of the sea called 'younger brother.' We're talking of the time when younger brother will reach the halfway point up the Sierra Nevada—when his mind arrives, with his ideas, to flood half of Gonawindua."

Gonawindua is our name for the Sierra Nevada de Santa Marta; the sea is Zalzhijwe. The sea was the first mother. And it is you, the non-natives, whom we call "the younger brothers," because you were born in the world a long time after we were. ... We come from the first semen. That is what Gonawindua means: *Go* is to enlighten, to give birth; *na* means to come; *wi* is the first movement of being, when the unborn child moves for the first time after two or three months in the womb; *du* means people by the millions; and *dua* stands for semen, the first semen. Serankua contemplated Gonawindua and then everything was born.

The first to be born were the Kagabba, the Wiwa, the Iku Kankuamos, the Chimilas, the Wayu, and other native peoples. Afterwards, from the last semen were born the French, the Germans, Spaniards, and people from faraway lands: all the younger brothers. It was there, in the Sierra Nevada de Santa Marta, that the semen was studied, and that is why it is the heart, the heart of everything. We, the native peoples of Gonawindua, were given the mission of looking after the heart of the world for everybody, older and younger brothers alike. Gonawindua, the Sierra Nevada, is the heart of the universe. That's the reason why this land is so sacred: it is the heart of every heart.

The earth is a live being. The wise ones say it's Mother Earth and we live on it. We feed on it; many animals and many lives feed on it, and we feed other lives and everything feeds others. Mother Earth can be as God is for you people; we call her Serankua—Mother/Father Serankua: something like a god, but woman in spirit; she has strength, force of gravity; she moves the earth.

This is how the earth was made by The Parents: Mother took a thread and broke it in two, and she lifted one part and turned it into a circumference. Then she crossed the thread to close the circle. The Gonawindua mount was left at the heart. The Mamas say that we are made of several lands, many circumferences, many planets ... the head is one; two others are the eyes; the heart is another earth. The mouth and our body are made of circumferences, of earths. When the woman is about to give birth, she becomes round. That's why the Mamas say that we are the earth too, and if the earth suffers—even if we do not feel it—we suffer as well.

Serankua made the earth, and it was difficult for Serankua. The first to be created was the white woman, then the red one, the brown and the green ones, and so on until nine women were created—the last one being the black one, the most fertile of all. All were women of the spirit. Each was an earth of a different color. When all nine existed, Serankua made four crosses; she threw soil over the four crosses, and in the end she fertilized them with the black soil. It wasn't easy to get the black soil. It was hidden, but that's another story.

This is a small world for Serankua. She sees it as a little ball. For us it does not seem small, since we can't see the whole of it. There are four corners of the earth, four cardinal points: the *schaquacara*. We call these four points *schaquacara*, *sayaschaquacara*, *mamaschaquacara* and *aramaschaquacara*. Serankua placed them in each corner to support the earth, and our law says that it is up to the Mamas to make offerings so that these things may remain as they have always been. Otherwise, the world would fall. The Mamas work for the whole world. It took Serankua a lot of effort to create the earth, and to create us. She went to great lengths to give us eyes, noses, fingernails, bones.

We are here to nourish nature. Jaba Aluna, Mother/Father Serankua left us here to nourish nature. We all breathe, and my breathing feeds the others. Breathing nourishes other lives, and others' breathing nourishes me. The earth itself breathes and nourishes. Serankua bequeathed us knowledge of how to make things: one must concentrate, search for a sacred place, purify the spirit, and then breathe and nourish nature.

In the old times we had great wisdom, given to us by Mother. We had the knowledge of everything we were and are. We knew, according to our law, not to kill too many animals, and not to cut down too many trees. We knew what complies with the law bequeathed us. The law is not written in books but in nature, which is itself a book.

When younger brother came, our compliance changed. We have lost the wisdom. There are stories from old times which announced the conquest, the arrival of the Spaniards. The Mamas knew that younger brother was coming five thousand years ago. The word of old says that around five thousand years ago there was a Kaggaba who could fly the way an airplane flies today. His name in our tradition is Kasuaka. Serankua looked at Kasuaka over and over until she found that, if Kasuaka remained in Gonawindua, he was going to create much danger. He was dangerous for Gonawindua, for the heart, and he could harm the sierra. Alterations and sickness would come upon us. The Mamas, the fathers, and the mothers got together with Serankua, and it was decided to send him to another side of the earth. They threw Kasuaka far away, together with the thought of invention. In Gonawindua, they left the masks, the gold, the glues, the dance, as well as the palm trees, the lagoons, the beliefs, marriage, and many other things which belong to our own days. Kasuaka was born here, but that intelligence, because of the understanding of the mothers and the fathers, was sent far away.

The Mamas used to say that Serankua told them, five thousand years ago: "The younger brother is going to come and harm us. The younger brother will come as a blind man; in his blindness, he will disrespect. For the sake of his business, he will use machetes, metals, and enterprises to change what's proper. He will come in order to replace the traditional thought with his businesses." The conquest came, and we were changed. Mother Serankua also said, "Another time will come, however, and they will see what they did. Then they will want to learn the word of old. It will be time to make it known."

The Mamas also say: "There have already been four histories of the world. We are at the end of the fourth one. In the first, the waters came and filled the earth all the way up to the sierra. Everyone died. Then came other peoples. There was evil, violence, and disrespect; and when the violence grew too strong, the sickness came, and so the second world came to an end. Afterwards, in the next age, the sun raised its heat, but not everyone died. Then the sun went dark, and although there was some light, there was no warmth. Still, there were survivors. It was then that an evil spirit came, and his name was Petiku Umabash Umahuaba. He would bite the people the way you bite a ripe, yellow plantain, and so it was that he finished them all off. The world ended for a third time.

In our age, the Mamas say that the sun will not be darkened. Signs will come first, and they are already visible. The wise ones say that one signal is the arrival of the younger brother's sea in the tundras of the sierra Gonawindua. The younger brothers are already among us, not only in the material sense, but also with their thoughts. They have changed us with different religions, and with other ideas about the truth. Harm is being done to the land. Nature is no longer The Mother: it is something to be sold. They pull out gold and oil, and go on selling without turning their eyes to Mother Earth. The *yuluka*, the harmony, traditional thought, and compliance with Mother and Father, has been lost. The Mamas say that the land will go dry and that the crops will no longer bear fruit. This is happening: the rivers and the creeks are going dry. ... Another end will come then, another change, with sicknesses and rains, or Kaloboco, the spirit that is the enemy of the sun, or even the spirit Noanase. Our wise ones say it's possible that Noanase has already broken loose. Many things are happening which appear to be his doing. ... Afterwards, another world will come. For that we have to cleanse, to purify.

There was a lot of wisdom on the earth before the arrival of the younger brother. From other planets resembling the earth, there came visitors to make payments of compliance and to gather knowledge. The old ones say that before there were cattle here, there were exchanges with those beings. The cattle scared them away. They came from earths called Mulkuaba, Guonquirra, Guonka, and Guelkaba. These are planets far from earth, inhabited by peoples who are different from the ones here. Some are neither masculine nor feminine; others are only masculine or feminine. There are nine planets, and there used to be a relationship between us, but it no longer exists. That is also part of what has been lost.

There are other signals too. The brakes which the law set upon us have been lost. The path of old lies in knowing how to master the eyes, the ears, the masculine, and the feminine. There are four brakes of the soul—that is, the brakes of energy. Now a lot of disorderly energy is being wasted. It is the same to do good or evil. We have broken off with nature. We are all like flowers: we bloom, and flowers are harvested which nourish nature. All of that is being broken. There are only disorders, many disorders. There are so many machines, also. There were no airplanes before, *orkuskiavi*, or motorcars, *hemojaqui*, so many inventions that bring about disorder. ... Now we pay only our material debts, with money, currency—but not our payments of compliance, our spiritual debts, or the debt of the ancient word. That is why the Mamas say: "Younger brother came and changed our heart. He gave us a lime heart, an eye of glass, a brain of cement. We must search for the ancient word."

Parabola
Volume: 22.1
Ways of Knowing

Tangible Visions

Allen Wardwell

Isaac Tens, a Gitksan Tsimshian shaman tells of his conversion:

Thirty years after my birth was the time when I began to be a *swanassu* (medicine man). I went up into the hills to get firewood. While I was cutting up the wood into lengths, it grew dark towards the evening. Before I finished my last stack of wood, a loud noise broke out over me, *chu*—, and a large owl appeared to me. The owl took hold of me, caught my face, and tried to lift me up. I lost consciousness. As soon as I came back to my senses I realized I had fallen into the snow. My head was coated with ice, and some blood was running out of my mouth.

I stood up and went down the trail, walking very fast, with some wood packed on my back. On the way, the trees seemed to shake and to lean over me; tall trees were crawling after me as if they had been snakes. I could see them. Before I arrived at my father's home, I told my folk what had happened to me, as soon as I walked in. I was very cold and warmed myself before going to bed. There I fell into a sort of trance. It seems that two *halaaits* (medicine men) were working over me to bring me back to health. But it is now all vague in my memory. When I woke up and opened my eyes, I thought that flies covered my face. I looked down, and instead of being on firm ground, I felt that I was drifting in a huge whirlpool. My heart was thumping fast.

While I was in a trance, one of [the medicine men working over me] … told me that the time had arrived for me to become a halaait … like them. But I did not agree; so I took no notice of the advice. The affair passed away as it had come, without results.

Another time, I went to my hunting grounds on the other side of the river here … after I reached there, I caught two fishers in my traps, took their pelts, and threw the flesh and bones away. Farther along I looked for a bear's den amid the tall trees. As I glanced upwards, I saw an owl, at the top of a high cedar; I shot it, and it fell down in the bushes close to me. When I went to pick it up, it had disappeared. Not a feather was left; this seemed very strange. I walked down to the river, crossed over the ice, and returned to the village of Gitenmaks.

Upon arriving at my fishing station on the point, I heard the noise of a crowd of people around the smokehouse, as if I were being chased away, pursued. I dared not look behind to find out what all this was about, but I hastened straight ahead. The voices followed in my tracks and came very close behind me. Then I wheeled round and looked back. There was no one in sight, only trees. A trance came over me once more, and I fell down, unconscious. When I came to, my head was buried in a snow bank. I got up and walked on the ice up the river to the village. There I met my father who had just come out to look for me, for he had missed me.

We went back together to my house. Then my heart started to beat fast, and I began to tremble, just as had happened a while before when the halaaits … were trying to fix me up. My flesh seemed to be boiling, and I could hear *Su*—. My body was quivering. While I remained in this state, I began to sing. A chant was coming out of me without my being able to do anything to stop it. Many things appeared to me presently: huge birds and other animals. They were calling me. I saw a *meskyawaw-derh* (a kind of bird) and a *mesquaggweeu* (bullhead fish). These were visible only to me, not to the others in my house. Such visions happen when a man is about to become a halaait; they occur of their own accord. The songs force themselves out without any attempt to compose them. But I learned and memorized these songs by repeating them.

From Allen Wardwell, *Tangible Visions: Northwest Coast Indian Shamanism and Its Art* (New York: The Monacelli Press Inc., 1996), pp. 36–37). Reprinted by permission of Sally Wardwell.

Parabola
Volume: 24.1
Nature

Spider Woman and the Twins

Hopi

Sótuknang went to the universe wherein was that to be Tokpela, the First World, and out of it he created her who was to remain on that earth and be his helper. Her name was Kókyangwúti, Spider Woman.

When she awoke to life and received her name, she asked, "Why am I here?"

"Look about you," answered Sótuknang. "Here is this earth we have created. It has shape and substance, direction and time, a beginning and an end. But there is no life upon it. We see no joyful movement. We hear no joyful sound. What is life without sound and movement? So you have been given the power to help us create this life. You have been given the knowledge, wisdom, and love to bless all the beings you create. That is why you are here."

Following his instructions, Spider Woman took some earth, mixed with it some *túchvala* (saliva), and molded it into two beings. Then she covered them with a cape made of white substance which was the creative wisdom itself, and sang the Creation Song over them. When she uncovered them the two beings, twins, sat up and asked, "Who are we? Why are we here?"

To the one on the right Spider Woman said, "You are Pöqánghoya and you are to help keep this world in order when life is put upon it. Go now around all the world and put your hands upon the earth so that it will become fully solidified. This is your duty."

Spider Woman then said to the twin on the left, "You are Palön-gawhoya and you are to help keep this world in order when life is put upon it. This is your duty now: go about all the world and send out sound so that it may be heard throughout all the land. When this is heard you will also be known as 'Echo,' for all sound echoes the Creator."

Pöqánghoya, traveling throughout the earth, solidified the higher reaches into great mountains. The lower reaches he made firm but still pliable enough to be used by those beings to be placed upon it and who would call it their mother.

Palöngawhoya, traveling throughout the earth, sounded out his call as he was bidden. All the vibratory centers along the earth's axis from pole to pole resounded his call; the whole earth trembled; the universe quivered in tune. Thus he made the whole world an instrument of sound, and sound an instrument for carrying messages, resounding praise to the Creator of all. ...

Spider Woman then created from the earth trees, bushes, plants, flowers, all kinds of seed-bearers and nut-bearers to clothe the earth, giving to each a life and name. In the same manner she created all kinds of birds and animals—molding them out of earth, covering them with her white-substance cape, and singing over them. Some she placed to her right, some to her left, others before and behind her, indicating how they should spread to all four corners of the earth to live.

Sótuknang was happy, seeing how beautiful it all was—the land, the plants, the birds and animals, and the power working through them all. Joyfully, he said to Taiowa, "Come see what our world looks like now!"

"It is very good," said Taiowa. "It is ready now for human life, the final touch to complete my plan."

Parabola
Volume: 13.2
Repetition and
Renewal

World Renewal

Thomas Buckley

> *Are bad the people is getting,*
> *   is getting afraid.*
> *Man, will be all right in the world.*
> *Don't be too afraid.*
>
> —Stone[1]

We don't know when people first settled the canyon of
the lower Klamath River and the Pacific coast above and
below its mouth, in northwestern California. The river
has perennially flooded, sometimes with devastating
effects along its margins where villages have always been
built. Winter rains loosen slides in the canyon and tidal
waves occasionally rise at sea, running inland. Because
of the massive changes in the land that such events have
brought, the archaeological record is shallow and incomplete. We know, however, that the people who are today
called the Yurok Indians are relative newcomers, probably
entering from the north between one and two thousand
years ago, settling the lower forty miles of the Klamath
and the coast near its mouth. When they arrived they
met others who had been there far longer, living in a way
that worked well in that place. The Yurok adopted their
own former ways to it.

It was a good and bountiful world despite its occasional upheavals. Spawning salmon came into the

Klamath reliably, several times a year, and there were seasons of Lamprey eels, sturgeon, and steelhead trout. Other cycles were reliable as well. The heavy winter rains nurtured abundant growth that fed large deer and elk populations, and acorns—a staple food—covered the sun-warmed oaks on slopes above the fogs of late summer. The rising Pacific tides brought surf fish and floated valuable timber and, occasionally, fat-rich whales ashore, and the falling tides revealed dense beds of mussels, clam flats and gardens of sea-lettuce. The Yurok were healthy, seldom if ever hungry, resourceful and independent, and many grew wealthy on the great bounty of their place.

These people felt that the seemingly steady pulse of goodness in the world was not due to their own merit. It was well within the range of the human spirit to become greedy in the face of abundance and arrogant in the independence that it permitted, rather than careful for the interdependence that underlay this autonomy. Unrestrained, people violated the pure and reliable order of things, polluting it, bringing death. "We know that we are not the good ones," said Jimmie James, a contemporary Yurok spiritual person; "we know that the Creator is the good one." His words are touched with a monotheism that came with Christianity, after the 1860s, but the essence of his conviction seems as old as the Yurok themselves.

As I came to understand it through Jimmie and others, the world or Creation, *ki wes'onah,* "that which exists," is balanced and pure: "Beautiful," *merwerkseryerh.* It is naturally in harmony with "the law," its own Way. Each being in Creation is linked with it through its own life-spirit, *wewolocek,* which is both a figment of *wes'onah* and unique. All things are thus at once independent and interdependent parts of Creation. Their unique spirits are not necessarily good; it takes all kinds.

In the beginning, when the world was new, it was inhabited by the Immortals, the *wo•gey,* myth-time people with pure spirits who lived in easy accordance with the law. When human beings—"the Indians"—came, the Immortals "went away." While the world itself remained perfect and beautiful, human beings had the capacity to violate and disrupt that beauty, to throw off the balance of Creation through, especially, their greed. Because people constantly broke the law, death threatened to outweigh life in the world. As violations of the law and deaths built up, their weight began to tip the earth-disk in the seas upon which it floated. The tides rose higher and higher and whales came far up the Klamath, a dire sign. The river flooded, the earth shook and diseases began to spread.

There was always a struggle, then, to keep the world balanced upon the waters, the rhythms of abundance steady, in accord with the law and despite human beings' breaches of it. Knowing that this would be so, before they left the wo•gey instructed certain people in what to do to put the world back in balance when the weight of human violations grew too great for it. These instructions were the basis of what the anthropologist A. L. Kroeber called the "world renewal cult" (why a "cult" I do not know) and of its central ceremonials, the "Jump Dance" and the "White Deerskin Dance." Like the runs of salmon or the flow of tides and seasons, these dances and a variety of other ritual events were repeated in a regular way and in accord with interlocking cycles at more than a dozen ritual centers in the territories of the Yurok and of their neighbors, most notably the Karuk and the Hupa. The cycles of dances and rituals were diverse. Some were repeated every year, some every two years, some every three, their cycles overlapping in intricate, regulated ways throughout the region, forming a generative background for human life within it.

Kroeber called the spiritual experts who were responsible for the ritual dimensions of these dances "priests" or "formulists." In Yurok, however, they are called the ones who "talk with the world" and also the "doctors of the world," the ones who "fix" it. These practitioners recited the myths of the wo•gey who had first shaped the rituals, quoting their speeches and performing acts of power that the wo•gey had dictated. In effect, they became the wo•gey, uniting their consciousness with that of the Immortals in the purity of the first times through language and through ascetic practice. Doing so they gained the power to return the world to its original condition.

The major dances that these people led were the focus of great festivals which lasted for many weeks and were attended by thousands from throughout the region. The medicine people prepared for the dances through long weeks of training and private ritual, cleaning themselves of impurity, bad thoughts, and transient concerns. All those who hoped to attend were expected to prepare as well. The metaphysics of renewal were accompanied by universal attention to the physics of social interrelationships—the concrete side of returning to balance and beauty.

Litigations and debts had to be settled, grudges laid aside, the grief of mourners assuaged. In the actual dances teams of dancers displayed the regalia amassed by the wealthy families of the area, valuable things that had "beauty," the fundamental quality of the world as it was in wo•gey times and was, now, to be again. So, in the minds of the ritual leaders, in the social relations of the spectators, in the singing and costumes of the dancers, everything was once more as it should be, beautiful, and the world was "doctored," "fixed," "balanced" once again, decay and death reversed, life affirmed.

Lucy Thompson, the first Yurok author, wrote about the 1876 White Deerskin Dance at Kepel: "I counted upwards of three thousand Indians there. . . . There were five different languages spoken among them." Thompson stresses the use of kinship terms among all of these spectators, who addressed each other as "sister" and "brother." The dance singing in such events, she wrote, "is most perfect in time and tune and makes one feel the love of the great Creator of all things." Of a Jump Dance at Pekwon shortly before the turn of the century, she writes that:

> *All Indians are invited to come, rich or poor, from any and all tribes, from far off and near by. Far away tribes are looked after, fed and asked to take part in the dance, even if they cannot speak the language. ... This is the time that the very poor and slave class of our own [Yurok] people are made jolly and contented. ... They are here allowed, both men and women, to put in whatever they may possess that is of value, that is used to dance with. The wealthy ones that own lands, hunting territory, fishing places, slaves, flints, white deer skins, fisher skins, otter skins, silver grey fox skins, and fine dresses made of dressed deerskins, with fringes or shells knotted and worked in the most beautiful styles, that clink and jingle as they walk and make one have a feeling of respect and admiration for them [sic.]. The eyes will strain to look on this most pleasant sight, which can never leave one's memory that has seen it in its flowery days.*

While Thompson's descriptions are of uncertain ethnographic accuracy (and reflect her aristocratic prejudices), certainly the feeling that underlies them is authentic and a reliable reflection of her own and others' experiences. The "festivals are held," she concludes, "for the purpose and equality of the whole people together, the rich, the poor and the slave, make themselves come together in peace and harmony as one family and to ... feel that there is some good to live for."[2]

> *Now it was toward evening. The old man went outside and my father followed. Then the old man sent him to bring down sweathouse wood. On the way he cried with nearly every step because now he was seeing with his own eyes how it was done, when before he had never thought much about it. Also he cried because this is the way the people of old had done from the beginning, and now they had chosen him for that part.*
>
> —Robert Spott[3]

People periodically had to be brought back into harmony with each other and with the world, lest the weight of their infractions against the law, of their selfishness, throw the whole off balance and destroy them. The repeating cycles of salmon and tides and seasons were accompanied by repeating cycles of renewal, of "dances," among people (they say that the Immortals in the Spirit World are *always* dancing). These renewals became, after the coming of human beings, as central to Creation, as much a part of the law, as anything else, and the "health" of the whole world depended upon them. So repetitions of dances joined other repetitions, interdependent with them. "We and the world, well, we very much support each other" say the wo•gey in a speech once quoted by leaders of the Wecpus White Deerskin Dance.[4]

In order to stay true to the law it was necessary that some people, at least, learn how to accomplish renewal, how to support the world, "talk to" it and "doctor" it, through yet other orders of repetition. Like seasons and dances, sacred knowledge had to be repeated in the minds of individual human beings, generation after generation. The repeated act of recreating this knowledge was itself of the essence of the sacred, like salmon runs or dance cycles.

My adoptive uncle and teacher, Harry Roberts, often repeated himself, too, in a more limited sense. There were a variety of phrases that he used didactically, again and again over the years. "I know what all real men have known for forty thousand years," he'd say, his gaze deep and alert, his stone talisman before him; "I know what I know—the law, Creation."

Harry repeated stories as well, often reminiscences. How, for instance, when he was a boy of eleven or twelve he'd gone down among the rocks on the ocean beach at the mouth of the Klamath River below Rekwoy and heard the Little People singing, and how he'd learned their song and come back up the hill to the village, to sing it to his uncle, the Yurok "high man" Robert Spott. It was the song that was needed to start sweeping out the Sacred Sweathouse at Rekwoy, to begin the Jump Dance. Robert began teaching him seriously then. Harry had heard "spirit language," the language of pure feeling, "just emotion." And he told me how, many years later when he was an "all-grown-up-person," he and Robert would speak to each other in this language of emotions, just making "little noises," pure sound, and how they had understood each other perfectly. There was no need to say more or to say it differently, their minds as one.

Other stories lead back through deeper generations and tell us more of how such men came to know what had always been known.

Harry's teacher, Robert Spott, was a famously conservative man, born in 1888 and so about twenty years Harry's senior. He was profoundly religious in a highly traditional, Yurok way, his gentleness nicely balanced by a well-honed intellect. As he had adopted and begun training Harry, just before the First World War, so Robert himself had been adopted and trained by Captain Spott, a forceful leader of the people of the lower Klamath, born around 1844, about six years before first massive contact with the invading Euro-Americans. Captain Spott was a tough, canny, and occasionally dangerous individual, from what we now know of him, but he was also a deeply spiritual man, even devout, and highly trained in the way that he was to train Robert, and Robert Harry.

A. L. Kroeber met Captain Spott when he first came to the Klamath, in 1900, and through him met his son Robert. Robert was to do considerable ethnographic work with Kroeber, over the years that followed, telling him many stories, probably repeating them; he "tried and tried to teach Kroeber," his nephew Harry said. In 1942 Robert Spott and Kroeber published a book together, *Yurok Narratives*, and one of Robert's stories in this book is about Captain Spott's training as the "assistant" to the First Salmon Ceremony "priest," Pegwolew Omegwimor, at Wellkwew in 1864 or shortly before. (The First Salmon Ceremony was apparently once accompanied by a White Deerskin Dance and was, in this and in many other ways, part of the renewal cycle.)

Captain Spott was a young man, not yet married. He trained ascetically for a month and a half in a sweathouse at Rekwoy before crossing the river to Wellkwew for another week of intensive ritual practice and the spearing and eating of the First Salmon. When Pegwolew Omegwimor, through his power and knowledge, speared the First Salmon a great cry went up from all of the people gathered along both sides of the river: "He's caught!" Jimmy Gensaw heard this as a boy and told his foster daughter, Florence Shaughnessy, about it: "I looked into the sky where I could hear a tinkling sound, and the mist that came down was as though the sky wept for the beauty of it."

When all was accomplished, the priest sent Captain Spott to gather sweathouse wood once again. "On the way he cried at nearly every step," Robert told Kroeber, quoting his father, "because now he was seeing with his own eyes how it was done, when before he had never thought much about it." After this the Captain continued his training at Wellkwew for a month before returning to Rekwoy, and for still another month when he got home.

Such knowledge could not be inherited, could not be "transmitted" in any usual sense, could only be acquired by determined individuals through their own stringent, exhausting efforts. The role of the teacher, usually an "uncle," was not to teach this truth, in our conventional sense, but to "keep you out of trouble" while you learned and to confirm your knowledge when you had gained it. Still, such truth had to be seen, the song had to be heard: " I can't learn *for* you, can I?" Harry asked, often. Yet what was seen or heard or known was precisely what had been perceived by all real men forever, back to the beginning of time, in the wo•gey all-time; "the way the people of old had done from the beginning." It was this process of repeated return to the pure knowledge of the myth-time that occurred individual by individual, generation to generation, and that permitted the continuation of existence even in the face of the inevitable and overwhelming, continual violations and depredations of people who, failing to learn, constantly threatened the world with their greed and selfishness.

Thus, from an old-time Yurok point of view, the seemingly reliable and automatic repetition of natural cycles, like the yearly return of the spring salmon, the ocean tides or the seasonal rains, were not quite that. In the face of human nature, these cycles were reliable only when they were accompanied by other, human orders of repetition: the return, generation by generation, of a very few gifted and very determined individuals, on their own as it were, to knowledge of how Creation actually is, when people don't interfere with it, and the cyclic, repetitive enactment of this knowledge in ritual. For it was only on the basis of such knowledge that the great rituals, like those of the First Salmon Ceremony or of the dances, could be performed and through them, the violations engendered by people's failings expunged, the world, unbalanced by the weight of these violations, set to rights again. Cycles enclosed cycles, all interdependent, all necessary, all successful: "the beauty way" Harry called it.

> *The winter moons are bastards. The sun is proud and will not travel with them; therefore he is alone in the daytime. Yet it is the bastard moons that bring the rains which make the growth in a good summer. So when I fasted and gathered sweathouse wood I cried out to the bastard moons as well as the others and they helped me.*
> —Kerner[5]

At the end of the Jump Dance at Rekwoy the priest's benediction was simple: "Keep up the old ways," he told the young.

When Harry Roberts heard the Little People sing the song to start the Rekwoy Jump Dance his uncle, Robert Spott, "spotted" Harry, then a child, as one who had the life-spirit of a Jump Dance "assistant," and started in to train him. Robert knew that Harry probably would never perform the ritual functions of the assistant, for the Rekwoy Jump Dance had not been given since 1904, before Harry was born. Still, Robert knew, it was essential that somebody younger than himself learn to see how the world is; that somebody know what all real men have known, lest it be utterly lost and the world lost, truly, with it.

Before 1904 the Jump Dance at Rekwoy had been put up every three years. In alternate performances—every six years—a structure in the village was rebuilt. This structure was called the "old" or "ugly" sweathouse, and also the "sacred sweathouse." It was the center of the world and it supported the world. It had been placed in Rekwoy at the beginning by the wo•gey and its center post reached up to the top of the sky, keeping it in place, its four beams extended to the edges of the world, holding them up. This structure was constantly getting dirty, dilapidated, and it had to be ritually swept out every three years and rebuilt entirely every six, as it had been from the beginning when the wo•gey first constructed it.

There were three parties to this reconstruction: the "priest" and leader; his "assistant" and senior student; and several "helpers," a sort of chorus of (originally) young men and unmarried women who were under the priest's guidance too, though junior in power and in training to the assistant. It would take long to argue the case, but it seems that these three positions encoded three human generations, as well as three degrees of knowledge and experience—grandfather, father, sons and daughters, for instance.

While the assistant worked alone, sweeping out the old structure and the sacred paths used in the ritual, the priest and the male helpers crossed the river to the Wellkwew side in a canoe. There the leader felled a living redwood tree—with the helpers' help—announcing that he would kill it: "I will have you for holding up the sky" he told the tree before making the first cut. The tree fell—uphill, on account of the priest's power, according to the late Dewey George—and the men split from it the post and four beams, burying all five in a grave that they had dug, as a human corpse would be buried. Then they exhumed the timbers, which they carried the way that corpses were carried *to* their graves, transporting them back across the river to Rekwoy where they installed them, rebuilding the old sweathouse around the new timbers. Death was reversed, the world renewed and life supported once again.

In this process every important action was initiated by the priest but completed by the youthful helpers; the assistant seems only to have prepared, as in sweeping and, in a graphic way, to have held the center while the others came and went. For example, when the post was ready the priest touched it and the helpers set it erect. Then the assistant steadied the post while the helpers put the four beams, each first touched by the priest, in place. It seems to me that what was being acted out in such sequences was the history of knowledge itself, and the history of the perfect, timeless world that that knowledge both embodied and assured.

I think that the reconstruction of this center of the world encoded the constant movement of time and of knowledge across the generations, as well as repetitive, cyclic renewal and return to the timeless. Of course the old leader would die—everyone dies. Yet his place would be taken by future generations, his "grandchildren" when they, too, had seen with their own eyes. In the meantime the center held, the world was made clean by those who had already seen and heard, like the assistant, however incomplete their power might now be, and who would, in their turns, return the world to balance, yet only starting that which must be completed, again and again, by those who would come after. "Ritual knowledge went ricocheting down the generations," as Bruce Chatwin has recently written about Aboriginal Australia.

Anthropologists have talked about peoples apparently caught in a mythic non-time, "closed societies," "without history," governed by an ethic of "eternal return." But I think that *we* have been caught by our own dualisms, here. The old-time Yurok knew perfectly well about what we call "history" (take a look at *Yurok Narratives*, for instance), but they knew something else along with it; that the world is at once an unfolding in time and timeless, when truly seen; that time and all-time are parts of each other and support each other. The priest's actions bear a double message: the world must be remade lest it die, but death is necessary to remake the world and sustain it.

"The price of a life is a life," said Harry Roberts. The price of life is to live it, and the price of timeless life is historical death, the Rekwoy ritual seems to say. Thus the tree was killed, I think, like the First Salmon. In spearing that fish, Erik Erikson wrote, the Yurok hoped "to perform the miracle of his existence, namely, to eat his salmon and have it too." The Salmon's death assured the life of both the salmon who were to follow, endlessly, and of the people who would eat them.

Overwhelming death that threatens to unbalance the world is the result of human selfishness and ignorance, on the one hand, but too, death is just death, the other side of life in Creation, in beauty. "The miracle of existence" performed by the Jump Dance priest was to take that death which tends toward the destruction of the world and convert it into those necessary deaths that support life, in accord with the law. "There're two sides to everything," Harry repeatedly said, patiently, laughing at himself and me alike: "keep 'em in balance."

After the Gold Rush of 1849 the Yurok and their neighbors were invaded by tens of thousands of gold prospectors. These were soon followed by white settlers and entrepreneurs and drifters of every sort. The

contact was violent and virulent. Between 1851 and 1910 Yurok population declined from roughly 2500 to 610, three out of every four people;
a wretched part of a regional decimation that was often much worse
and that the Hupa historian Jack Norton has termed "genocide." Great
floods exacerbated these losses in the mid-1860s. As the whites co-opted
more and more land and laid to waste greater and greater quantities of
available food resources, malnutrition became a commonplace among
Indians. Military resistance all but ceased after 1865 and the defeat of
the Chilula, to the south of the Klamath. Among the Yurok, the great
dances disappeared one by one. Rekwoy held out until 1904. Wecpus
until 1912, efforts to keep the Kepel rites going faltered in the 1920s.
What seemed to be the last Yurok Jump Dance was held at Pekwon in
1939. "What's the point of dreaming of elk," Harry Roberts remembered
an old and discouraged hunter asking in the 1920s, "when there are no
elk left to hunt?" A way that had worked for millennia seemed to have
been ended in less than ninety years. The whites had brought a different,
single-sided kind of time.

Before their coming the world renewals of the peoples of the northwest found symbolic parallels throughout native California. Center posts
and mythic enactments, rituals of generational continuity and of return
to the pristine, pre-human world, the sacrificial cost of this return, were
all variously represented in the Kuksu, Hesi, and Ghost Society dances of
northern California, in the Mourning Anniversaries and Toloache mysteries to the south, and in many other local traditions. They depended on
people, as different as you and I, coming to shared understandings of the
real nature of the world, repeating this knowledge in heart after heart,
generation upon generation. This world was perfect, but only because
people continued to see it to be so, each with their own eyes, as Mohave
men along the Colorado River, at the other end of the Californian world
from the Yurok, were initiated only when they had learned the chants of
their clan origin myths, correctly, in their own dreams.

In the Yurok case at least, that the ways of world renewal were good
was constantly demonstrated by the long survival of the people themselves. Those people's fear that human beings might bring about world
imbalance, which underlay the therapies they instituted to "doctor" the
world, were hardly "hypochondriac," as Kroeber thought them to be. The
First Salmon Ceremony at Welkwew in which Captain Spott acted as

assistant was the last one ever performed. By 1865, fifteen years after they first came into that country, the hydraulic gold miners, driven by greed and armed with ever-changing technical know-how, had so silted in the spawning grounds that there were no more runs of spring salmon. With no First Salmon to be speared, not even the strong medicine of the high men could bring them back. It was, as people said at the time, "the end of the world."

Well, yes and no. Although it took a long time, the spring salmon eventually did begin to run again in the Klamath. And the 1939 Jump Dance at Pekwon that was viewed by many old-timers as marking "the end of the real Indian way" marked, rather, the beginning of a long hiatus. In 1984, forty-five years later, the dance was again put up, under the guidance of Dewey George who had danced in 1939. Dewey died a short time later, having instructed a new generation, but the dance was repeated in two years, on schedule, in 1986, and it will be given again this year, 1988. Yurok world renewal itself has been renewed.

My thanks to the Yurok people and especially to the elders who discussed these things with me in the 1970s. *"World Renewal: A cult system of native northwest California"* by A. L. Kroeber and E. W. Gifford (University of California Anthropological Records 13[1], 1949) is an important written source. I draw on it often, without citation, throughout this essay.

Notes:

1. Stone, Yurok, gave this translation of a part of the Wecpus White Deerskin Dance "medicine" to A. L. Kroeber in 1904. The "medicine" is among the Kroeber Papers in the Bancroft Library at the University of California, Berkeley.

2. Lucy Thompson, *To the American Indian* (Eureka, CA: Cummins Print Shop, 1916) 112-19.

3. Robert Spott and A. L. Kroeber, "Yurok Narratives," *University of California Publications in American Archaeology and Etymology* 35 (9), 1942: 177.

4. Kroeber Papers. Again, the informant was Stone but the translation from Yurok, here, is my own.

5. Kerner was a contemporary of Captain Spott. He is quoted by Robert Spott in *Yurok Narratives*, 226.

Parabola
Volume: 18.1
Healing

Saving Mother Earth to Save Ourselves

Joel Monture

At a time when the world was covered with water, it is said that a race of spirit people lived above the great sky dome which envelops the world. A woman, the wife of a Chief, was digging at the base of a great tree, when she opened up a hole and fell through the sky dome, clutching seeds in her hand. Large white birds saw her falling, and also saw that she was fat with an unborn child inside her. These birds (some say the snow goose, whose wing is used to symbolically sweep away old business in the council area) caught her between their outstretched wings and brought her safely to lie on the back of a big turtle. There, the water creatures and sky creatures endeavored to help the woman, who needed earth to plant her seeds, by diving under the water in an attempt to find some soil.

Muskrat was successful, finally touching bottom and picking up a speck of earth under his nail. Sky Dome Woman spread the earth all over Turtle's back until the world was fertile for planting. Her seeds began to grow and the world became lush and green with the sacred plants from the heavens.

Soon the woman gave birth to a daughter, who grew to young womanhood in the fertile, clean world. One night as the daughter lay sleeping, a man came (some say he came down from the sky), and he placed two arrows—one blunt and one sharp—on her stomach, and she became pregnant with twin sons. One was born the normal way, and was right-handed. The other, who had argued with his brother even before they were born, broke out through their mother's side, killing her. He was left-handed.

Grandmother, Sky Dome Woman, raised the twins, but first she buried her daughter. Plants sprouted out of the earth where the daughter was buried: From her head came three plants (corn, beans, and squash), which are known as *The Three Sisters*, and sustain life. Tobacco grew out of her heart, and was used to make blessings and offer thanks to the Creator for all the gifts of life. Strawberries grew from her feet, and are regarded as the leader of the plants. Also from her feet grew many medicines which would cure illness.

From that time on the twins regarded the earth as their mother, because she continued to provide the means to nourish and feed, heal, and give thanks.

Meanwhile, Grandmother gave the twins names, calling the right-handed one Teharonhiawako, meaning *Holder of the Heavens*. The left-handed twin was called Sawiskera, meaning *Mischievous One*. Grandmother also made a mistake, favoring the mischievous one because she thought it was his brother who had killed their mother.

Even though Grandmother ignored him, the right-handed twin loved her right up to the time when she grew old and died. Sawiskera wanted to throw her body off the world, but Teharonhiawako would not permit this and they tugged and fought over the body. The left-handed one finally pulled off the head of his Grandmother and flung it into the sky near the spot she had originally fallen from. There her head began to glow and it became our Grandmother, the moon, who watches over all of earth's people, just as grandmothers watch over sleeping children.

Now Teharonhiawako busied himself, making all manner of things in honor of Mother Earth. He created the animals, and all of them were of similar and of peaceful minds; he created all the flowers, and fruits, and more medicines. Sawiskera tried to create things but he was no good at it, making things that were ugly. He altered the minds of some animals, so that the wolf fell upon the deer; he put thorns on roses, and poison on ivy. For every single thing the right-handed twin made, the left-handed twin made something ugly, or dangerous, or bad-smelling, until the world was completely in balance, with neither too much good nor too much bad.

The twins decided to stop arguing and divide the world. Teharonhiawako would occupy the day of the world, and Sawiskera would occupy the night, where Grandmother who favored him would always be.

However, Teharonhiawako's work was not finished. He decided to create a being in his own image who would have intelligence and a custodial relationship over the other creatures, to look after his world. He made people from tree bark, from white sea foam, from red earth and black earth, and he placed them all over the world, instructing them to be of the *Good Mind*. He expected them to take care of the world, because their mother made up the world and provided for them.

Eventually the left-handed twin went off to become the Great Rim Dweller, who was given the power to cure diseases.

The right-handed twin is known now as Sonkwaiatison, *Our Creator*, who continues to influence people's minds, and who is always pleased when people live by his teachings, burning tobacco in blessing and giving thanks. Sometimes, however, Sonkwaiatison needs to remind people of their obligation to maintain life, and he chooses people who are clear and willing to bring his original message of respect.

One group of people created by Sonkwaiatison were the Hotinonshonni, *The People of the Longhouse*, (called the *Iroquois* by the French and the *Six Nations* by the British). Comprised of the Mohawk, Oneida, Onondaga, Cayuga, Seneca, and later the Tuscarora Nations, they were united by the efforts of the Peacemaker, Tekahnahwita (who was aided by Haiawentha). The Hotinonshonni's confederacy eventually declined, the populations reduced by war, disease, alcohol, and Christianity. At this time, it is said, Skanientariio (*Handsome Lake*) was sent to reveal the message of Sonkwaiatison, by bringing a *Code of Conduct* to live by, which also contained dire warnings about the future.

Today, it is as if the left-handed twin were continuing his work, and the world is becoming unbalanced. Is there any way for the right-handed twin to keep up with the damage or to repair it? Degradation to Mother Earth is done not by spirits, but by humans, who have ignored the original teachings. It is believed by Native American nations that sickness, both of the mind and the body, can come from spiritual forces, and can be directed to those who are out of balance and harmony with the natural world. However, it is also known that innocent people are harmed by the degradation done to the earth. There are good people in the world, but there are now bad places to live.

At one time every place was fit for life, and all life had an equal chance to survive. But mankind, who was charged with the particular responsibility to care for the earth, has taken great steps to alter it in many ways. Do shooting rockets to the moon and Mars tear holes in the Sky Dome? Do we leave our planet in the hopes of finding a better place away from our Mother? It is natural to part from Mother, but not because she is toxic. A parallel in western culture is the increasing number of children being removed from unfit homes by social service agencies. Is it possible that some other planet will eventually become a foster mother for the neglected and abused children of earth, while the original mother shrinks in loneliness and abandonment?

Skanientariio's prophecies provide insight into the current state of the world. He told us the Council of Chiefs would weaken, and would no longer be of one mind.

It was also predicted that the worlds of Skanientariio would be ignored, a sign that the Creator would make big changes in the world. We were told that the sky would be filled with flying objects made of metal. Women past the age of childbearing would bear children. Young children would bear children of their own. Trees would die from the top down, dead fish would float on top of the water, and the water, even from the deepest wells, would be undrinkable. Our language would vanish, and people would change shape and openly practice bad things in public. There would be diseases with no cure, people would go to bed well and die before morning—a sign that the Creator is recalling his children. Strawberries would disappear. We would build homes like white people. Wild animals would no longer be with us. We would raise animals, but have to treat them with respect. Our Grandfather Thunderer would come out of the west, never to return, and then strange creatures and insects would emerge from the earth. Our vegetable plants would be stunted. Sonkwaiatison would stop all life on earth to begin again.

These are some of the prophecies, but the *Code of Handsome Lake* contains messages about how to live in accord with the old ways. Perhaps the most important message regards the unborn generations.

Specifically, we are always to think of the effects of our actions on the unborn who will come into being seven generations from now. What world will the seventh generation be born into, what will be the quality of their lives, water, air, food? No mistakes can be made, nothing should be left to clean up. We are to keep our homes and our world clean from the start. We are also warned about using anything that will alter our minds, such as alcohol; about using witchcraft or negative thoughts towards each other; or mistreating our children, or our elderly who convey wisdom.

From a Native perspective, the world now is in a crazy state, and it has become almost normal for people to be crazy. There seems to be a direct correlation between the degradation of the environment and the breakdown of society. As the natural world reels against the onslaught of unnatural abuse—the overuse of poisonous chemicals or the practice of clear-cutting timber—cultures begin to disintegrate. The very essence of spirituality is found in nature, in accepting the coming and passing of generations and the knowledge that is transmitted. As more and more harm is done to nature, we find more and more people devoid of healthy feelings, and filled instead with feelings of self-doubt, anger, and disrespect. On individual levels this creates a suspicious and uncooperative world.

It is somewhat comforting to know that seven generations ago the people were thinking of us today, but sometime between then and now, someone forgot the message. So now we are charged, not only with thinking far, far ahead, but with recognizing today's problems in an attempt to stave off what may soon become unresolvable.

The problem is almost like the chicken/egg controversy, but, instead of being a matter of what came first, it is a conscious choice about what *should* come first! Will saving the earth heal our minds and souls, or must a healing of the mind precede any real cure for our mother planet? And is it even possible to do one first? Can simultaneous healing, restoration, and cure take place?

It is evident from the interest taken in Native ways by non-Native society that much of western culture is spiritually bankrupt. Organized western religions, based not so much on spiritual values as on the power bases created by micro-national economies, do not bind as ligaments but instead pull people apart. Thus, Native people are now being approached for answers to solve problems not of Native making. The disturbing trend of corporate North America is to disregard Native values, lands, issues, and lifeways in attempts to broaden its hold on western dependency, from Hydro-Quebec's slaughter of thousands of migrating caribou which sustain northern Native life, to foresters and national politicians who dismiss the spotted owl as an inconvenience to loggers in the United States' Northwest. The problem is that western culture has an overwhelming, seemingly paranoid, desire to control nature beyond human ability, and the death of a species pales against "progress."

The thinking is, and has been for a long time, that only today is important. Whether it is seeing one's psychiatrist or jumping into a hot tub made from California redwood, there is no time for patience, real talk, or thought. As in an Orwellian nightmare, we need telephones in commercial airlines because we inflate the importance of time, and have to know immediately if the *deal went through!* We need voices, buzzers, and blinking lights in automobiles to remind us that we are our own unsafest friend. We don't need wisdom, we need subpoenas. We are encouraged to create miles of paper trails to safeguard ourselves against the behavior of others, while we play phone tag with answering machines. Somewhere, somehow, sometime, some of us actually walk outside, slowly, taking time to wonder about the shooting star. Don't worry, it's just a piece of space junk falling from orbit, *but* it will burn up before it hits you in the head.

It seems as if Sawiskera is always at work, inside us, undoing all the good deeds of Teharonhiawako, who is also inside us. The twins are you and I. The battle to keep the world in balance rages continually. Light competes with dark, east with west and north with south. If there was ever a sign of hope, it is that single blade of grass splitting through concrete.

Brave *Old* World!

CHAPTER THREE

Place: The Land Is Our Religion

These are stories and essays that "rest on the edge of creation." Mapping the inner terrain together with the outer, tribal people maintain a spiritual connection to the land of their ancestors, stories of the land, and a significant knowledge of place. The land is the altar. It is precious. The medicines live there. Place defines who we are as people, and we locate ourselves within its realms. Mythic narratives often come from our Native earth, and those narratives keep the people connected with the land and the cosmos. The earth itself has created the cultures and indigenous ways of knowing. Many stories are based on location and the recounting of events in that place. This creates how we view and understand the outer and inner worlds. For aboriginal peoples across the world, the physical world is viewed and known as alive, embodied, and sometimes as having the power to assist human lives. It is our job to take care of and love the land. We are participants in the earth's becoming and it participates in ours.

Parabola
Volume: 3.1
Sacred Space

The Sacred Pipe

Black Elk

The chief priest, Kablaya, prayed:

"O Grandfather, Wakan-Tanka, I shall now make this Your sacred place. In making this altar, all the birds of the air and all creatures of the earth will rejoice, and they will come from all directions to behold it! All the generations of my people will rejoice! This place will be the center of the paths of the four great Powers. The dawn of the day will see this holy place! When Your Light approaches, O Wakan-Tanka, all that moves in the universe will rejoice!"

A pinch of the purified earth was offered above and to the ground and was then placed at the center of the sacred place. Another pinch of earth was offered to the west, north, east, and south and was placed at the west of the circle. In the same manner, earth was placed at the other three directions, and then it was spread evenly all around within the circle. This earth represents the two-leggeds, the four-leggeds, the wingeds, and really all that moves, and all that is in the universe. Upon this sacred place Kablaya then began to construct the altar. He first took up a stick, pointed it to the six directions, and then, bringing it down, he made a small circle at the center; and this we understand to be the home of Wakan-Tanka. Again, after pointing the stick to the six directions, Kablaya made a mark starting from the west and leading to the edge of the circle. In the same manner he drew a line from the east to the edge of the circle, from the north to the circle, and from the south to the circle. By constructing the altar in this manner, we see that everything leads into, or returns to, the center; and this center, which is here, but which we know is really everywhere is Wakan-Tanka.

From *The Sacred Pipe: Black Elk's Account of the Seven Rites of the Oglala Sioux*, recorded and edited by Joseph Epes Brown. Copyright © 1953, 1989 by the University of Oklahoma Press. All rights reserved. Reprinted by permission of the publisher.

Parabola
Volume: 13.4
The Mountain

The Four Sacred Mountains of the Navajos

Trebbe Johnson

The construction of the hogan, the Navajo's traditional dome-shaped dwelling made of earth, is a reenactment of First Man's and First Woman's creation of the four sacred mountains that define the boundaries of Navajo country. In the act of building their hogan, the family takes part in the dynamic, ongoing process of bringing into being the sacred cosmos.

Starting at the east, and moving in a sun-wise, or clockwise, direction, they set into the earth the four main poles of the framework, just as First Man and First Woman placed a sacred mountain at each of the four cardinal points. They fill the spaces between the poles with bark and smaller sticks, and pat a covering of soil into place around the frame, thus enclosing the sacred space, as Navajo land and life is secured within the circle of the sacred mountains. The door of the hogan faces the rising sun. In the center is the fire, representative of the Emergence Place through which the Navajo ancestors long ago climbed into this world from the one preceding it. Directly above the fire is the smoke-hole, passageway for prayers traveling up to the skies.

When construction is complete, a medicine man comes to consecrate the hogan as a sacred place. The hogan songs he sings, which are part of the Blessingway ceremony, were first performed before the mountains to make them holy and strong. The ceremony connects the family home to the tribal home, affirming both as the enclosed, protected center of the universe.

> *Of origins I have full knowledge.*
> *Of Earth's origin I have full knowledge.*
> *Of plant origins I have full knowledge.*
> *Of various fabrics' origins I have full knowledge.*[1]

It is in the hogan that blessed events are expected to occur—births, weddings, healing ceremonies, the daily awakening to life-giving sun, long talks under lamplight about sheep, neighbors, legends, dreams. In the hogan, as in the land between sacred mountains, Navajo people have nothing to fear, for they are in a holy place of "long life and happiness."

Today, even though many families on the reservation prefer to live in modern, electrified homes made rectangular by cinderblocks, aluminum or wood siding, they often have a traditional hogan, symbol of what it means to be Navajo, just a few steps away.

The first hogan was made of the four sacred mountains and the space between them. Having made their way to the top of a hollow reed to escape the flood that was devouring the previous world, First Man and First Woman looked around and determined to mark their hopes of remaining here, in the Fifth World, by embellishing the land for the generations to come. First Man took out a bundle of mountain soil he had brought from the four worlds below, and proceeded to create the mountains that are the foundation of Navajo culture and consciousness.

In the east they placed *Sisnaajini*, "Black-Belted One," or Sierra Blanca Peak in the Sangre de Cristo Range, near Alamosa, Colorado. They fastened it to the earth with a bolt of lightning and decorated it with white shells, white corn and white lightning, and with the dark clouds that give rise to the strong, hard male rain. The feathered beings they settled here were the white-winged wild pigeons. They covered the mountain with a sheet of daylight and set within it, as guardians, Rock Crystal Boy and Rock Crystal Girl.

In the south First Man and First Woman fashioned *Tsoodzil*, "Tongue Mountain," or Mount Taylor, near Grants, New Mexico. This mountain they fixed firm to earth with a great stone knife. Upon it, to beautify it and give it a character all its own, they placed turquoise, many different kinds of animals, and the dark mist that brings the soft, gentle female rain. They made it possible for bluebirds to nest there. They wrapped their creation in blue sky. Finally, to dwell on this mountain forever, they formed Boy Who Is Bringing Back Turquoise and Girl Who Is Bringing Back Many Ears of Corn.

Dook'o'oosliid, "Light Shines From It," or Mount Humphrey in the San Francisco Peaks north of Flagstaff, Arizona, they set in the west, attaching it to the firmament with a sunbeam. This mountain they embellished with abalone shell, with animals, and with the black clouds that bring the male rain. They made conditions right for the yellow warbler to live there. They blanketed their creation in a yellow cloud, and stationed to live there White Corn Boy and Yellow Corn Girl.

Dibé nitsaa, "Mountain Sheep," or Hesperus Peak in Colorado's San Juan Range, is the mountain First Man and First Woman created for the north. They made it firm to earth with a rainbow, and adorned it with beads of black jet, with plants of many different varieties, and with the gray mist that engenders the female rain. On the top of the mountain they placed eggs that would hatch to become the blackbirds that still thrive there today. They enfolded the mountain in a blanket of darkness, and made Pollen Boy and Grasshopper Girl to live within it.[2]

The four sacred mountains rest on the very edge of creation; the Navajo world cannot extend outside them. That is not to say that a person who works, or even lives, beyond the mountains ceases to be Navajo, or that the things he holds sacred are profaned. But it does mean that a vital balance, implicit in the mountains' creation, goes askew. Within the bastion of the sacred mountains, the Navajo man or woman lives in intricate reciprocity with sacred beings—rocks, springs, animals, canyons, mountains, plants—all of which were placed there for his use and benefit. He, in turn, serves as the caretaker of these, the earth's blessings, for the duration of his life. His primary responsibility is to pass along the creation stories and the principles of living in a sacred manner, just as they were given to him by the generations that came before.

Of his bond to the place between the sacred mountains a young Navajo friend once said to me: "The land is our religion, and our religion is our life." Unlike the Judeo-Christian religion, Navajo spirituality is based not upon historical events that occurred in time, but upon the manifestation of spirit in a particular place. The mountains, and countless other sites of myth and legend, are real places on the reservation that sprawl over much of the northeast corner of Arizona, and through parts of western New Mexico and a narrow strip of Utah. To pass by these places, to be in their presence, is to be reminded anew of how they were created, how they came to have their characteristic shape and color, and what has happened around them ever since—not only to the Holy People, but to one's cousins and grandparents as well. Navajo stories, told in the hogan on long, cold winter nights, are necessarily stories about places between the sacred mountains.

Joseph Epes Brown has written:

> Native American experiences of place are infused with mythic themes. These express events of sacred time, which are as real now as at any other time. They are experienced through landmarks in each people's immediate natural environment. ... Further, each being of nature, every particular form of the land, is experienced as the locus of qualitatively differentiated spirit beings, whose individual and collective presence sanctifies and gives meaning to the land in all its details and contours.[3]

The land, quite literally, is alive.

As it is now, so was it intended to be, for First Man and First Woman took care to imbue all of their creations with inner, animating forms. According to Blessingway singer Frank Mitchell, after they had set the sacred mountains in their places, First Woman paused to consider:

> I wonder by what means [the mountains] will be made to be alive! ... Let some beings take standing positions within them! In matter of fact, if there be none standing within them they are but things that lie around without a purpose.[4]

The responsibility of the Holy People is to be the life of the forms in which they themselves dwell. Regarded as actual people with tempers, hungers, and plans, and garbed in the jewels and mists which are their natural features, they are the means by which the Navajo taps for himself the vital essence of the natural world. Holy People, or *diyinii*, are not gods and goddesses; they do not reign over the mountains, or cause weathers and encounters to happen there. Instead they are the mountains, expressions of the Earth's spiritual being, just as a smile and a softening of the eyes is one expression of the human spirit.

First Man's and First Woman's creation of the sacred mountains was a profoundly thoughtful and imaginative act. Paul G. Zolbrod, translator and interpreter of the great Navajo creation story, *Diné bahane'*, has remarked that the mental effort attributed to the progenitors "reflects both observation and thought on the part of those who were instrumental in the composition of the creation cycle."[5] The choice of where to place the mountains, the elaborate details for their adornment, and the final act of invigorating each mountain with beings representative of animals, minerals and plants the Navajos value highly—all were phases of a creative act that was sophisticated, deliberate, and beautiful. First Man and First Woman did not simply picture the mountains in their minds, and then transform the image, whole and complete, to the waiting earth; they gave fullest attention to their work.

Theirs, moreover, was a fully loving act, for along with the mountains, First Man and First Woman also gave to the *Diné*, The People, as the Navajos refer to themselves, the principles for continually recreating beauty, harmony, and fruitfulness in the land between the sacred mountains. In prayer, song, and ceremony, and in his attention to the performance of all daily tasks as meaningful sacred acts, the Navajo communes with the inner forms of the earth, and hence taps the inner forms of beauty within himself.

Perhaps the foundation of the Navajo world view is the people's perception of themselves and their land as indivisible parts of the intricate, vital web that is life. That is why traditional Navajos will always ask permission of a plant before plucking or cutting it, and why they are careful to put things back in place after they have used them, so as to show no trace of their interference. Inherent in the placement of forms on earth was the placement of order. If the order is disturbed, imbalance and disharmony can fester and spread.

Injuries done to the land in the name of economy, progress, or mere recreation cause extreme spiritual distress to the Navajos. Ella Bedonie, who grew up at Coal Mine Mesa, just north of the San Francisco Peaks, has witnessed the scarring of this sacred mountain by the ski trails of Arizona's Snow Bowl. A Navajo would never take a casual outing to a sacred mountain, she said. "The only time you would climb one of the mountains is if you had a special purpose—to gather herbs for ceremonies, or get a jar of water from a sacred spring, or if you really needed a blessing from the Holy People who live there. We do not go to the sacred mountains just to be there. They are our churches and our pharmacies."

For Ella Bedonie, the San Francisco Peaks have always been a source of strength, a presence from which she draws comfort and sustenance in times of need. She would like to take her three children to the top of the mountain one day. They would make offerings and say prayers at sacred sites along the way, and perhaps request permission of the Holy People to take away a small bundle of mountain soil. In times past, many Navajos aspired to make such a pilgrimage just once in their lifetime. Today it is a journey few except the dwindling number of medicine men are likely to take. "My grandfather has gone to the top of the San Francisco Peak," Ella told me. "He said you feel very different at the top of the sacred mountain, very humble and grateful for your life." In the late seventies, she herself traveled to Mount Taylor with a group of Navajos who had banded together to protest—in vain, as it turned out—the uranium mining that had begun to pierce the living flesh of the sacred mountain of the south.

The Navajo does not even have to be in direct sight of the sacred mountains to be ever mindful of their influence upon him. Shimmering around each of the mountains, as smoke wafts around the roofs of the hogan, are particular kinds of light phenomena, also wrought by First Man's medicine bundle. By paying attention to these lights, whose colors correspond to those of the fixed forms below them, the Navajos receive sacred instructions as to the conduct of their day.

Dawn, the white first light of the east, tells the sleeper to awaken, to prepare food that will strengthen him for the day's work ahead. Throughout the daylight hours, every task—weaving, tending flocks, repairing an old pick-up, hauling water—is overseen by the sky-blue light that shines over the sacred mountain of the south. This is the time when all things grow and multiply, not just children, plants and animals, but jewels, fabrics, language and plans as well. It is the time, too, when death, the complement of fruitfulness, can be expected to take its toll.

Twilight, yellow in the western sky, reminds the family to put aside their work and come together again in the hogan, for the evening meal and for reflection on the day's events and accomplishments. Night, black as the jet of the northern mountain, extinguishes light, bringing sleep and dreams.

Thus the mountains are inextricably connected to the cycles of the day, the months, the seasons, and to people's behavior within the cycles. Together they are an ever-present teacher of beauty, balance and the interrelatedness of all things.

Integral to the Navajo attentiveness to balance is the imminent possibility of imbalance. In the time long ago, monsters plagued the Navajo ancestors and upset the harmony that First Man and First Woman had so carefully instilled in the land at the center of the earth. Even after Monster Slayer killed or transformed all the enemies, still the people could not rest. The earth quaked, the mountains weakened, and the failing energy of the land infected the people, who became ill and confused. Not until proper ceremony was observed, and the bodies buried, did harmony return to the land.

Even today, most Navajos regard physical or emotional illness as merely symptomatic of a more deep-seated spiritual ailment that is ultimately linked to the health of the earth. There are many curative ceremonies that can be performed over a person to restore the balance; one ceremony, Blessingway, is preventative.

Blessingway is concerned with the building of the hogan, the formation of the sacred mountains, the placement of the inner forms within all the natural phenomena of earth, and the gathering of the ancient Diné into clans. This great ceremony, which takes place over part of one night, the next morning, and all of the following night, was given to the people by First Man at the time he created the sacred mountains. He told them:

Those songs with which you originated back there [in the previous worlds], all of these, without exception, you will sing. ... This you will somehow decide for yourselves.[6]

In other words, it was the responsibility of the Navajo people themselves to determine how they would use the ceremony which they were actually in the process of receiving at that very moment, as the life of the earth came into being all around them.

Blessingway is sung at the consecration of a hogan, at a young girl's puberty rite, for a soldier returning home from war, or to revitalize the ceremonies of other medicine men. The Blessingway singer himself needs it sung over him every so often. As Frank Mitchell explains in his autobiography:

It is a custom with the People that even though everything may be going all right with a family and nothing is wrong, that family still may say, "Well, let's have a Blessingway to freshen things up, to renew ourselves again." So they do. ... That is the reason it is called the peaceful way, the healing way, the blessing way.[7]

The only religious item that is absolutely essential to the performance of Blessingway is the mountain soil bundle, made of earth that has been gathered from the peaks of each of the four sacred mountains and wrapped in ritually prepared buckskin. Once tied, the mountain soil bundle is never opened or disturbed in any way, never laid down casually or indiscriminately handed about. Ella Bedonie described it as "a representation of everything you have and everything you are, all tied up in that one bundle."

Daniel Deschinney, a Blessingway singer from Oak Springs, in the eastern part of the reservation, pointed out to me that the Navajo word for mountain, *dzitl*, is the root of *adzitl*, strength. Like the mountains themselves, with their male-female pairs of guardians, the concept of strength encompasses a pair of complementary concepts: invincibility and beauty. When a Navajo experiences the sacred mountains' inner forms kindling new strength within himself, Daniel explained, then,

He says, "I am invincible. I am beautified." To be invincible is masculine. To be beautified is feminine. These two concepts together are a powerful entity. There is no strength from only one. Power comes from the interaction between them. When you have strength, you recognize your opportunity, you know what you must do, and you have the grace to do it. Our strengths as Navajos are placed on these landmarks which are the four sacred mountains.

The attainment of adzitl involves an inner, spiritual journeying that is tantamount to making an actual pilgrimage, on foot, to the sacred mountains. Through prayers and songs, a person can make the journey on his own at any time. For a special occasion, and to obtain a concentration of benefits, he can follow the path with a trained guide, a Blesssingway singer.

Every medicine man has his own way of performing the ceremony, and his own interpretation of its intricately connected parts. Moreover, Blessingway changes according to the circumstances, and to the person for whom it is being sung. "When you are a child and you listen to the medicine man tell about the creation of the sacred mountains," Daniel said, "you see those mountains. Then you grow up and you become more sophisticated. You begin to see the nuances in the prayers. Today, my image of the mountains is something deeper. It is that inner strength." He added, "It's all a process. It's about learning how to calm your nerves, and how to *have* nerve!"

To be Diné is to be supremely conscious of one's relation to the ultimate reality that is the place between the four sacred mountains. Navajos and Holy People, who embody the inner forms of all the natural features in this place, are jointly engaged in perpetuating the welfare of the earth. When the people are strong, making offerings at sacred places, attentive to their sacred responsibilities, then the Holy People increase in beauty and invincibility. They, in turn, bless and fortify the Navajos. And so the process is ongoing. To go to the sacred mountains, in prayer, song, or ceremony, is to acquire the means for activating harmony on earth. This divine gift the Navajo carries forth into his daily life, like a mountain soil bundle.

Notes:

1. Leland Wyman, *Blessingway* (Tucson: University of Arizona Press, 1970), 113.

2. There are as many accounts of the formation of the sacred mountains as there are Navajo people to relate them. This one is taken primarily from Paul G. Zolbrod, *Diné bahane': The Navajo Creation Story* (Albuquerque: University of New Mexico Press, 1984), 84–89, and from personal conversation with Navajo people.

3. Joseph Epes Brown, *The Spiritual Legacy of the American Indian* (New York: Crossroad, 1985), 51.

4. Wyman, 357.

5. Zolbrod, 362.

6. Wyman, 112.

7. Frank Mitchell, *Navajo Blessingway Singer* (Tucson: University of Arizona Press, 1978), 218.

Parabola
Volume: 2.3
Cosmology

The Spiritual Landscape

Elaine Jahner

Wakan-Tanka, the Great Spirit. This one word is known by innumerable persons who are not even aware that its tribal origin is Lakota. Although the word is widely known, its meaning, like that of *Yahweh* in the Old Testament, remains a mystery that reverent members of the Lakota tribe continue to meditate on. One Lakota asked older members of the tribe about the meaning and origin of the word. He received a story as his answer.

> *Way back many years ago, two men went walking. It was on the prairies. As they walked, they decided, "Let's go up the hill way towards the west; let's see what's over the hill."*

So they walked and they came to the top of this hill and they looked west and it was the same. Same thing as they saw before; there was nothing. They just kept going like that, all day and it was the same. They came to a big hill and there was another big hill further back. Finally they stopped and they said, 'You know, this is Wakan-Tanka.'"

This story needs to be situated within the context of the Lakota worldview, but once it is, its nuances of meaning seem almost endless. In the years since I first heard it I have come to appreciate a few of its many dimensions and, for me, these revolve around three different features of the episode: 1) the searchers are exploring the *physical* universe when they sense the mysterious depth of the spiritual one; 2) the search is not an individual one—*two* people wander toward the west; 3) the searchers' response to their new insight is an awed response to mystery.

Anyone who has lived in the American plains region knows something about the way in which the landscape can shape modes of thinking and feeling. There are the extending lands where occasionally buttes rise from the level stretches and seem sharp, assertive definitions of form. Then there are the winds, those permanent presences that vary in intensity and direction but are always there. All combine to demand a response from inhabitants that require them to go beyond the trivial. It takes time and courage for people to find themselves at home in such an environment, and perhaps only the American Indians have succeeded not only in feeling at home but also in learning to see in it a set of symbols for a personal and cultural self-understanding that makes them genuinely present to the environment. By means of their basic cultural symbols and the corresponding social organization, the Lakota have taught that the physical world is spirit seen from without and that the spiritual world is the physical viewed from another dimension. During the two hundred years since the Lakota moved from the woodlands into the plains, they have found in the area's natural rhythms and demands an effective design for their own lives and movements. Their sensitive accommodation to the environment is an essential chapter in the story of human efforts to relate creatively to the rest of nature.

The Lakota worldview facilitates presence to oneself, to nature and to the community; Lakota religious symbols represent ways of thinking that dramatize that mode of presence. To understand the basis of the imagery we have to turn to the ancient sacred stories—the myths. Fragments of the sacred story have been preserved in oral tradition and in the fieldwork notes of various scholars who sought to record Lakota traditions. J. R. Walker's unpublished manuscripts contain parts of a Lakota creation myth that show the intimate relation between the physical and the spiritual worlds. This powerfully moving story deserves extensive quotation, especially since it is not yet generally available. In this version, Creation begins with Inyan, the rock, an effective symbol of power in a plains setting.

Inyan (Rock) had no beginning for he was when there was no other. His spirit was Wakan-Tanka (The Great Mystery), and he was the first of the superior gods. Then he was soft and shapeless like a cloud, but he had powers and was everywhere. Han was then, but she is not a being; she is only the black of darkness.

Inyan longed to exercise his powers, but could not do so for there was no other that he might use his powers upon. If there were to be another, he must create it of that which he must take from himself, and he must give to it a spirit and a portion of his blood. As much of his blood as would go from him, so much of his powers would go with it, for his powers were in his blood, and his blood was blue. He decided to create another as a part of himself so that he might keep control of all the powers.

To do this he took from himself that which he spread around himself in the shape of a great disk whose edge is where there can be no beyond. This disk he named Maka (earth). He gave to Maka a spirit that is Maka-akan (Earth-goddess). She is the second of the superior gods, but she is a part of Inyan.

To create Maka, Inyan took so much from himself that he opened his veins, and all his blood flowed from him so that he shrank and became hard and powerless. As his blood flowed from him, it became blue waters, which are the waters upon the earth. But the powers cannot abide in waters, and, when the blood of Inyan became the waters, the powers separated themselves from it and assumed another shape. This other being took the form of a great blue dome whose edge is at, but not upon, the edge of Maka.

Inyan, Maka, and the waters are material or that which can be held together, and they are the world; the blue dome above the world, which is tanka (the Sky), is not material, but spirit. Nagi Tanka (Supreme-god or Sky-god) is the great Spirit who is all powerful and the source of all power, and his name is Skan (Almighty or Most Holy).

Thus in the beginning there were Inyan, Maka, and the waters, all of which are the world, and Nagi Tanka, named Skan, the blue dome which is the sky above the world. The world is matter and has no powers except those bestowed by Nagi Tanka.

When these powers assumed one shape, a voice spoke, saying, 'I am the source of energy, I am Skan.'

This was the beginning of the third superior god, who is superior to all because he is spirit. This was the beginning before there was time. This was the beginning of the world and of the sky over the world.[1]

When we study this version of a creation myth, we see how it is that a journey of exploration into the physical world can be a meditation on the interdependence of consciousness and the environment, an interdependence that is manifested in the course of life itself. The myth defines the purpose of life as a progression from unity, through existential encounters with the meaning of diversity, toward renewed experience of unity. The physical universe flows from Inyan's need to exercise power, so Creation begins because the very nature of power requires relationship and sharing. The initial exercise of power reveals the contrast between materiality and spirituality and shows that power's mode of functioning is through reciprocity. Materiality is represented by the earth and spirituality by the Sky—one feminine and one masculine. Walker translates *Skan* as "Almighty or Most Holy." A far more accurate translation is "Movement." "I am the source of energy, I am Skan." Movement seen as creative power and its relationship to the Rock, an image of movement held in abeyance, is an important motif in the Lakota worldview. When Ella Deloria tried to validate the Walker version of the myth by collecting other versions in oral tradition, she heard the following comment, "there is only one thing like that which I have heard; it runs thus: It is belief in the God of Movement. That thing, they say, is stone ... And that Stone was all-powerful, like nothing else; so whenever the race had to pursue anything very difficult, then faith was placed on It in prayer."[2]

The dialectic between movement and rest is a major element of Sioux sacred story but it is not the only important cultural concept articulated in the myth. Light and Darkness (metaphorically related to knowledge and ignorance in Sioux ritual) are shown to be aspects of the same reality. "Skan divided Han (darkness) into two halves—one remained darkness ... From the other Skan created the light (Anp)." The Lakota considered movement in nature and learned to see in it an imperative pattern for their social organization that derived its authority from the belief that it was basic to the nature and structure of the universe itself. It is in this context that we can see the importance of my concentration on the second aspect of the story that introduces this essay—the exploration of the universe is not an individual one; *two* people wander toward the west. The camp circle and the surrounding environment are not mere juxtaposed elements of space; they are coordinated patterns of life. The response to the movements of nature is to coordinate human movements so that they correspond to the universal pattern, and the effort to understand that pattern is a shared effort. The Walker version of the myth justifies the close link between social life and environment.

The gods in Lakota sacred story established their patterns of movement in specific spatial domains only gradually; and the story of the four winds establishing their directions constitutes a major part of the Walker collection of narratives. Tate, the wind, had five sons; Yata was the first-born, then came Iya, Yanpa, Okaga, and Yum. The youngest did not grow strong and brave but remained like a child. All the sons lived with Tate, their father until Woope (later represented in Lakota story as White Buffalo Woman) came to them with a message from Wakan-Tanka about their tasks.

> *His message is this. Now there is no direction in the world, and your four sons must each fix a direction, and establish it so that it will forever be known. When each one has fixed a direction, it shall be his living place. The directions must be on the edge of the world, and each an equal distance from the one next to it. They must divide the edge of the world into four equal parts, and one part shall belong to each of them. They must go around the world on its edge. From when they start on this journey to when they finish it will be the fourth time, the year.*

The events that occur as the brothers establish the four directions and the fourth time are prototypes for Sioux ritual and for heroic action. The first part of their journey takes the brothers to the west where Wakinyan lives, the powerfully beneficent, winged god. Only Iya, the second born, dares to demand to look at Wakinyan, and the sight causes him to become a heyoka, a "contrary," who does and says everything in reverse, because this is the only way to approach the creative force. Thus Iya gains the right to establish himself in the first direction and Yata loses his birthright. Yata has to establish his place in the north from whence he continues to send his cold, sometimes cruel winds from his loveless home. The east is left to Yanpa and the south to the warm, generous

Okaga, the one loved by Woope. In all Sioux ritual, the four directions are greeted with the usual order for the greeting being the same as the myth's order for the establishment of directions.

The positions of the four directions make the world a mandala and every place of ceremony a center of the world. This idea is visualized in the fundamental image of Sioux religion, the image of the crossroads within a circle, an image that still retains its expressive content and power because its immense structuring power has helped the Lakota people reorganize their lives in a reservation environment. The road from the south to the north is the red road of growth and advancement that the people try to follow while the road from west to east is the black road of change and disruption that inevitably crosses the red road at times. The circle that contains the crossroads has a wide range of cultural references and all other major symbols are related to the circle image.

Joseph Flying By, a Standing Rock Sioux, explained the image and its range of meaning in the following way:

> ... the sun from the east and the moon from the west are all symbolic of a circle. Likewise, our Lakota people are also symbolic of a strong circle. Whenever you see our people camp, it is always in a circle. When they sit and have a parley or in a council of many fires, the pattern of their sitting is always in a circle. From this circle of our Lakota people comes the extended family. Whether they are cousins, brothers, sisters, or distant cousins, they are still bound by love, honor, respect, and strong ties which symbolize a circle.

As a symbol of social unity, the circle receives consistent emphasis because its reference is extended to the way social organization is articulated. The circle refers to the organization of the camp and of the tipi. Within the tipi, all space and all positions were meaningful and it represented a plan of order that directed the family's movements. The central area of the tipi held the place of honor for guests. The area to the right was allocated to family members and the left central portion was for guests undeserving of the place of honor. Nearest to the left of the tipi's doorway was the area where the old people begging for food could rest. The pattern of order that directed all movement within the tipi helped the family to visualize it as the cosmos in miniature where movement had to follow culturally prescribed patterns. In commenting on the importance of the tipi as a microcosm, Joseph Brown has said, "Since for every Sioux, every tipi is the world in an image, the fire at the center represents Wakan-Tanka within the world."[3] In such a dwelling it is easy to integrate images of the universe with images related to one's personal life. The great myths and legends take on concrete meaning when the fire that draws the attention of all participants in the story-telling session represents Wakan-Tanka.

The camp circle also had its prescribed movements. Each tipi had its place within the circle and thus it automatically identified the role of its inhabitants relative to that of other members of the group. As a family gained in prestige, a tipi could be moved but whenever a family could not contribute to the group's welfare, its tipi had to be moved outside the circle.

Because the Sioux visualized every level of social organization as a circle that unified members of the group and marked out the circumference of a prescribed pattern of movement, they could think of their personal identity as a function of the particular place occupied in the circles of social organization. But no one's place was ever static. All of life's activities caused movement among the various circles of being. The one inescapable movement that every person had to submit to was the constant progression of time. The Lakota used spatial imagery to articulate their concept of time. Black Elk has explained this idea.

> *Is not the south the source of life, and does not the flowering stick truly come from there? And does not man advance from there toward the setting sun of his life? And does he not arrive, if he lives, at the source of light and understanding which is in the east? Then does he not return to where he began, to his second childhood, there to give back his life to all life and his flesh to the earth whence it came?[4]*

As the Lakota questioned the forces that govern the natural world, they found symbols, images and patterns of meaning that gave them a relationship to immense creative energies. They could see that the macrocosm and the microcosm stay alive in the same ways. But there was and is still the sense that much has yet to be learned. There is still the sense that the ways of the Great Spirit are a mystery that compels human beings to continue their search in both the physical and the spiritual worlds. And this search for the future brings us to my third point about the introductory narrative: the searchers' response to their new insight is an awed response to mystery. If one gives one's entire being over to exploring the patterns and possibilities in the environment, then new possibilities are always in the making and one is caught up in a forward momentum just as the two characters in the introductory narrative are. They keep going on and on just to see what might be beyond the next hill. This is the restlessness in the search for the unknown that gives creative strength to a person and to a culture. But such restlessness can lead to anarchy as well as to new life for the individual and the group, so the Lakota found ways to safeguard the search for the new without destroying the structure of the old. The individual was taught to penetrate farther and farther into the incomprehensible and marvelous mystery of both the physical and spiritual worlds but always to come back to the group with his or her finding so that the group could integrate the new knowledge with the old.

If we look at the vision quest as a way of responding to the mystery that must intrude upon every individual life, then we can see that the Lakota way of relating the known and the unknown makes the image of two men moving from hill to hill, horizon to horizon, a symbol of every Lakota's journey through life. The vision quest was a journey to the inner, spiritual landscape that showed the questor the direction to follow in the travels through the physical landscape. "Hanblecheyapi" or "Crying for a Vision" is among the most ancient Lakota rites. As with all of the ceremonies, some of the details varied according to time and place, but the essentials of the rite were part of the life of all the Lakota bands. The person who wanted a vision sought the guidance and instruction of a holy man who tested the strength of character and the knowledge of the person about spiritual matters. Just before leaving camp, the seeker underwent a purification ceremony as protection against evil influences. The actual crying for a dream occurred in isolation usually atop a high butte or hill. Upon arrival at the chosen place, the seeker ritually prepared an area of earth making it a "center of the earth." The person remained on or near the place until a dream came or a mentor advised giving up the quest. Generally the quest included the gift of some object representing a spirit that would be the visionary's helper throughout life.

The events that occurred in isolation definitely enhanced the individual's prestige and they were believed to be evidence of unique powers. But the individual could not actualize even the unique powers of the dream without the help of the community. In most bands, the dreamer had to enact the dream for the tribe before it could become efficacious. In this way the powers of the dream were made part of the general economy of spiritual power and the person was dramatically reminded that he acted on behalf of the group.

The vision gave its seeker the courage to face the mysterious dimensions of life with the calm foreknowledge that comes from a personal relationship to mystery and an inner point of departure for the continuing journey of exploration that is life itself. The light of the vision illumines some of the night of uncertainty for both the individual and the group. Or, to use another set of images, the vision is a way of climbing a hill so high that the visionary has a perspective from which to view the many lower hills stretching toward the horizon of death.

Much has changed in Lakota life since the establishment of reservations, but the people have not lost the sense that their spiritual journey is linked with their travels through their plains environment. In the Lakota world, the west is a direction of change and occasional destruction. Perhaps the brief story about Wakan-Tanka can even be interpreted as a comment on the last hundred years of history. Using different words, of course, dozens of leaders have said to their people, "Let's go up the hill towards the west; let's see what's over the hill." What they have seen has been a mystery that could have crushed people with less spiritual strength. But the Lakota go on climbing hill after hill in order to see what is over the horizon.

Notes:

1   J. R. Walker, "Legends of the Oglala Sioux," American Philosophical Society, Phila.delphia. Franz Boas Collection of American Indian Linguistics; 15. Freeman Guide 824, Film 372, Reel 1.

2. Ella Deloria, "Dakota Commentary on Walker's Texts." American Philosophical Society, Philadelphia. Franz Boas Collection of American Indian Linguistics; Freeman Guide 824, Film 372.

3. Joseph Brown, *The Sacred Pipe* (Norman, 1953), 23.

4. John Neihardt, *Black Elk Speaks* (Lincoln, 1961), 203-204.

Parabola
Volume: 5.1
Old Ones

I Climb the Black Rock Mountain

Leslie Silko

I climb the black rock mountain
    stepping from day to day
    silently.
I smell the wind for my ancestors
    pale blue leaves
    crushed wild mountain smell.
Returning
    up the gray stone cliff
    where I descended
    a thousand years ago.
Returning to faded black stone
    where mountain lion laid down with deer.
It is better to stay up here
    watching wind's reflection
    in tall yellow flowers.
The old ones who remember me are gone
    the old songs are all forgotten
    and the story of my birth.
How I danced in snow-frost moonlight
    distant stars to the end of the Earth,
When I swam away
    in freezing mountain water
    narrow mossy canyon tumbling down
    out of the mountain

out of deep canyon stone
down
the memory
spilling out
into the world.

Parabola
Volume: 19.2
Twins

THE WAYS OF A NAVAJO WARRIOR

Trebbe Johnson

Several years ago, I met a Navajo elder, Roberta Blackgoat, whose traditional life in the high desert country of
northeastern Arizona had been thrown into upheaval by
a federal law ordering her and thousands of other Navajos off their land. Roberta was determined to fight the
law. She did so in two ways: first, by refusing to capitu-
late to pressures to "relocate" and, second, by speaking
publicly about how the loss of the land would destroy
the spirit of the Navajo people. Thus, for days or weeks
at a time, she would stay on the land, practicing the ways
she had learned from her grandmother—herding sheep,
weaving their wool into rugs whose patterns reflect the
forms of earth and sky, going out to remote valleys and
mountaintops to gather plants for ceremonial use, and
starting each day with prayers and an offering of sacred
corn pollen to the sun. Then, when necessary, she would
get into her pickup and leave the reservation to do the
things political activism demanded. She picketed in
front of federal agencies; spoke, in her eloquent, if halt-
ing, English at college rallies; posed for photographs in
her long skirt, velveteen blouse and silver and turquoise
jewelry; and gave interviews to reporters.

Like many non-Indians, I imagined that her attempt
to straddle two such different worlds must be difficult,
and I asked her once if she minded being away from

home so often. Or, I suggested, maybe she enjoyed the excitement of travel, the new sights and people, the sympathetic attention to her cause. Her reply I found cryptic at the time.

"Our Creator has planted us here on this earth, where we could use this land for generation to generation on down, so that's how we should take care of the land. My roots is way down deep and can't be pulled out."

I assumed I had posed one of those questions an outsider is not supposed to ask and that Roberta, wishing not to be impolite, was shifting the subject away from herself and back to the issue in general. Later, however, I came to understand that she had answered me pointedly. What she was telling me was that defending her homeland for future generations was a sacred responsibility and that her way of doing so entailed no contradiction whatsoever. To accomplish her task she needed to be a fighter of the enemy and a protector of the home, two warriors in one, and willingly, she assumed both roles.

In taking this approach to a long, difficult task, she had a pair of formidable role models—the holy Twins who killed the monsters that ravaged the land and whose story is part of the Navajo cosmology. The Twins are the sons of Changing Woman, the primary holy being of the Navajos and the personification of the eternal cycle of aging and rejuvenation in all things on earth. By most accounts, the boys had two fathers, the sun and the water of a stream. Drawn by the sensuous touch of each of these natural forces on her skin, Changing Woman lies in their midst and, opening her legs to their potent energy, becomes pregnant. In some versions of the myth, it is Changing Woman who makes love with the sun, while her sister, White Shell Woman, conceives by the water. In nearly all versions, however, Changing Woman gradually emerges as the sole mother of the boys, and the Sun as their father. In any case, the boys are always known as the Twins, for their paths are entwined from the moment they are born.

The boys mature quickly. Two holy beings, Talking God and Rain God, who midwifed them to life and fashioned beautiful cradleboards for them out of cosmic elements, now come to give them a rigorous physical training. Every day the gods push them to run farther and faster, to endure fatigue, cold and aching muscles, and to build their strength. The holy people's method is a blend of encouragement and good-natured teasing; clearly they are grooming these children for important work.

As soon as they've been deemed hardy and fit, the boys start asking questions about their father and about the world beyond the lodge. Their mother puts them off. Ever since Navajos began to inhabit this world, they have been plagued by monsters. For instance, there is a Monster Who Kicks People off Cliffs, another who Kills With His Eyes. Big Giant is so huge the hills quake when he walks and when he is thirsty he can drain a lake. But even though Changing Woman wants to keep the boys safe at home, she, too, is obviously aware of their destiny, for she makes them bows and arrows so they can go out hunting.[1] The boys return from their hunting trips full of curiosity about the animals and birds they have met, but so great is the danger throughout the land that Changing Woman suspects even familiar presences like Coyote and Raven of being spies for the monsters that stalk and devour people.

Eventually the Twins meet Spider Woman, who tells them who their father is and counsels them how to reach him. They set off eagerly and, using Spider Woman's wiles to overcome the obstacles they encounter, such as some malicious cactus plants that hurl knives at them, they arrive at the Sun's sky-top home. Rather than embrace them as his sons or cast them out as frauds, the Sun insists that the boys undergo several trials, all of which they pass impressively thanks to the prompting of the Wind, who whispers ploys and crafty answers in their ears. Finally, the sun is convinced that it is the duty of the Twins to kill the monsters, and he outfits them with resplendent armor and weapons—a helmet and shirt of flint scales; deadly arrows made of chain lightning, sheet lightning, sunbeam, and rainbow; and two stone knives.

And streaks of fire and lightning reflected from their every limb and joint once they were dressed for battle. Indeed, they looked like warriors.[2]

Now their father has one more test for them. He takes them high above the earth, to the place where noon shines down, and asks them to point to the place on that vast landscape where their own home lies. In their responses they show that, although they are both warriors, they each have distinct and individual strengths and weaknesses. The older brother is unable to recognize any landmarks whatsoever from such a distance. The younger brother, however, hears once again the voice of the Wind in his ear and confidently names all the sacred mountains and rivers that define the homeland. Now the Sun is truly satisfied that these are his sons.

When the two young warriors confront their first monster, Big Giant, it is the older brother's turn to show his prowess. He mimics Big Giant's queries, baiting and taunting it with brash cleverness. Together the boys kill the creature and cut off its scalp, and then, to solemnize this first act of courage that will make the land safe for all people, they bestow names on each other. The oldest will henceforth be called Monster Slayer; the youngest is named He Who Cuts the Life Out of the Enemy.

Changing Woman is jubilant about the death of the monster, and joins her sons in a victory dance, but she can't help urging them to quit while they're ahead. Monster Slayer, however, is through with caution. "I want to continue fighting the monsters," he declares. Together the brothers hold a council to determine what should be done next. They make two prayer sticks and attach a sunbeam to each one, then place the sticks in a turquoise dish. The prayer sticks, which have a prophetic quality, apparently reveal some aspect of the divine plan at this time, for Monster Slayer says:

> My brother, I shall go alone to fight [the next monster]. Mean-while, you stay here and watch the holy [prayer sticks]. If a sunbeam should light either one, you will know that I am in danger. If that should happen, you must hasten to find me and to help me. Other-wise, know that I am safe and do nothing but wait here and guard the others.[3]

No doubt the Wind knew, when he selected the younger Twin to recount the holy places of his homeland to the Sun, that the role of the guardian has always been his. And so, with this compact, the brothers tacitly acknowledge that, although their responsibilities in safeguarding their home will differ from now on, each will embody something of the other's role, just as each of the curling shapes in the yin and the yang symbols contains the eye of the other. Through the prayer sticks, a kind of sacred channel between them, the younger brother will follow the fighter's path even as he remains at home, while the older brother remains in good care at home, though he wanders far and faces great danger. From this point on, in most versions of the story, we hear almost nothing about the younger Twin.[4] It is as if he has become part of the landscape, while the myth follows the exploits of his brother.

Monster Slayer ventures forth six more times to destroy various terrifying enemies and to bring about important transformations. Each time, he carries a piece of the creature back home, as proof that he has killed it. The claws, blood, hair, or bones of the monster turn into prominent landforms, and he changes either the monster or its offspring into something beneficial. According to the myth, for example, Monster Slayer is to thank for turning a fledgling Rock Bird Monster into the owl, bird of prophecy, and an offspring of the monsters Who Kill With their Eyes into the whippoorwill, whose nighttime song is a promise of dawn. A truly visionary hero, Monster Slayer understands that in order to bring about peace in a troubled place it is not enough just to destroy the enemy. Only by incorporating into their daily lives a new aspect of what was formerly feared and hated can the community accept both the power of the enemy and their own power to defeat it. What is gained on the journey away from home belongs, in a vital way, *to* the home, which holds the place of the journeyer during his absence and welcomes his safe return.

In the midst of these journeys, another, more subtle transformation occurs. When Monster Slayer returns home after one of his exploits, his twin tells him that he has watched over the prayer sticks "every moment of your absence," and once saw one of them burst into flame. The fire went out quickly, however, he continues, so he realized that his brother probably did not need rescuing. What is significant here is that it is not a boy named He Who Cuts the Life Out of the Enemy who relates this news, but one called, suddenly and inexplicably, Born for Water. No longer known by what he achieved in battle, he now has a name that tokens the manner of his conception and his relationship to the land he looks after.

When the Twins next visit the Sun, their father accords both of them the respect due to warriors. Changing Woman now lives in the west with the Sun, while the Twins make their home at a place in the

San Juan Mountains where two rivers, sometimes believed to be the Los Pinos and the San Juan, run together. It is said that people still go there to this day to pray, not for fertility or health, but for help in overcoming enemies.

The Navajo word for monster is *nayéé*, a term anthropologist John R. Farella argues is more properly translated as "anything that gets in the way of a person living his life."[5] The "monsters" that contemporary Navajos confront are usually not external entities, but inner fears, worries, and preoccupations that skew a balanced life. Some early ethnographers and anthropologists who made their way to the southwest noticed the attention Navajo people paid to the complementary aspects of things, and took it for granted that this was akin to the Judeo-Christian preoccupation with the polarities of good and evil. In truth, however, what Navajos aim for is not the conquest of "evil" and the triumph of "good," but balance, a flexible interplay between two mutually dependent, living principles, such as male/female, moist/dry, warm/cool. The balance between such pairs—in essence, the partnership between twins—is central to every aspect of Navajo life. Never static or complete, the two sides bend and flow. In the myth, the home, the human heart, first one takes precedence, and then the other. And within each member of the pair is a smaller pair and so on, endlessly and in all things.

Monster Slayer's transformation of the warlike power of the monsters into serviceable, domestic attributes mirrors the complementarity that the two warriors have with each other. Monster Slayer is a part of Born for Water, Born for Water is embodied in Monster Slayer. Today, Roberta Blackgoat knows that it is as crucial for a hero to be at home, protecting the boundaries, performing daily tasks, and offering up prayers for any community monster slayers who work away from home, as it is to be a monster slayer—taunting the enemy, boldly spearing it, and taming a part of it to bring back to the community. And so, for her, it is no betrayal of tradition to safeguard her home by leaving it periodically to go out into the world and confront her enemy in public. Nor is she retreating from the fight when she stays at home to attend to more traditional work. She summons the twins, the fighter and protector, as her allies, knowing she needs them both to be complete and that she must be complete to protect her homeland.

Notes:

1. There are as many versions of this myth as there are Navajo storytellers. The one I use primarily from this point on is from Paul G. Zolbrod, *Diné bahane: The Navajo Creation Story* (Albuquerque: University of New Mexico Press, 1984), 179–278. Zolbrod's translation is a beautiful and exhaustively researched blend of past texts and firsthand interviews with Navajo elders.

2. *Ibid.*

3. *Ibid.*

4. One Blessingway singer, River Junction Curly, tells a version of the story in which the younger Twin, seeing one of the prayer sticks burst into flame, goes out to help his brother overcome the Traveling Rock monster. See Leland Wyman, *Blessingway* (Tucson: University of Arizona Press, 1987), 568–69.

5. John R. Farella, *The Main Stalk: A Synthesis of Navajo Philosophy* (Tucson: University of Arizona Press, 1984), 51.

Parabola
Volume: 5.4
Woman

A Woman's Ways

An Interview with Judy Swamp

Judy Swamp is the wife of Jake Swamp, a Mohawk leader at Akwesasne.

The traditional Mohawks, people of the Longhouse, see themselves as a separate nation, by treaty, under no other jurisdiction than that of their own council and their own constitution, the Great Law of Peace (dating from the fifteenth century or earlier) of the Iroquois Confederacy, of which the Mohawks are one of the original Five Nations. Their chiefs, men, are chosen and advised (and can be deposed) by certain women who have attained the position of Clan Mothers. The "elected" or "tribal" people, on the other hand, recognize and cooperate with the laws and governmental agencies of New York State and the United States, and their Tribal Council is elected, American fashion, by political processes and popular vote—a custom abhorrent to the traditional Iroquois. The two groups on the reservation are often in conflict over the values that govern their lives and their lands. The Longhouse people do not wish to impose their traditional ways on anyone else, but they want to be allowed to practice them in peace.

The Mohawk reservation straddles the St. Lawrence River near the head of the seaway, one part in New York State, one part in Canada. That river is now lined with industry—aluminum and chemical plants, paper mills and the like—and its waters are heavily polluted with fluorides, mercury, and PCBs.

Judy's existence is informed by something which, as she says, can't always be described in English. It is something we saw, felt, and were deeply struck by, when we visited Akwesasne: perhaps "respect" is the nearest word to express the relationship that is evident there between man and woman and child and earth; something connected with a sense of the sacred in all things. The potency of this respect, and its almost total absence from our society, can only be appreciated when it is seen in operation. All around the camp people sit together in twos and threes, talking, often laughing: the young people asking older ones for comfort and advice; men consulting with women; and everyone listening to everyone else.

The women play a special and vital role. They are guardians of the home and the children, the support and counsel of their husbands and friends; they carry the lineage of the tribe; they maintain the social and moral order. They are the caretakers of life. And the Mohawk people see themselves in general (and very specifically) as caretakers of the earth and its progeny. They are responsible, they say, for keeping this earth sacred and safe for seven generations to come. This seemingly impossible concept enters all their practical thinking and planning. For the Mohawks, it would be equally impossible to reject the evident fact that the earth is our mother, and that we and our children are part of an inescapable relationship.

As they describe it, they are all only ordinary people ("We don't hold anyone high," says Jake Swamp) whose varying qualities make them more or less suited to a particular task, whether that of chief, Clan Mother, or a member of the community. Ordinary people—with an extraordinary sense of themselves and their place and their duty on earth. We offer a talk with an extraordinary ordinary woman, Judy Swamp.

Judy Swamp: Our ways are quite different from the ways of the white women. White people would consider us as "liberated" women. But it's not that we've been liberated. It's just that we've always had rights. We've always had an equal voice in the Council. And we have our own Women's Council.

We have talked with many different women, but they don't get the full meaning of how it is with us. There are different words that I know in Mohawk that I couldn't translate into English, and a lot of the meaning of what we are as Indian women is just lost. We have our homemaking and living—the way we are in this community. We don't just look out for our own; we have to look out for all the children. When they need help, like when they're eating, you just take the time and help them out. If a young girl or guy has problems, you sit down with them and try to sort out their feelings and get them back on the right path. And that's always been our way, not just of our Clan Mother, but of our older women. As for myself, being the wife of a chief, I'm not any higher in position; it's just that I feel at times that I have to be more outgoing when I have to meet with people. It is not a very heavy position. It is more like being a mother to all of them.

Parabola: *That's quite a job!*

JS: People come in here, the young people and say, "Hi, Ma." It's rather funny. It doesn't embarrass me; it's just that that's who I am to them. They're mine. There are a lot of young people here that don't have their parents with them. They come to me to talk.

P: *If it weren't for the encampment, and you were living in your own house, would you still see all the young people the way you do now?*

JS: I would, because that has been my position even before my husband took his position as a chief. That is me. I have been to a lot of other reserves, and that's always been my concern, the young. I have noticed how they go astray with liquor and drugs, and other things that go against our ways. I've always felt it was my place to try to help.

You can't treat all the young alike. You have to treat each in terms of his own ways and in terms of his own feelings. At one time I thought that you could discipline children all the same. It's not like that. Some are sensitive, and some will only get straightened out by getting a good stick after them once in a while. It's the last thing you would want to do to them, but after so many lectures you get to the point where you have to get that twig, one that doesn't break easy, but is very skinny, and use it!

P: *How many children do you have?*

JS: I've got seven. They are 17, 16, and 13. And there's the middle one, he's 10. Then I have like a small ladder.

[Laughter]

It wasn't so hard bringing them up, because I found that just when I got used to not having them, I would have a new one, and start all over again.

I'll never forget the day that I came home from a convention in Maine to find that things had changed in our home: I sensed Jake wanted to talk. I thought that something happened. So I was unpacking, and about one o'clock in the morning, he finally hit me with a bombshell: "I adopted three kids while you were gone."

If any person ever felt like packing right up and walking out that door …

[Laughter]

… and he said it as calm as anything! I couldn't argue when he said, "I have so much faith in you, that you will accept and respect my decision when I'd said I'd take them." Then what can you say?

[Laughter]

P: *He's a very smart man!*

JS: How can you turn your back on that?

The father was white; they were left by the mother to the grandmother. When they started coming to the Longhouse, the grandmother booted them out of her house, and they were of our clan, so we took them. It worked out, I guess; the mother eventually took them back.

P: *You said something about a Women's Council. Is there a regular official council of women?*

JS: We have a Women's Council if things need to be organized or if just too many problems arise concerning our young or the children, the small ones. All the women get together, even the very young.

P: *From what age up?*

JS: There is really no age limit. We've had a Council where there was an eight-year-old that spoke out. It is very sad that the young look at life knowing that there is not much of a future for them. They are being sent to white schools from the time that they are three or four years old, and by the time they get out of there, when they are past high school, their interest is not where it should be. It has already gone to the point where they have to learn all over again to try to reach out. They don't know what they want; they have to learn their true identity. That is something they are not taught in school. They have language classes, culture classes, but the one thing they are not allowed is to be aware of the Great Law, which is our true form of government. The schools want them to be taught their culture, but to them that's making baskets, bead work, and the like. The children are not told of their own history.

P: *And their own language?*

JS: There are quite a few that know their own language. All my own children have an understanding of it.

P: *But they learn that at home, don't they, not in school?*

JS: There are a lot that don't know it at all, and are not taught at home. It has only been lately that the awareness has come back that we should teach our young their language, and it came from the young themselves; it didn't come from the parents.

"Who am I?" is a big question today. "Who am I?" And you can't answer them. It has been so long that that identity has been taken over. It is hard for them. They have to learn it for themselves before they can teach their own. It's sad; it's really sad.

I was asked one time to teach our language in one of the high schools, and I refused, because I can't even get my own children, except for the older ones, to speak it. They understand it fully, but they won't speak it. I didn't feel right being in a school trying to teach other Indian children their language when my own wouldn't even speak it.

P: *What keeps you going in the face of all this? When you say an eight-year-old stands up and asks a question you can't answer? When you say that they see no hope?*

JS: They lose a lot of faith as they're growing up. But a big problem with the young often happens when they want to go back to the traditional way, and the parents won't allow it. They allow them a lot of other things; they are too lenient. And yet there is one thing they fight against; their own background.

I asked Jake the other night, "When our Great Law was made, did you ever think that it could be for all mankind?" All he said was, "If the Law is so great, how can it harm *any*one? How can it do damage if people go by it? The only thing is that the others can't interfere with us in our ceremonies, how we conduct *our*selves." He sees that people are human, that we're all paying for other people's mistakes. We can't be prejudiced in a way to say, "Well, you're white. Get over there!" And yet we can't live together because when we do, it gets all mixed up and there is confusion and hurting the little ones that are born out of it.

P: *Do you think that being in the encampment has made relationships stronger?*

JS: I think in a sense, yes. It wasn't easy at first, different people, different ideas. Your own ways are not always necessarily the best. There are different ways even in cooking and sewing.

Like everybody thinks that there's only one way of cooking beans, and we found out different when we got the women together to talk about it when it came to planning meals!

P: *There isn't too much food raised on the reservations now, I suppose.*

JS: With all the pollution in the water and the earth from the paper and aluminum plants, the people tend to keep away from it. But the young ones are coming back to it—raising their own food. Younger people have come in and tried to have what we call "nation gardens"; they have different gardens set up in different places and everybody just goes and works. It's been done for the last few years.

If we had the land, we would have more animals. We tend to shy away from raising them, not knowing whether they will live. Whole litters of pigs died, and we never connected it with the pollution. None of us even thought of bringing a vet in and having them checked out. It wasn't until the next year when the same thing happened again, when a litter of what looked like a healthy brood of nine, just all went like nothing again. When we started back up again, we see what happens: they miscarry.

P: *Is that a big worry for human mothers too?*

JS: Yes. They say, "If this is what is happening to the animals, what of our children?" We've got one ourselves that has a skin problem, developed it one day. I mean it wasn't something that came gradually; it just happened one day. And we've had a problem with it going on about three years. I treated it at first with Indian medicine, and it helped, but winter came, and we couldn't get to the plant that we were using, so I had to go back to a white doctor. I was sent to a skin specialist, and he claimed it is psoriasis.

Just yesterday, I was across the river to my mother's and the fog from the pollution was hard to believe! I've been there almost every day this week, and I've had a sore throat every day. It goes away after a while, but comes right back again. It's like a burning thing you have to breathe.

They are telling us it is supposed to be safe.

P: *Is it the women who have the knowledge of the plants? Or does everybody have it?*

JS: It's not really who has it, I guess. Years back, that was something you were born with. I have one son who was always like that. He would find something, some roots and herbs, and seem to know what it was. If it's there for me to use, I know how to fix it, but as for going out and looking, that's something else. I guess that medicine is just not in me. At one time, my father used to say that that was part of getting to a certain stage when you raise your own family—what can you do for your young? What can you use to help them when they are sick?

That is another thing that we find is going. I grew up being aware of different prophecies. One of our prophecies tells that our own medicine will come to our door crying, because we tend to turn away from it. You go to any of the homes now, and if you are aware of medicines, you would find them right in the back yard. But it's not being used.

And at this time that is another thing: who wants to use something that's polluted and full of fluoride? What are we supposed to do? Where are we supposed to turn? I've had two of my boys born with teeth with a grayish color. They weren't white at all.

They don't want to admit to what they are doing. It is harming our people. But no one seems to care.

If the animal life is damaged, then the plants will be, and our children will be too. I don't know where this all will go.

You know, they say that you need the sun's rays to make things grow. I'll be teaching the oldest one something—different words to say—the moon and the sun. And that makes me think of—the time hasn't come about yet—but the prophecies say there would be a time when the cloud would just start, and there would be no sun rays to go through, and no life would be able to survive it—no plants, nothing at all. And from that no vegetation will be left, no oxygen. They're killing us! Not just the Indian people.

P: *We are all killing ourselves.*

JS: We've tried to get land back so that we would have a base where we could do planting that would be somewhere away from here.

P: *Where would it be that would be free from this? Of course, there are some spots that are worse than others, but where is there now where there is no pollution?*

JS: As far as I'm concerned, I watch the prophecies, and they're just fulfilling themselves. We're to the point where it's toward the end. There's something that's there: you can't touch it, you can't feel it—no, you *can* feel it. It's not just us, it's not just the Indian people.

P: *And yet you go on. We heard that a woman had gone to Six Nations Reservations to participate in the ceremonies. Is it the planting ceremony, the sun and the moon?*

JS: Yes. Part of our ceremony here among the Mohawk people was what we call the Moon Ceremony. We had it at one time, but it was more or less lost to us. It's one thing we want to bring back.

P: *And does that have to do with planting?*

JS: It does. You plant in the spring, and harvest in the fall. My husband found out that that's why those ceremonies are held at those times. Most of the time they try to have it either at the time that the trees start to bud or late in the fall. That's what they go by, not the month or the date.

P: *Do you hope it will have an effect, or do you see it as a celebration?*

JS: A celebration. But I think it will, in the future, have a big effect on our people. There was something about things that just wasn't complete, but we weren't sure what it was. It has been accepted, and our young girls are really anxious to participate. They are told of the role they have from the age of puberty on; they're no longer little children.

I know how my daughters feel. Now one that's only just turned seven says, "I can hardly wait." Of course, she gets rather shy about what comes with it.

P: *And only women attend that?*

JS: The men come to it too. They do the singing. There are different parts they have to participate in. Of course, my daughter and myself, we wanted to go real bad, and we just weren't able to participate, because at that time of the month we don't attend ceremonies. We stay by ourselves for a few days.

P: *That's always been that way?*

JS: Yes, but it gets hard at times, even before this encampment started.

P: *You see that as a duty to fulfill, keeping to yourselves at certain times?*

JS: Yes—even after bearing children. I have always been told that it is not up to us to break a life cycle. That's another thing that's happened today to our people. Some are getting married and saying, "I don't want to be bothered with kids."

In our wedding ceremony in the Longhouse, it's very serious, and they're told of their role. Strong words are used that you don't forget easy.

P: *Do the Longhouse people divorce at all?*

JS: Never. When the wedding ceremony takes place, they make their pledge to the Creator and to those bearing witness to the ceremony. I don't think it's easy for any person to make promises to another and to Him and think they can turn around and break them. If a couple have trouble, it's up to the people who witnessed the marriage to try to talk to them and get them back together.

P: *If one of them commits a crime, or one of them goes mad, or something of that sort . . .*

JS: It's still not allowed. Once you commit yourself, it's for life.

P: *No breaking of the bond?*

JS: No. They have a session—I guess you could call it—that they go through even before the marriage ceremony is performed. If the Clan Mothers and chiefs see that they are not ready for it, they won't perform it. It's too bad, but if it sometimes happens that there's a breakup, it's lack of communication between the people involved. And you try. You don't give up. You keep trying, even if it's for them to stay together for the children's sake. Every child needs a set of parents. It's funny too, in our way, it's usually an uncle that will talk to them. They usually respect him. The young say, "Isn't it funny that whenever he talks to us, we'd better listen." That has always been the way, within the clan, when any type of problem develops—it is up to the clan to straighten them out.

P: *How do you explain to a girl in this day and age where girls are brought up not to pay attention, really, to their cycles—how do you explain that it is their duty to be quiet at that time?*

JS: It depends, I guess, on how much you believe in it. When you believe in something, you know it's just natural for you. I find that if a mother isn't strict enough with her young, they tend to kind of jump back into something that they try to get out of.

P: *Youngsters of that age … it matters to them so terribly much what their friends do and think, and how they dress and all that. For children who are mixed with white children and other Indians who don't have the same evaluation of things, it must be really, really tough.*

JS: I guess it is at times. It's up to each individual. That's why we feel, when people are prejudiced against us, it is not always easy to be gentle with your words. It took me a while, but I learned—you don't get through to the people by shouting at them, by telling them off. It gives you a good feeling when you know you can clear the air, and you can sit down and talk, instead of bickering about your differences.

P: *Do you have time to go to the Longhouse to the meetings?*

JS: Yes. I found that with Jake's sitting in Council, I have to be there to understand what went on before *we* can sit down and discuss different things. Sometimes we don't see eye to eye on things, but at least I can be aware of what he decides.

P: *But he listens to you too?*

JS: He listens to me, but he doesn't use my comments when he decides something. When he took that position as chief, one of the sort of rules that we were given was that we were not to go to him to just complain or gossip.

He says you can't tell people how to think, what to say. They have to realize for themselves when they are in the wrong. That's when it gets rough—when it comes to the feelings of people. You have to talk to people in such a way that you don't hurt their feelings. If you want to get something across, you have to know how to talk to them. Jake's known in the camp for that—a gentle man.

And they tease him about his not so gentle wife!

Well, when you have seven children, you have to deal with that, and politics, and whatever else! [Laughs]

I don't feel so gentle sometimes.

P: *Maybe that's why you're with him.*

JS: My mother says there's always a balance; opposites attract.

P: *When a chief is chosen, he's chosen for life, isn't he?*

JS: He is. When the chief accepts the position there are different things he has to be qualified for, and a lot of strong words are given to them when they are chosen. One of them is that they have to be able to decide in a way that won't hurt any future unborn generation, seven generations to come. You have to have a very good head to be able to sit in that position. At times, just within our family, the children kind of miss their father, when he has been away for quite long spells. There are things he has to do that we aren't really able to participate in. You see, he has his position, and we can't interfere in it. But they have faith; they think a lot of him. They know that he can't just work for them—he has to work for everybody else's children—even the unborn ones. I'm glad that I brought them up in a way that they do understand that.

P: *How does a woman become a Clan Mother?*

JS: In Mohawk we do have three clans, and if we were to go about choosing a Clan Mother, it would be the people who would choose her. Somebody that they know would have the qualifications to be able to be a very strong person and be able to look after the nation.

P: *All the clans elect the Clan Mother of one clan?*

JS: No. If we were to choose a Wolf Clan Mother, which is my clan, it would be the people who would decide, from within that clan. The same for the Turtle Clan and for the Bear Clan: they have their own big family. To be a Clan Mother, I find, is almost like a mother. You raise your children; you have to guide them—to me it's a big responsibility. I mean it's one thing to be able to more or less discipline a child; it's another to actively discipline somebody that may even be older than you. And yet, the respect is there because they know what position you have to fill. The Clan Mother has a lot of control over the young in the way that she has to watch over her women-folk, and if there's any problems with our young, it is mostly to her that they go for advice. She has to be a very compassionate person, and very understanding—where everybody would refer to her as their grandmother. That's the Indian way, that's how we are about our grandmother. When you have problems you can't solve, somehow the feelings are that she is wiser. You can go to her to get your answers. They don't always just give out advice; they just lay down different facts, and from there you have to use your own judgment and mind and figure things out for yourself.

P: *And they actively do reprove and advise the chiefs when they feel it's necessary?*

JS: They do.

P: *And the chiefs come and ask them for advice when they want it? I mean, when they feel the need of advice?*

JS: Yes.

P: *It is not the kind of relationship between men and women that is very common among us.*

JS: When people have come here to observe, that's another thing that they felt was different. They see two people sitting there, a man and a woman, talking, just talking, discussing different things about camp, or making different plans. They say, "Well, that must be his wife sitting there discussing this." And it isn't. We all know we have to work together in order to make whatever we're doing a success.

I was always told by the older ones; keep your people together; keep them constantly alert to what goes on, and don't let them stray.

P: *Sometimes you get quite a lot from straying away, as long as you come back to your roots again …*

JS: Yes, yes. I went to the city; I worked; then I got married. We traveled a lot after we got married, and wherever Jake's work was, that's where we were … until we came back, back into our Longhouse. And there were people that I grew up with, still there! A lot of us came back, more or less in the same situation—with families, married … And now we watch our own families come back again.

Parabola
Volume: 6.1
Earth and Spirit

Our Mother Earth

Oren Lyons

A thousand years ago a man came from the west. And he came across the water, and he brought a great message of peace. He came across the water, the great lake that you now call Ontario; he stopped on the shores, and he visited the various nations who were at war and who had forgotten how to live together. He came with a great message of peace; and he gathered the strongest and the fiercest of leaders in the Great Council.

And it took many years; but with the help of Hiawentah, whom you call Hiawatha, together they created the Houdenosaunee, the great league of peace—one thousand years ago. And the principles were set down, at that time, of how to conduct ourselves, of how to raise the chiefs, how to raise the clan mothers; and how to set men in council, so that they could first perform the ceremonies as the spiritual being, the center, of the nation. The ceremonies were the first obligation of the chiefs, and the faith keepers, and the clan mothers. And then they were to sit in council for the welfare of the people.

A thousand years ago we were given this message by the Creator; we were given a government by the Creator. This government was not manufactured from the minds of men, it was *given* to us; and we were to cherish it. And each generation was to raise its chiefs and to look out for the welfare of the seventh generation to come. We were to understand the principles of living together; we were to protect the life that surrounds us; and we were to give what we had to the elders and to the children. The men were to provide; and the women were to care for the family, and be the center, the heart, of the home. And so our nation was built on the spiritual family, and we were given clans: the turtle—the eel—the deer—the beaver—the wolf—the bear—the snipe—the hawk—the heron: symbols of freedom. We were given an understanding of how free people live. And we were told to protect the freedom of every individual; we were told that sovereignty began with the individual, and you protect that. And so a free nation stood, and a great peace prevailed.

Many years later there landed, on our shores to the east, our white brother. And he brought with him things that we could not contend with. We were told at an earlier time that the name Ga-nya-di-yo, whom you call Handsome Lake, would be important; and so it came to pass that in the year 1800 we were given a third and final message of how to deal with the things that were brought across the water—when our men were drunk; when our home fires were out; when the dogs walked in the ashes; and the children and the women hid in the woods because of what the whisky and the liquor did to our men. And we were given a message at that time; and this message told us about Ga-nya-di-yo; and again the Creator took pity on us, He felt sorry for us, and He gave the third message of how to deal with the whisky and with gambling, how to deal with the Bible and the missionaries. We were told at that time what would happen to this earth. And as Ga-nya-di-yo walked with the Four Beings, the Four Protectors, who had been sent by the Creator to look out for mankind, they pointed out to him, here and there, "What do you see?" "I see a woman, so fat that she can't rise, yet she continues to stuff her mouth, she continues to eat like a glutton." And they never said whether that was right or wrong; they asked him, what did he see? And so they went, and he was given this opportunity to see, and to be told that one day the water would not be fit to drink, that indeed the water would burn, that the trees would begin to die from the tops down; that the chief of all trees, the maple, would signal to us the time of the deterioration of life, when the end would be near. He told us, and pointed out the variety of events that would occur: the sickness of our children and of the elders, and of what money would do—the greatest sickness of all.

Now we are faced with these things, as leaders of our people, as people given a great responsibility; we in this generation must deal with all of these elements.

When the Creator gave His Great Law and planted the great tree of peace, He uprooted it, and He threw under it all the weapons of war. He said: You are now a nation of peace; and I will give to you *oyankgwa-oohway*, the sacred tobacco; and that will be your strength. That will be what you depend on, the spiritual power of prayer, a belief: the belief of your people. And if you have one mind, and you consider this again, it is the power that you have. So it happens when you burn the tobacco and use the sacred cornmeal that all of the animals stop and they listen; they turn, and they listen to these words.

Our brothers, the bears and the wolves and the eagles, are Indians. They are Natives, as we are. At one time we spoke their language; at one time we conversed, a long time ago. The two-leggeds have fallen from grace. Those animals and those wingeds, they live in a state of absolute grace; they can do no wrong. It is only we who have been given a choice, so clearly pointed out by the Four Beings: this is the way it is, they said, and what do you see here? They did not tell him: Do this or do that; they said, This is the way it is: what you do will be up to you. And that is what the Creator gave to us, the choice: a great gift, the mentality that we have. And among us there are even people with other gifts—a gift of art, or a gift of speech, or a gift of a smile that can make everyone laugh. Whatever it is, each of us was born with a mission. We were born with a mission, and we must know what it is and develop it and *do* it. And that's a choice—that is *your* choice.

We went to Geneva—the Six Nations, and the great Lakota nation—as representatives of the indigenous people of the Western Hemisphere. We went to Geneva, and we spoke in the forum of the United Nations. For a short time we stood equal among the people and the nations of the world. And what was the message that we gave? There is a hue and cry for human rights—human rights, they said, for all people. And the Indigenous people said: What of the rights of the natural world? Where is the seat for the buffalo or the eagle? Who is representing them here in this forum? Who is speaking for the waters of the earth? Who is speaking for the trees and the forests? Who is speaking for the fish—for the whales—for the beavers—for our children? *We* said: Given this opportunity to speak in this international forum, then it is our duty to say that we must stand for these people, and the natural world and its rights; and also for the generations to come. We would not fulfill our duty if we did not say that. It becomes important because without the water, without the trees, there is no life.

New York City—you live here; you can't get a clean drink of water here. You don't know what clear spring water is like, because you have to drink what comes out of the tap. And eventually it will kill you. Eventually you will not be able to clean that water, nor your children, nor your grandfather, nor your grandmother. …You think about it. …When you are sick and when you children are sick, you remember what the Indian said to you about water.

We are indigenous people to this land. We are like a conscience. We are small, but we are not a minority. We are the landholders, we are the landkeepers; we are not a minority. For our brothers are all the natural world, and by that we are by far the majority. We want you to understand the opportunity now. It is no time to be afraid—there is no time for fear. It is only a time to be strong, only a time to think of the future, and to challenge the destruction of your grandchildren, and to move away from the four-year cycle of living that this country goes through, from one election to another, and think about the coming generations.

We spoke about human rights and we spoke in defense of all people and of all children. But remember that as long as we are burning tobacco, as long as the Indian nations exist, so will you. But when we are gone, you too will go.

Dahnato. ("Now I am finished" is the translation of "Dahnato.")

Acknowledgment: The preceding was first delivered as a talk at the Cathedral of St. John the Divine, New York City, May 24, 1978. Reprinted by permission of the author.

CHAPTER FOUR

MERE HUMAN

Pity me, I am just a man, says Lakota Arthur Amiotte in his vision quest poem. Native peoples are often seen by non-Indians as something more than mere humans. We are sought out for our knowledge and spirituality. Yet we have our lessons to learn in life as well as others do. It is by learning compassion and diminishing the ego that we become participants with creation. Sometimes people need to be in the world just like they are, as in the Tom Harmer essay: It is by taking away the falseness of ourselves that we grow. Even the animals know this about humans. Perhaps that's why in the wilderness they now live without us. We need to be a human who dwells in a body, and without politics, as Tony Black Feather knew when he wrote how distortions, as he understood from his life, can seem real. Many of us come from great leaders and they, too, were merely human. Historical trauma, poverty, and illness, as Black Feather mentions, are part of daily life for Native peoples. We must learn to live for the community more than ourselves. That is the tribal manner of being. Through it, spiritual growth is enabled. Sometimes we fail, but thrown down to the ground, perhaps we find hope, peace, and the true spiritual life.

Parabola
Volume: 6.1
Earth and Spirit

Dead Man's Song

Copper Eskimo

I'm filled with joy
when the day dawns quietly
over the roof of the sky,
    aji, jai ja.

I'm filled with joy
when the sun rises slowly
over the roof of the sky,
    aji, jai ja.

But other times, I choke with fear:
a greedy swarm of maggots
eats into the hollows
of my collar-bone and eyes,
    aji, jai ja.

I lie here dreaming
how I choked with fear
when they shut me
in an ice-hut on the lake,
    aji, jai ja.

And I could not see
my soul would ever free itself
and get to the hunting-grounds

of the sky,
    aji, jai ja.

Fear grew, and grew.
Fear overwhelmed me
when the fresh-water ice
snapped in the cold,
and the booming crack of the frost
grew into the sky,
    aji, jai ja.

Life was wonderful in winter.
But did winter make me happy?
No, I always worried
about hides for boot-soles and for boots:
and if there'd be enough for all of us.
Yes, I worried constantly,
    aji, jai ja.

Life was wonderful in summer.
But did summer make me happy?
No, I always worried
about reindeer skins and rugs for the platform.
Yes, I worried constantly,
    aji, jai ja.

No, I always worried
for my little hook,
in case it never got a bite.
Yes, I worried constantly,
    aji, jai ja.

Life was wonderful
when you danced in the feasting house.
But did this make me any happier?
No, I always worried
I'd forget my song.

Yes, I worried constantly,
    aji, jai ja.

Life was wonderful . . .
And I still feel joy
each time the day-break
whitens the dark sky,
each time the sun
climbs over the roof of the sky,
    aji, jai ja.

Parabola
Volume: 1.1
The Hero

PRAYER TO THE WEST

Arthur Amiotte

Oh you to the West
   the first direction
   home of Wakiyan and of the setting sun:
   hear my prayer.
Pity me.

I am just a man, but of the people
It is for them that I make this prayer.
It is that we may live that I make this prayer.
My voice is weak but it comes from my heart.
Hear my voice and be merciful to me.

Oh you where the thunder and lightning live
   home of the rain and hail
   your powers to give life are those of the storm
   that comes in fury but leaves peace in its wake.
You shake the world with the voice of thunder
   and your eye of lightning
      eagles fly before you
   you bless the world with your lifegiving rain
   and dancing hail
      eagles fly after you.

Oh you from where comes the blessing wind
   the wind of answers to prayers

bring to the people the rain of washing away blindness
    that we and our land and our faith may be renewed
    made whole and wholesome again.
Shower us that we may wash away our ignorance
    and once more look upon you that we may see you
    with a pure heart.
Wash from our eyes the blindness of unholy ways
    that we may see again the good red road and walk it with pride
    knowing that dignity in this life is being in harmony
    with a proud creation with humble origins.

Oh you where the lightning lives and the day is red
    cast your dancing eye of light
    and in its power strike the nation with enlightenment
    that we may realize that we are
    but as momentary as that flash yet as powerful
    for that power which is the lightning
    is also the power that makes us live.
Enable us to understand
    and live with that power in a holy way.
Remind us that we are of one creation
    yet below it and above it
    and that our duty to pray to you should be as faithful
    as the thunder that follows the lightning.

Oh you where the daytime rests
    bring solace and peace to the people in their weariness
    for we cry and are hungry
    strangers in our own land
    deprived of survival
    and losing the strength of mind and body
    to see our way in this changing world.
Give us the healing light
    and the beauty of your setting sun to see that way
    so we may live in health and beauty and peace.
Send us the living rain
    so we may grow again as the plant people do

reaching fruition in our time
and bearing the fruit and seeds for generations of good people.
Send us the living rain
that we may relearn for ourselves
the meaning of all that grows from the land
for we too are of the land
and must be reminded of how we are to live with it
and from it and take
care of it.

Open our ears that we may listen to the whole creation
and hear again the voices that are one voice.
Open our ears that we may hear the wisdom of our teacher
who is the universe
and once more listen to the message of the red way.
Help us to learn
that the voice of Wakan Tanka is continually around us
and it is our duty to listen when the voice calls
and to recognize the voice.

Oh you where the thunder lives
sound your voice that all may hear
and ears will be opened to the sound of voices.

Oh you to the West
hear my prayer.
I am only a man and I now cry and weep before you.
I cry to you for the people and for myself.
Pity me.

Parabola
Volume: 29.2
Web of Life

LIVING LIKE A NATURAL PERSON

Tom Harmer

Driving home from work earlier than usual, I'd been thinking about what happened to me when I almost froze to death. Only when the edge had worn off in the familiar routine of going to work did I remember the voices I'd heard, and how they came at critical moments to wake me up and get me to build a fire. Something momentous had happened, something that made me feel different. On a whim, I'd turned off the highway to drive up in the mountains and see if I could find my old friend, the Okanogan Indian elder Clayton Tommy, Jr. He was the one person who'd always made sense of my strange experiences.

Miles of plowed country roads even my old Ford Falcon could negotiate without having to chain up brought me to the old homestead where Clayton's sister, Annie, told me he'd gone off shortly before, on foot into the hills. Even though I was dressed for work, I dug out my boots and set off following his tracks. ...

I found Clayton sitting by a hot fire of pine branches, sheltered from the cold and wet under a sloping ceiling of rock. Once inside the low, wide opening in snow, I could see it was the bottom of an ancient avalanche pile of enormous angular granite slabs, with passageways leading off to other hidden recesses. As my eyes grew accustomed to the dim firelight, I saw the walls were covered in weathered pictographs, the red ocher paintings of nature spirits Clayton's people left behind in the old days, after quests for power in remote spots like this.

Since I hadn't seen him in a long time—maybe six months—I was a little self-conscious about blundering into his presence, invading what looked like a sacred place for elders like him. Fortunately there was an etiquette for chance meetings in the bush, and Clayton predictably made no sign of noticing me as I moved to warm myself at his fire. Long used to the Native preference for easing indirectly into meeting someone, I sat down across from him and stayed quiet, too, holding my bare hands up to the welcome heat. ... After the usual minutes of feeling things out, he finally glanced up at me.

"So ... you still comin' around, eh?" he said indifferently, stirring the fire with a stick.

"Yeah, well, barely made it."

My jeans began to steam.

"What for?" His eyes inspected my unlikely clothes for traipsing around the mountains in snow.

"Been a long time, Clayton," I said, wondering why he sounded so harsh after our years of friendship. "Got off work early and drove up to see if you were around. Annie said you just took off somewhere, so I tracked you. Somethin' happened to me and ... well, I wanted to ask you about it."...

I told him about my experience of almost freezing to death. It was the first time I'd tried to put into words what had happened. I faltered at certain points, correcting myself to be more exact. Talking about it made me aware how disturbed I was at how real my mother's voice had been, and how familiar the other voice had seemed. I finished by saying how dismayed I was that I could miscalculate the weather so badly.

"Well, that maybe happen to anybody, get caught out in the hard cold comin' on," Clayton said. "But not to be saved like that. Not anybody be warned and told what to do. Only the power man." He seemed surprised and pleased by what I'd told him.

"I don't get it."

"They do that, the *shumíx*, the spirit partners. This how they do, speak in the voice of someone close, like your parent. When things are bad, to save your life. Make you listen, wake you up. Many stories handed down tell you how they done that. And then, when you see how bad it is, how pitiful you are, tell you what to do. What you got don't fool around, say, 'Don't die, make a fire!' So this show you still got somethin'. That power still stickin' with you. Maybe I figure wrong about you after all."

He piled more pine branches on the fire, then stared off thoughtfully.

"But now, my want to know, you just another stranger like all the rest, or you maybe an earth person after all?"

"What can I say, Clayton? I don't know what you're getting at."

"*Tiskélux kul temxúlaux*, somebody who come alive on this earth, wake up here, live like a natural person. You know what I mean—White or Indian don't matter. How all people used to know how to live here." He patted the ground at his side.

"I don't know. I think I'm trying to. That's why I like to learn from you. How would I know?"

He shook his head slowly, staring into the fire, rubbing the stubble of hair on the back of his wrinkled neck. A flock of chickadees came flitting and peeping from limb to limb in the lower branches of a fir tree just outside, foraging in the snow-heavy tips of needles, displacing the burdens in cascades of glittery powder drifting down. Clayton watched them going about their ancient business, then spoke with unexpected sadness.

"There's a war going on. A war against the earth, against mother earth. I wonder whose side you on?"

I didn't know what to say.

"Ever since your people come here. But now, everybody in on it. Not many left to be on the earth's side. Just the few."

One of the chickadees flew down and landed just under the overhang, on the tip of a dry limb in Clayton's pile of firewood. A tiny black and white ball of fluff tamely studying us.

"You either on the earth's side, or you not. One or the other. If you are, everything in the world knows it, eh? Every animal, every tree, they know it. And they show themself to you. Open things up to you, watch over you, make things happen for you. Whisper in your ear so you feel in your heart what to do.

"But if you not on the earth's side, why, the earth don't even know you here. Don't even see you, feel your steps, know you breathin'. Just like you don't mean nothin' to her, ain't it?"

The chickadee fluffed out its feathers and continued to perch, watching us in profile. Clayton turned to the bird and said gently, *"Aaaa, sits'kakána, alá ch'xóoyux uhl kwu ask'amúten* (So, chicka-dee, you came here to sit with us)." Then to me: "Yah, this one listen to what we sayin', eh? Can carry the message to the whole world. Wonder whose side you on? Wonder if you livin' in the same world I am. Where this not just some little birdie that come to the bird feeder in the back yard, but is someone powerful and can know what we say."

"I want to be on the earth's side," I said with sudden conviction.

"Aaaa," Clayton said.

I felt a flutter in my chest at how immediately the chickadee flew up into the fir tree with the others. A clear song burst out, "Chick chick chick-a-dee-dee-dee!" There was a cloud of snow powder as they all flew off. ...

"You ponder on what you say to the earth this day. They always waitin' for us to make up our mind, hear what we say, words from the heart. Then maybe they show themselves, come and look at you, see if you mean what you say."

"Who?"

"Chip'choptikxwl, the Animal People, the ones the old stories tell about. One of 'em already done it. Maybe you remember? That time we comin' back from Wenatchee, and we stop at the dam on the river. Go down where we see the fish go by. Maybe you remember that one salmon, the chief of all the salmon, how he come and look at you that time, eh?"

I remembered we stopped at Rocky Reach Dam on the Columbia River one afternoon, and went down to a dimly lit public-viewing room with rows of benches. We sat with tourists watching a long window, the glassed-in side of where the fish ladder opened out to the lake. It was like looking into a huge, long aquarium, the greenish water rushing by left to right, with occasional salmon, in ones or twos, darting quickly across from right to left. There were long lapses of nothing to see between the infrequent, sudden appearances of fish that made it up the ladder from the river below and swam by toward open water. The tourists would ooh and ahh when a fish or two went by, then get bored and leave. Only Clayton and I remained while tourists came and went.

The dams on the Columbia had decimated what once had been one of the world's largest salmon runs. Clayton sat brooding and uncommunicative beside me, sighing occasionally at what had become of the run since his childhood. At one point, all the other visitors left and we were alone in the viewing room for about five minutes. It was silent and dim, and the only thing to look at was the rush of water behind glass. Something big appeared from the right, the biggest salmon I'd ever seen, maybe three feet long. It was so thick around the middle it looked like the granddaddy of all salmon compared to all the smaller, slimmer ones that had gone by. The salmon actually came to a halt just inside the glassed-in channel, as if warily looking things over before going on. The look of its great eye in profile was startling. Then with preposterous ease, as if the current was nothing to something so big and powerful, the salmon glided by slowly and effortlessly, and disappeared out the opening. Clayton said something to the salmon in Salish when it paused. After it was gone, he said, jokingly I thought at the time, "He come to check you out, see this White man who wanna be the Indian!"

Now he said, "That how they do. Come and show themself to somebody who want to be in the world like they are. Come to see what is in your heart. Maybe you watch for that. That bird, sits'kakána, he spread the word, eh?"

There seemed nothing more to say. I sat in silence with him as the fire burned and the light outside the rock overhang faded into evening.

Parabola
Volume: 29.4
Friendship

OYATE OLOTAPI:
THE PEOPLE BORROW HIM

Kent Lebsock

After a long struggle with cancer, Lakota elder Tony Black Feather went home to the spirit world. Tony had lived his life in a good way; struggling against injustice, working for future generations, transforming suffering into hope and smiles.

Kent Lebsock, Lakota activist and Director of the American Indian Law Alliance, worked closely with Tony for over a decade.

Politics makes lies sound truthful and murder reasonable.

—Tony Black Feather

Tony was born and raised on Pine Ridge Reservation in South Dakota. His ancestors were warriors from the battle at the Little Big Horn, and included White Cow Bull, Long Wolf, Black Feather, Red Cloud, and Yellow Boy. On his father's side of the family he is a descendant of Sitting Bull. He is also related to Red Cloud. There's leadership in his blood. Treaty meetings had been going on since the Fort Laramie treaties were signed in 1851 and 1868 in our territories. The treaties recognize the Lakota as a sovereign nation, acknowledge our right to self-determination, and delineate our homelands.

Unfortunately, it only took about two weeks for the U. S. government to break the treaties. When they found gold it made the problems worse. In 1877 the U. S. Congress annexed the Black Hills, which had been recognized as part of the Great Sioux Nation territory; in 1890 was the Massacre at Wounded Knee. In 1894 Chief He Dog founded the Tetuwan Oyate, or Teton Sioux Nation Treaty Council. Tony was the spokesperson for the Tetuwan Oyate for over twenty years.

Our ancestors signed the Fort Laramie treaties believing that they would be respected. For almost one hundred years our elders and leaders fought the case through the U. S. court system until, finally, in 1980 the Supreme Court came down with a decision. They actually agreed with the Lakota. They said "[a] more ripe and rank case of dishonorable dealings will never, in all probability, be found in our history. ..." Yet, they said there was nothing that they could do about it, and they offered the Lakota people money (now over five hundred million dollars) as compensation. The Lakota people turned down the money. For us, the Black Hills are sacred.

It was about that time that Tony went to the elders with the idea of taking the treaty issues to the International Court of Justice. "These are international treaties," he said, "they always have been, it's where we should have gone in the first place." The elders liked his idea and agreed to support him. One of the elders, Pete Fills Pipe, went to a junkyard and bought Tony an old typewriter and with this typewriter Tony got to work. He began to write letters, to look for support, to find a way to have our grievances heard by the international community. In 1982 someone from England sent two plane tickets from Rapid City to Geneva for the first meeting of the United Nations Working Group on Indigenous Populations, which had just been established.

So Tony got these two tickets and, with Garfield Grass Rope, who was a chief from Lower Brule and is also my godfather and name-giver, took a plane to Geneva. Two guys from the reservation and they had no idea... you see, Pine Ridge is the poorest country in America, there's about ninety percent unemployment, historical trauma, lots of problems. Tony lived and worked out of a little wooden shack with no indoor plumbing, no kitchen facilities, heated with a wood stove; and in the Dakotas it can get down to sixty below zero. It was pretty amazing that he could get this whole process going. And then there they are in Europe. ...

They arrived in Paris and had no idea how to change planes and they were hungry. They saw a McDonald's in the airport and, as he told it, they charged him "thirty dollars for a cheeseburger." I think it was actually thirty francs, but that was about all they had. When they made it to Geneva they had no money. They stayed in what Tony called the "Homeless People's Hotel," which was actually an abandoned building occupied by squatters who took them in. They would walk to the United Nations every day to participate in the meetings and, in Tony's words, "represent the forgotten people of the world." That trip began a twenty-year journey that would bring Tony into the hearts and minds of indigenous and non-indigenous peoples all over the world. His legacy at the United Nations is one of wisdom, compassion, courage, warmth, and, most significantly, humor. You'd see him in the halls, joking with people with whom he didn't even share a common language.

Even though he only had a third-grade education, Tony made a significant contribution to the development of an international body of law relative to the rights of indigenous peoples. He took a very active role in the process of drafting the United Nations Draft Declaration on the Rights of Indigenous Peoples and submitted dozens of interventions over the years with specific language on treaty rights, self-determination, sovereignty, self-government, and resources. He also contributed to the work of U. N. Special Rapporteurs Professor Dr. Erica-Irene Daes, for her report on intellectual property, and Dr. Miguel Alphonso Martinez for his report on treaties and constructive agreements.

Tony would always tell me "building our friendships is the most important thing we can do." That's how he approached life. At the U. N. in Geneva he knew everybody from the security guards to the secretaries, to the translators, to the working-group members, the diplomats, and all of the indigenous people. They would all stop and chat with him and he would be equally friendly and equally amicable with everybody. Even the U. S. representatives had a pretty good chance with Tony, although he would not hesitate to tell them to "stop acting like children" when they used insignificant details to delay the passage of the Draft Declaration on the Rights of Indigenous Peoples.

Tony would remind us that first and foremost we have to remember that this is not a political movement—it's a spiritual movement. He was our conscience. There was no compromise. Tony was fearless in his work.

He wasn't afraid of power, or poverty, or scorn, or threats. You see this in all of the indigenous leaders from around the world who are doing this work. Because it's very unrewarding—the achievements that we make can be measured in centimeters, over decades. He always pointed out that this was really work for generations yet unborn. He believed that, ultimately, this was not simply about justice for indigenous peoples, but a solution to many of the problems of the whole human family.

Tony led an exemplary life. He lived and died in a way that is completely consistent with all of our great leaders. He never thought about his own comfort or even considered it an issue. He thought only of the people. He never got paid. He lived on his pension from the army (he was in the 82nd Airborne Division during the Korean conflict), which was about seventy-five dollars per month for the last twenty years. I never quite understood how he did it. Friends that he met in different parts of the world would help pay the phone bills and travel expenses. He was notorious for giving things away. We'd go to Geneva and I'd give him fifty dollars and then I'd see him sitting there giving it all away and I'd say "Tony, that's for you to eat!" I literally had to buy him food or else he wouldn't eat. Same thing with gifts; people would give him watches and clothing and stuff and he would go home and give it all away.

Even though Tony is gone, the work is going to carry on. What he started is not just going to continue, but it's going to grow. We are still working on bringing our case before the International Court of Justice, and, in time, it will be heard. Tony fulfilled his commitment to the elders and to future generations. I have no doubt that stories will be told about him long into the future.

When he was a small child his grandfather, Dan Long Wolf, gave him the name Oyate Olotapi, which means "The People Borrow Him." Now his life has come full circle, and we give thanks to the Creator for having lent him to us.

In the 1960s a baby died on the reservation, and they wouldn't let the baby be buried in any of the Christian cemeteries, so Tony started a cemetery on his family land in Wolf Creek and the child was buried there. The cemetery then became a gathering place for his people and his community, and that's where he was buried, in the little cemetery that he founded, and that is where I hope to be buried someday.

—Mitaku Oyasin (All My Relations)

Parabola
Volume: 23.1
Millennium

CROSSING THE RIVER

Linda Hogan

Within time, there are mysteries that humans search to understand: mysteries of stones that were moved or worked by human hands, of time itself in all its facets. Stonehenge with its cherished blue megaliths is only one of these. There are ancient stone circles still unexplained, a pyramid said to have been built in one night by a dwarf in the Yucatan, and walls in the Southwest seamlessly fitted together in places far from where the stones had originally come from. We can't say how humans transported these stones. No one knows how stones move.

There is a story I once read. In this story there was a moving stone. One night a large stone rolled across the river and took up residence on the other side of the water. The people did not know how it happened that a stone had crossed the river. They agreed it was the desire of the stone to cross the river, yet the people thought it impossible for a stone to move of its own accord. Finally, one curious man decided to sleep on the stone in order to learn its mysteries. Every night he climbed on the stone and went to sleep. Every morning he found himself thrown off, lying instead on the ground.

At night, it seemed, the rock shrugged him off, shed him in the way a human might brush away an insect.

I don't remember the source of this story, but I think often of what it contains. The story of the rock that crossed the river is more than the story of a man devoted to understanding a mystery; it is surely about time in all its formulations. The most obvious kind of time, and the first level that the story addresses, is geologic; rock itself is another word for time. The mineral world is time's first cousin. We read earth's history and changes by the measuring devices of stone, fossil, lava, the sediment of ancient rivers.

The story also enters the realm of sacred time. It is something of a spiritual geology. Perhaps our only escape from other kinds of time that hold dominion over our lives is sacred time. Within this time and its mythic layers, a person can leave the straight, uncurved line of the time we think we understand, and enter another dimension. Inside it is a connection with the ancestral people, with the earth, and with stones. Entering, there is a quality of being that is not wholly of the body, but of the unbound parts of a human being. For most of our days and nights, sacred time is as distant from ordinary human experience as the concept of geologic time. "Once upon a time there was no time" is a statement that arises from inside this place.

Most especially the story is about daily measured human time, in which a night or a day is an increment of our ever-diminishing life spans. And like the man who slept on the rock, daily we are thrown back to earth from our night journeys and excursions into mystery. Against the mystery we seek to know, we fall into ordinary life. For most of us, existing as we do in human time, rock seems solid and unyielding, and it is time that throws us to the ground. And yet, having fallen, we are at the bottom of life, the feet of creation, bedrock. It is the falling to earth that is important—even more so than progressing from day to day, year to year, century to century.

Now, in our time, perhaps a century later than the story of the rock, we know that it is not unusual for a stone to cross a river. The old story holds up for us a knowledge about the worlds of time and matter. Now we know that earth moves easily—a mountain becomes a seashore, a hurricane picks up sand and takes it to form another beach across the ocean. Lava flows downward, islands rise. In a matter of seconds the plates of the earth shift. Rocks fall from mountains, and new stones rise to the surface of the earth with freeze and thaw. Now we say it and know it is true; stones are always crossing rivers.

Perhaps what is most significant about the story of the rock crossing the river is not time, nor the movement of the stone itself. What is unusual in this story is for a man to sleep night after night on the stone, searching for its secrets in moonlight, in open air, listening to the water. Unlike the story in which Sisyphus struggled daily to push a stone uphill, the sleeper's work was not a chore so much as it was an entering into all kinds of time—sacred, geologic, and human—in order to understand mystery. He took up residence to learn the unknowable.

And yet, with what was he rewarded? He was tossed back into life. Daily he found himself at the foot of earth, returned to ordinary human time. Like the man who slept on the rock, daily we are thrown back into ordinary time against the mystery we seek to know.

Like the stone, we are traveling, it seems, through time, through space, crossing other elements. We are moving toward something unknown, a landmark or destination, toward another century, a better future. We rarely think of what we've left behind, except in how it proves us (such as when we search the past for evidence of human origin), or to fulfill human stories, as if the stories will keep us whole. Sometimes they do. And even when we travel backward looking for the rock called Mount Ararat in search of the ark, or when we seek out the frozen history of past life in the Arctic, we are moving in two directions at once. We believe that progress is a motion toward better things and that the future holds the greatest hope of all. Surely it is not time that gave us this mistaken notion, but the unseen human organs of need and desire, those that try to explain the world. Even so, in all our human searches we are only crossing a river, and water, which is as eternal as time, keeps flowing alongside us. Like the man who slept on the rock, we are thrown down into something significant, thrown to the ground, and nothing else, no measure as large as a century, will lead us to any other kind of hope than this.

Parabola
Volume: 21.2
Home

Going Home

Bernard A. Hoehner

When an American Indian in the San Francisco Bay
Area asks another, "Are you going home?" he or she is not
referring to a home in Concord, San Jose, or Fremont, but
to the reservation. People from reservations never really
leave their home grounds but regard themselves as "on
loan" to various cities, and they stay in touch with their
reservation relatives by phone, letter, and periodic visits.
When "at home," they re-enter community life without
a ripple, taking part in activities and ceremonies as they
occur. Some return specifically for certain ceremonies.

When my older brother died suddenly, we went home
for the funeral, and immediately afterward my sister and I
declared our families to be in mourning and started planning for the feast and giveaway to be held a year from
the date of his death. Upon returning to California, I
explained to my family the customs involved in the death
of a close relative: I would have to forego all my powwow
activities, give up going to movies, and keep my thoughts
on the upcoming event.

In the old days, a lock of hair would have been taken
from the deceased and kept in a quilled case in its own
special tipi. It was symbolically fed, and on pleasant days
it was taken outside and hung on a tripod with a war-
bonnet at the peak. A member of the family would be
designated as the Keeper, for the whole event was a holy

undertaking called "Keeping the Soul." The soul was believed to stay in the quilled packet and to have a special status until it was ceremoniously released. It then went straight to the Spirit World.

In those days, the Keeper could not hunt, nor touch blood, knives, or weapons. He or she would accompany the hunters on a buffalo hunt, but sat on a hill nearby and watched while the hunters chased and killed the great beasts. The buffalo killed nearest the Keeper would be given to him or her, to be butchered by relatives and friends. The hide of the buffalo was tanned and hung over the Spirit Post of the tipi in which the Soul was being kept. The Keeper and his or her family had to lead solemn and exemplary lives away from all social pleasures, and would not be free to re-enter tribal life until the release of the Soul.

On the day of the release people gathered together, and amid prayers, speeches by Elders, and ceremonial activity by spiritual leaders, the Soul was set free. Immediately the mood changed from solemn to celebratory, and gifts were distributed by the family. There would be feasting as well, beginning with *wasna* (a traditional food made of toasted, dried buffalo meat, tallow, and mashed chokeberries) being passed out among the people, starting with the Elders. This was followed by the soups and stews, broiled meats, and other foods that had been prepared by the Keeper's relatives, until all present had had their fill.

This sacred rite was banished, along with the Sun Dance, by the U. S. government, which ordered that by a certain date "all souls currently being kept" must be released. Our people complied with the order and stopped the Sun Dance, but continued mourning their dead in the old-fashioned way, simply dropping some of the trappings and changing the name to "Memorial Feast." The withdrawal from social life, the accumulation of giveaway goods, the preparation of the feast are all still the same. The presence of drum, singers, and spiritual practitioner are also the same, as are the prayers, the speeches, and the solemn remembrances.

The release of the Soul now occurs with the singing of the Memorial Song by the drum, while all rise and the family quietly dances around the arena. Some weep as the honor song rings in their ears. When the dance ends, the mood changes abruptly as of old, and easy laughter and goodwill wash over all the participants. The local priest and clergymen of all denominations are always invited and asked to say a prayer, and each one is presented with a star quilt or other handsome gift by the family.

At my brother's Memorial Feast, the program starts with a prayer, followed by remembrances of the deceased by friends and relatives. When all have had their say, the drum begins to sing its song, and we all dance slowly around. I cannot keep the tears back when I hear my sister cry.

When this is over, a female cousin puts a shawl on my sister's shoulders and says, "Your days of mourning are over." Then she gently wipes my sister's eyes and leads her to her seat. As the cousin comes over to me carrying a pipe, I hear the announcer say that the family has decided that my brother's name, Peji, is to be bestowed on me. This is somewhat of a shock, for Peji was my Grandma's father, a chief. Now I'm to be Peji, the fourth to carry the name, though I already have a name given to me by Grandma, in honor of a wound her father suffered at the hands of an enemy. It doesn't seem to matter, for all rise, and the drum sings the naming song. When it is done, I donate money to the drum and go back to my seat, my emotions heaving and roiling like the bubbling, steaming GI cans of stew now heating on the stove.

Later, when all have been fed and the gifts distributed, and even the GI cans and soup ladles have been given away, we get into cars and head back out to the ranch. Suddenly, I can scarcely keep my eyes open. There's a deep sense of accomplishment, a deep sense of contentment, a deep feeling of ancestral approval. I feel as though I'm floating or drifting through the atmosphere like a cloud.

I sleep a deep, dreamless sleep that night.

Parabola
Volume: 21.3
Peace

THE PEACEMAKER'S JOURNEY

Haudenosaunee

The oral history of the Haudenosaunee (the original five nations of the Iroquois) is traditionally told at five-year intervals, a telling that can last six to nine days. The following selection, retold here by Mohawk Chief Jake Swamp (Wolf Clan), describes the quest of the Peacemaker.

The Peacemaker, whose birth had miraculous origins, sets out in a canoe of white stone to unite five warring nations and teach them the ways of peace. He journeys from the area of the Great Lakes to the east, where the most warlike people live, where bodies lie on the ground and streams run red with blood. There he proves himself by surviving a fall from a cliff and into a swift river, and the people accept his message of peace. First to do so is the woman Jigonsaseh, and to her the Peacemaker promises that she shall be remembered as the Mother of Nations. But the people are not happy, for they grieve over those they had lost in their warlike days.

The Peacemaker is troubled by this, but does not know how to banish their grief. The answer is provided by Ayonwentha, a man who eventually learned the way of relieving sorrow after losing his own family: Wipe the tears from the grieving one's eyes, brush the dust of death from their ears, give medicine water so that the voice could be returned to their throats, and ask the Great Spirit to let them wake the next morning able to see and hear and speak clearly once again.

And so the Peacemaker and Ayonwentha decided to go back to the village to console the people, because at that time the women seemed as though they were always in pain for the losses that they had felt, the sons they had lost. They were always remembering what had happened to them, and it affected the way they lived. After they gave the condolence ceremony to the people, the Peacemaker and Ayonwentha stayed back and just watched. It wasn't too long before things started to change. The women went back into their gardens and their fields. They started to communicate with one another and their laughter started to come back. The children started to play different games, and the men in the village became energetic once more. And so the people were healed.

The Peacemaker faced Ayonwentha and he said, "It is now time to build a great long house. This longhouse will extend from the rising sun to the setting sun and all the nations will live in this long house as one people. We must now leave here and approach those people towards the west." They started out and soon they were arriving near the villages of the Oneida. There they confronted the leaders, and they wanted them to give in to the peace also. These leaders had already heard that peace was coming and so it was not too difficult for them to accept, although some of them had misgivings about this peace. But in the end, they, too, accepted.

And so they went on, going towards the west, and there they arrived in the territory of the Onondaga Nation. Now this is where they ran into a problem. This evil man, Tadadaho, lived there. He had snakes mixed in with his hair, representative of all the evil things that he used to do. Even his fingers were all twisted up. His whole being was all crooked. He was not very handsome, for all the things that he had done, those evil things, showed on him, on his very person. When the Peacemaker and Ayonwentha went to their villages, the people started to give in, accepting this peace. Soon they all desired this peace, but in the distance Tadadaho lived, and he kept refusing. Each time they would approach him he would just snarl at them. He had accumulated so much power in his life, and this is the reason why he kept refusing. He didn't want to lose that power. They tried different methods, but nothing could faze his evil mind. They would go to him and sing beautiful songs to him, but he would not give in. They would use nice words to him, but he would not listen. So finally one day they made a decision. They said, "We cannot wait here any longer. We must go on to approach those other nations towards the west. We will come back this way later on and we will deal with him then."

So they went on towards the west, and soon they arrived at the place where the Cayuga people lived. The Peacemaker and Ayonwentha explained the whole plan of peace to them, and soon they agreed to this peace. And then they traveled on and finally they arrived where the Seneca people lived in the big hill country. There they confronted the men, who did not want to give in. Those war leaders did not want to lose their power, but finally one day they all agreed to live in peace as well.

The Peacemaker and Ayonwentha sent some runners all the way back to the rising sun in the east, saying: "You tell them when you arrive that peace is now here. You tell them to come to the center and everybody will meet there in the territory of the Onondaga Nation."

And so they traveled back towards the center, and when they arrived at the place, Onondaga, they waited there. Soon the other ones were arriving—the ones from the east, the Oneida, the Mohawk, and the Cayugas—and all their work was cut out for them, for now they all had to work together on the evil mind of Tadadaho. He was the only one holding out on this peace; he was the only one holding out on all these nations to be formed into one heart, one body, one mind. Each time they would try something to take away his evil mind they failed, and it was very frustrating for them. So one day the Peacemaker said, "In the future we are going to put together five nations of people, five nations together into one body, one heart, one mind. And we need a fire, a counsel fire that will burn for all, and we need someone to watch over this fire." They went to Tadadaho and they said, "We want you to watch over the counsel fire for all of the five nations who want to live in peace." Then Tadadaho got excited, for he felt that he would still have control over all of the five nations, and he accepted. But in this manner they really tricked him, for now he had to live in peace. It didn't matter if he felt that he still had control, as long as he was peaceful.

Now the people were so happy that finally peace had arrived. The Peacemaker stood there as the men gathered from all directions, the warriors that used to fight with one another. As he observed them, he noticed they all were carrying weapons, although they had all promised that they were not going to fight anymore. He turned to them and he said, "What would happen in the future if weapons were allowed to exist among you? Isn't it true that an accident might happen in the future, someone would get cut and blood would start to flow? And then you would go back to that condition you just came out of." He looked around and there he saw a tall white pine. Because of its height, it seemed as though it went into the sky. He said, "We'll choose this tree standing here, which can be seen from long distances. We shall uproot this tree, and we challenge you men who used to fight one another to bury your weapons of war beneath it, so that they will be carried away forever by the strong currents underneath the ground."

The men were reluctant at first to do this, but finally one by one they came forward and cast their weapons into the hole. He also instructed them to take their feelings of hatred, greed, and jealousy, and to bury them also in this ground. After this was done they replanted the tree on top of the weapons. Then he turned back to them and said, "From the base of this tree will come four white roots. They will go into the four directions. In the future maybe many nations will come and recognize the tree's purpose. Maybe individuals will see it and they will have to take shelter underneath this tree. And now what we're going to do is place an eagle on the tree as a symbol of the future. Everyone who is living underneath this Tree of Peace will be entrusted with the responsibility that they must always look into the future like the eagle that sees afar. The greenery of this tree will represent the peace you have made between yourselves, that this peace must always stay fresh and green year 'round, for this tree does not turn colors through the season."

And so as the men gathered there, they appointed all the leaders, and Jigonsaseh was there at the final day. As the Peacemaker had promised, she was the one who put the emblem of the chieftainship titles, the deer horns, on these leaders' heads. He instructed them to stand in a circle around the Tree of Peace, and he brought an arrow forward. He said, "When you're only one nation like this one arrow, you are easily broken," and he broke it in half. Then he took one arrow from each of the nations and he bound the five arrows together. He passed them out amongst the strongest men, but no one could break them. And so he said, "This will be the symbol of your union, your unity in the future. You must never, as one nation, pull your arrow out. You must always be together as one.

In that way, you will always be strong." And so that was the symbol of their union.

Now he told the leaders to hold hands in a circle, and he made some predictions. He said, "In the future, this is what's going to happen: there will be a people coming from somewhere, and they will not understand the meaning of these roots. They will hack at these roots and try to kill the tree, and the tree will weaken and it will start to fall. What is going to happen in those times is that you, the leaders, will be burdened with its heaviness. As this tree falls, it will land on your joined hands. It will rest there for a period of time on your arms, but you must never lose your grip. You must never let it touch the ground, for if you do, peace will come no more.

"When you are burdened with its heaviness and its weight, near the time when you're about to give up, when you're about ready to lose your grip, there will be children born. And when these children observe the leaders burdened with the heaviness and the weight of this tree, they will come forward. One by one they will notice and they will lend a hand, and they will help to raise this tree again. And after it has risen again, a great calm will come and a great peace will arrive, but it will be for the last time." And that is what was predicted.

—Retold by Tekaronianekon (Chief Jake Swamp, Wolf Clan/Mohawk)

Adapted from *The Peacemaker's Journey*, told by Chief Jake Swamp (Parabola Audio, 1996).

CHAPTER FIVE

DOING YOUR THINKING: INDIGENOUS KNOWLEDGE

Native intellectuals, and there are many, have not been well respected by Euro-American scholars until relatively recently, when we have all had to look to the old wisdom and knowledge in hopes of restoring broken ecologies. The ancient knowledge of this world still exists, though it was dismissed by the new people who arrived. Matthiessen writes that for Indian people, an unbroken knowledge was passed down century after century, while in Europe traditions were ruptured and the relationship with nature forgotten in a human-centered world. His essay covers much ground, or should we say "Earth." He knows "the earth and myself are of one mind." We are now sought for our knowledge. Survival may depend on the people Columbus first called "People of God," *In Dios*.

Parabola
Volume: 6.1
Earth and Spirit

NATIVE EARTH

Peter Matthiessen

Christopher Columbus, going ashore in the Antilles, was struck by the profound well-being of the island Arawak. He called them *indios*, not because he imagined them to be inhabitants of India (which in the fifteenth century was still called Hindustan) but because he recognized that these friendly, generous Taino people, soon to be extinct, lived in blessed harmony with their surroundings—*"una gente in Dios,"* a People in God.[1]

Columbus's perception was shared by many Europeans, before and after, although the Vikings soon skirmished with the *skraelings*, and so did the English colonists farther south, despite the great kindness and assistance they received from the Algongkin peoples. Though the Europeans recognized the abundance of the land and waters, they were appalled by the sheer might of nature in a huge land without the mark of man, and with the departure of their ships, they felt homeless, cast away. They had not been prepared for the fierce extremes of climate, and they were dismayed by the huge dark wall of virgin forest; hiding unknown dangers from their view, it was perceived as oppressive and dangerous, even malevolent. As William Bradford wrote from the Plymouth Colony, "What could they see but a hideous and desolate wilderness, full of wild beasts and wild men? And what multitudes there might be of them, they knew not." Daniel Boone, breaking the so-called Wilderness Trail across the Cumberland Gap into Kentucky well over a century later, was still referring to "the horror" of this wilderness, which was everywhere met with a frenzy of land-clearing far beyond any practical need. In the nineteenth century, among intellectuals, an identity of "God" and "Nature" was perceived, but the idea made small impression on the frontier. To judge from the ruthless treatment of "the wild men" and the wasteful and destructive exploitation of the North American continent, the view of primordial nature as a "wilderness" to be tamed and dominated has persisted as part of the American sensibility to the present day.

The American Indian, of course, had no such concept. In fact, it was the Indians' lack of interest in modifying nature, their ability to live happily at one with it, that seemed to the beleaguered colonists the most savage thing about them. In 1796, an Indian told the Governor of Pennsylvania, "We love quiet. We suffer the mouse to play. When the woods are rustled by the wind, we fear not."[2] As far south as the cold, hard plateaus of Tierra del Fuego, where landmarks were commemorated by the white men with such names as "Famine" and "Desolation," the Indian understood the *rightness* of nature, in which nothing is out of place; one astonished missionary heard an Ona, gazing out across the windswept barrens, murmur rapturously, "*Yak haruin*"—my country. A northern land described by whites in recent years as "barren, uninhabited, fit only for flooding" is known to the Cree as *Kistikani*, "the Garden." In the Pacific Northwest, a chief declared, "Every part of this earth is sacred to my people. Every shining pine needle, every sandy shore, every mist in the dark woods, every clearing and humming insect is holy in the memory and experience of my people."[.]

An Indian friend in California once told me how much she hated the phrase "wild Indian" in the American History books that she was given to read in school: "We were never 'wild,'" as she said. "We were just natural." Traditional people, still in harmony with the world around them, do not isolate themselves from other living things, nor consider one creature superior to another. This was also true of Europeans, before the discoveries of science made them observers, manipulators of the natural world, instead of unselfconscious participants. By seeking to dominate it, the white men set themselves in opposition to a vital, healing force of which they were a part and thereby mislaid a whole dimension of existence.

One thing we know which the white man may one day discover. Our God is the same God. You may think now that you own him as you wish to own our land. But you cannot. He is the Body of man. And his compassion is equal for the red man and the white. This earth is precious to him. And to harm the earth is to heap contempt on its creator. The whites, too, shall pass—perhaps sooner than other tribes. Continue to contaminate your bed, and you will one night suffocate in your own waste. When the buffalo are all slaughtered, the wild horses all tamed, the secret corners of the forest heavy with the scent of many men, and the view of the ripe hills blotted by talking wires, where is the thicket? Gone. Where is the eagle? Gone. And what is it to say goodbye to the swift and the hunt, the end of living and the beginning of survival?³

In such utterances as these, and many many others, there is a clarity and a quiet beauty that is stunning, and I wonder if it isn't this very suggestion of a vision of existence more universal than our own that makes the Indian way of life so fascinating to all people of the Western world. We can no longer pretend—as we did for so long—that Indians are a primitive people: no, they are a traditional people, that is, a "first" or "original" people, a primal people. And it isn't just that we admire the teachings that are implicit in their vision but that we *need* them, if we are to live our lives in a complete way as whole beings, not seeking to dominate but to live in harmony with the natural world. The Indian concept of earth and spirit has been patronizingly dismissed as simple-hearted "naturalism," or "animism," when in fact it derives from a holistic vision known to all mystics and great teachers, the most ancient and venerated religion in the world. How ironic it seems that so many Americans, alienated from the earth that gives them life, have turned to Eastern religions for a healing vision, instead of learning from a similar vision which has always existed right beside us. "There are hundreds of religions in this country, and still you white people are searching for something else. We are not searching—we are already there. And you don't have to join us: you are already there, too. You just have to realize it." These words of a Pueblo Indian, an uneducated man from the streets of Los Angeles, might have been used by a Zen master in regard to the enlightened state of Buddhahood: "You are already there; you just have to realize it." Or as an old holy man of the Ute Indians has said, "You are becoming what you have always been."[4] Yet to this day, we dismiss Indian belief as something archaic, picturesque, to be pushed aside by that lunatic insistence on "progress," on "growth," on gross national product, that is destroying the land and air and water, the countryside, small towns and small businesses and small farmers, not to speak of quality and craftsmanship, the human habitat, birdsong, quiet, harmony, the night, and the very soul of man. Recently I saw an old John Wayne movie called *Hondo*; at the end, as the Apaches are defeated, Wayne says, "It's the end of a way of life—a good way. NOW GET THOSE WAGONS MOVING!" Those wagons of Progress are still moving, riding roughshod over what is left of the beautiful American Canaan. Not only have we failed to learn from the Indians' "good way of life," we are still in the process of destroying it through acculturation, the bureaucracies, the so-called termination legislation, and land claim settlements that prepare the way for seizing and polluting the last remnants of Indian Land.

> *Only to the white man was nature a "wilderness" and only to him was the land "infested" with "wild" animals and "savage" people. To us it was tame. Earth was bountiful and we were surrounded with the blessings of the Great Mystery. Not until the hairy man from the east came and with brutal frenzy heaped injustices upon us and our families that we loved was it "wild" for us. When the very animals of the forest began fleeing from his approach, then it was that for us "the Wild West" began.*[5]

Some rudimental understanding of Indian attitudes toward earth and spirit may be gained from such statements to the white man. However, one must keep in mind that the vast majority of Indian "sayings" were transcribed by white men, and are apt to be more literary—though no more eloquent—than the original.

The well-known words quoted above, for example, were transcribed by chief Standing Bear's acculturated niece; Black Elk was interpreted by a white man. Much authentic material has been documented in ethnographic publications, but excepting a few early works by "educated" Indians, such as the study of the Iroquois by the Tuscarora scholar, J. N.

B. Hewitt, and *The Soul of the Indian* by a Lakota, Dr. Charles Eastman, very little has been made available to the public; until recent years, when a number of gifted young Indian writers have emerged, it was very rare to hear an Indian in his own voice. Even now, the term "Indian literature" is limiting, even patronizing, carrying the suggestion that the writing is not mature enough to be called "literature" on its own merits. And the term is hollow: the images and rhythms, even the content, may be "Indian" to the degree that they provide at least an echo of the oral tradition, with its chants and dancing, but the narrative techniques will nonetheless be "Western"—that is, the techniques of the written word.

The oral tale, the ritual drama, on the other hand, are part of a poetic and dramatic tradition that goes back for centuries, beyond the earliest memory of the people. When the white man first appeared in North America, Indian lyric poetry, long epic narratives—such as the Creation Cycles of the Iroquois and Hopi—and a kind of ritual-drama (the Hako Ceremony of the Pawnee) were already well developed. Of these, the most fascinating is the controversial Wallum Olum or "Red Record," written in red ochre pictographs on bone and bark; the Wallum Olum is the immigration myth of the Lenape (the "Delaware") which may date back many thousands of years. But committed to print, these long and sustained narratives, without the ritual dance and chanting that invite the observer to suspend his thoughts and enter another world, read rather like opera might read without the music and stage business. And there are elements missing even in short poems, like these pure, spare songs of the Ojibwa:

> *Butterfly Song: In the coming heat of the*
> *day I stood there*
> *Mide Song: Drifting snow—why do*
> *I sing?*
> *Song of the Thunders: Sometimes I go*
> *about in pity for myself*
> *And all the while*
> *A great wind is bearing me across the sky.*

So much resonance in so few words, in the way of *haiku*! But are we hearing them as they were conceived? What we are reading may be beautiful, but more often it is prettified; how "Indian" it is by the time it appears in print is a good question. Perhaps there were syllables to be sung and danced that are no longer present in the written form. Very likely—to our ear, at least—the original might have seemed repetitive, monotonous, staccato. Only rarely is the original provided, with a literal translation, and the white man's "interpretations" identified as such. Many of the original languages are lost; the "interpreter" may "improve" the old translations as he pleases. Perhaps these poems represent the spirit if not the letter of the song, but we cannot be sure. Even what has been presented as Indian thought—books such as *Black Elk Speaks* or *Land of the Spotted Eagle*, or even a more earthy and less "literary" book like *Lame Deer: Seeker of Visions*—represents selective interpretations by the white man, with the strong rhetorical overtones of the white man's voice. And however poetic or mystical, however true to the original spirit of what was said, these interpretations all mislead us in being presented as the creative vision of one Indian, who at best is no more than the eloquent spokesman of a distilled vision of the world that has come down through the oral tradition, century after century; it is a whole people that is speaking (or singing, or painting). Only recently, in imitation of the white man, have Indians signed their work; they would approve of Georgia O'Keeffe, who when asked, "Why don't you sign your work?" responded, "Why don't you sign your face?" Nor is it the Indian who regards these sayings or these tales or songs as literature or poetry, far less "art," but the white man or woman who compiled them, edited them, and read them, applying his Western standards all the way.

There are exceptions, of course, and one of them is a recent collection of songs and tales of the Swampy Cree called *The Wishing Bone Cycle*;[6] they are fresh and amazing, earthy, very funny—so much so that I suspect they come much closer to the original than the more lyrical interpretations we are accustomed to, in which too much imagination has been used to bridge the cultures. And perhaps this is because the translator was raised among the Cree, speaks several dialects, and still returns there every year to visit. There is little attempt to be "poetic"; he is content with the pure spare beauty of the event. Thus, he tells me, the single Cree word *kooko-westiminkwe-neeshke* means "owl drifting down on a single snowflake, without noise."

Whether poem, narrative, or drama, works in the oral tradition were chanted or sung, usually to the accompaniment of a dance, and meaningless syllables were added, to conform the chanting to the rhythm. Though often poetic, these songs were rarely if ever composed for their own sake, any more than costumes or weavings or baskets were simply "decorated." They were aspects of ritual, in which the mystical reality was made visible through symbolic action, an interaction of forces out of which the mystery arises for those who are ready to see.

Among Indians, the concept of an art separate from the nature of which life is part is as unnatural as the idea of a life separated from religion. Rock painting, tent symbols, body paint, sand paintings, blankets, moccasins, belts, baskets, even jewelry, had signs that transmitted a teaching, and the most sacred signs were withheld from objects manufactured for the white man; for in a life that is not separate from religious experience, such objects may be dangerous, containing the power of a world in which there are no accidents. This power is not to be corrupted. To weave a basket is to re-enact the process of creation, and the finished basket is the image of the universe.

Since an art (or an artist) as something apart from daily existence is not recognized, "the basis for aesthetic judgment is mystical"; that is, it is rich or poor in quality according to the amount of power it can bring about. The words of songs were less important than the state of mind evoked, since these elevated states were protective and curative; in other words, these poem/songs were valued as much for the reaction in oneself as for the effect on others. All songs had a certain power, returning the singer to harmony with the life force, the Great Mystery, that permeates all of creation.

As a Blackfoot says,

> *I meditated often upon the powers in the air, water and earth. They are the great mysteries. Everything is done by them. ... I spent hours on the hilltop and near the waters, meditating and watching the birds, animals, and heavens.*[7]

All nature is sacred, therefore even "nature songs" are sacred. Songs and tales that are apparently recounted to entertain also help to account for strange things seen in daily life, or to reinforce the tribal history, or illustrate it; they are apt to be instructive, cautionary, practical. A Cree says, "The best storyteller is one who lets you live if the weather is bad"— in other words, if the story is about ice-fishing, there should be some instruction in it that the hungry listener might one day put to use. Even if the story is just funny, the laughter and happiness it brings are precious gifts in the long winter night, or in time of famine; among the Big Mountain Navajo, tales are only told in winter, when they are most needed.

The songs, too, whether vengeance songs or lullabies, were dedicated to specific ceremonies or occasions in order to bring a desired influence upon the outcome. For example, a man setting out upon a hunt might have a hunting song, and a song for the first sighting of his quarry, a song to be sung by his wife for his safekeeping, and many others. In addition, many Indians had a personal song, which was used to elevate the possessor to a plane of awareness and spiritual power.

Even the love songs are practical as well as lyrical—more often than not, they are invocations to assure *success* in love—and many of the so-called love songs "are actually songs of *seeking*, the mystical quest for the Great Mystery."[8] This seeking manifests itself to the very end, as in the Death Song of a Yokuts man (California):

> *All my life*
> *I have been seeking,*
> *Seeking!*

This is not an expression of despair, as (I suspect) the white interpreter has understood it, but on the contrary, a celebration of existence. The death song helps him to achieve a transcendent state of mind in order to face death, whether in famine or in battle or in plain old age; it was very important to the Indian to die well, for one's dying was not only a part of living but an expression of one's life, completing the circle. For traditional Indians, death is an initiation, a *becoming*, not a return into the cosmic void, and it promises the beauty of fulfillment, as in this Zuni death song:

> Hi-ithia, naiho-o
> *It is finished*
> *In beauty it is finished.*

This is the transcendental beauty that the Yurok know as *merwer serger*—"the pure and the complete." *Nih-Zhoni-go*, or "Go in beauty," say the Navajo.

Indian existence is not separable from Indian religion, which is not separable from the natural world. It is not a matter of "worshiping nature," as anthropologists suggest. Nature itself is the primordial religion, and man is an aspect of nature; the word "religion" itself makes an unnecessary separation. Nature itself is "the Great Mystery," the "religion before religion," the profound intuitive apprehension of the true nature of existence attained by mystics of all ages, everywhere on earth: the whole universe is sacred, man is the whole universe, and the religious ceremony is life itself, the miraculous common acts of every day. Respect for nature is respect for oneself; to revere it is self-respecting, since man and nature, though not the same thing, are not different. Plants and animals that must be taken are thanked with ceremony and respect, and rocks are not moved carelessly from their own places. Every day, blessings are offered to the sun, air, and wind of the four directions, the water that brings life, the mother earth, and nothing is wasted. And this respectful awareness of the world around, of its warnings and its affirmations, brings a joyous humility, a *simplicity*, that is also respect for the Great Mystery, or the "Great Spirit."

"Great Mystery" is a better translation of the power of nature than "Great Spirit," which reflects an attempt of missionary origin to give the red man our own sort of externalized "God." "God" comes from the German "Gut" and means "the Good One," but at one time we did not externalize this concept. Even Christian mystics recognized "the Lord who is seen within": Meister Eckhart said, "The eye with which I see God is the eye with which God sees me." In Aramaic, the language of Jesus, the word for God is "Alaha"—to the Arabs "Allah"—which means "Essence." And this is also the meaning of "Great Mystery"—which Iroquoian peoples call *orenda*, the invisible creative power, the life essence that permeates everything from the outermost stars to the smallest stone. "It represents the unused earth force," Lame Deer says. … "(Wakan Tanka) pours a great, unimaginable amount of force into all things—pebbles, ants, leaves, whirlwinds—whatever you will."

The Medicine Wheel of the Plains tribes is very similar in concept to the Asian mandala, which reflects all of existence.

*This Medicine Wheel can best be understood if you think of it
as a mirror in which everything is reflected. ... Any idea, person
or object, can be a Medicine Wheel, a Mirror for Man. The tiniest flower can be such a Mirror, as can a wolf, a story, a touch, a
religion, or a mountain top.*[9]

Mitakuye Iyasin, the Lakota, says: All my Relations! meaning all one's
relations with everything on earth. Indian healing ceremonies are based on
the idea of restoring those relations, including the balance of a body and
spirit—they are not different—that are out of harmony with the world
around. For Indians know, as all traditional peoples have known, that
"there is one flow, one common breathing, all things are in sympathy"—
so wrote the Greek Hippocrates, four centuries before Christ—in other
words, before the Western world had lost touch with the Old Ways. Listen to Dersu the Trapper, a forest Tungus tribesman of Siberia, awed by
rainy mist: "Ground, hill, forest, all same Man. He sweating now. Hark."
And he listened. "Hear Him breathe? All same Man!"

"The Indian," says a Cheyenne elder, "is a manifestation of the breath
or energy of God. He is earth, but the earth part is only that which
makes him visible; the part which is his real life ... is that which we call
the breath of God. Man, because he partakes of this spiritual essence, has
a mind reaching beyond the conscious mind. It is that which flows into
him from the deity."[10]

Breath is this essence or power or orenda, and the wind that animates
the leaves is the invisible breath of God. "*N'leheleche*," the Delaware say.
"I exist, I breathe." Or better, perhaps, "I am breathed." To the Mikasuki,
the Creator is "the Breath-maker," and a Navajo has said:

*It is the wind that comes out of our mouths now that gives us life.
When this ceases to blow, we die. In the skin of our fingers we can
see the trail of the wind; it shows us where the wind blew when our
ancestors were created.*[11]

The wind, the breath, relates us to all other things, which are not
inferior, nor even separate from us; the humblest stone is a manifestation
of life energy, and the smallest creature has something to teach us in its
accommodations; this is why a turtle or a chickadee may appear during

a vision quest as a spirit helper. In the Western world today, few understand natural matters that are taken for granted by traditional peoples, and few among the Indians themselves know how to listen to animals, to respect the earth; for the majority of the Indians, the traditional people say, the world is a dead thing. Like the white man, they have no home.

> When the last red man has vanished from the earth, and the memory is only the shadow of a cloud moving across the prairie, these shores and forests will still hold the spirits of my people, for they love this earth as the newborn loves its mother's heartbeat. If we sell you our land, love it as we've loved it. Care for it, as we've cared for it. Hold in your mind the memory of the land, as it is when you take it. And with all your strength, with all your might, and with all your heart— preserve it for your children, and love it as God loves us all. One thing we know—our God is the same. This earth is precious to him. Even the white man cannot be exempt from the common destiny.[12]

Chief Joseph of the Nez Perce declared: "The Earth and myself are of one mind"—a fundamental realization of all mystics, and a widespread intuition among traditional peoples: true knowledge of the mother earth becomes true knowledge of the self. A Zen master says, "If you have truly understood a frog, you have understood everything."[13] Western man, having lost touch with the earth, tends to belittle such ideas as Oriental mystification, but who has not had the sense at least once in his life that the trees were watching, or the mountains waiting? In our deepest being, where we still know that we are made of the same elements, the same minerals as trees and mountains, we are all animists. Like it or not, we are manifestations of the Great Mystery, but we no longer pay attention in the way that traditional people do, and so we miss seeing the threads that bind together the temporary accumulations of energy that we call matter—seeing, that is, into the shadows of things, seeing with every sense, with a third eye. Shamans, like Zen masters, encourage disciples to drop all accumulation of mind, to see what is really there, freshly, and without preconceptions. An old Pueblo man says:

> You must learn to look at the world twice. … First you must bring your eyes together in front so you can see the smoke rising from an

ant hill in the sunshine. Nothing *should escape your notice. But you must learn to look again, with your eyes at the very edge of what is visible. Now you must see dimly if you wish to see things that are dim—visions, mist, and cloud people ... animals which hurry past you in the dark. You must learn to look at the world twice if you wish to see all that there is to see.*[14]

Today, physicists are rediscovering these threads, and their views of the *real* nature of existence seem to draw closer every year not only to ancient teachings of the Eastern sages but to the way of traditional people all around the world.

Einstein once remarked that, among all people, twelve-year-old children of the Uto-Aztecan language groups (which include the Hopi) were probably the best prepared to grasp his Theory of Relativity. The Hopi have no expression for "time," far less "past" or "future"; time is not linear but a circulating space where past, present, and future are always together. A Cheyenne elder:

> *Indians do not speak of the beginning as Christians do. They know nothing of the beginning, nor will they say that there is to be an ending.*

Similarly, Chief Crazy Horse did not say, "Today is a good day to die." What he said was, "Today is a good day to die, for all of the things of my life are here." Or (as Zen says), "Everything is right here now."

Indians do not make our life-killing distinctions between mind and body, between the sacred and profane. In many Indian tribes, teachings analogous to Tibetan Tantra are expressed by sacred clowns or dancers who manifest the obscene and the perverse, the upside-down aspects of existence, in order to knock down the barriers of preconceived ideas and permit the initiated, at least, to glimpse the whole flux and interpenetration of existence; thus, they are the messengers between one way of seeing and another. For example, Hopi clowns wearing huge sex organs may simulate copulation right on top of a sacred shrine, as a demonstration of non-attachment to man's preconceived forms and ideas of religion; they break down the structure, the *appearances* of things, to reveal the essence within.

To the same end, a Zen master may shout at his students, "Kill the Buddha!" And the flow of energy between linear reality and the timeless, circular reality behind it, between one way of seeing and the other, is taken for granted by the Indians, who allow that silence that is needed for receiving perceptions that logic and mere words cannot explain—that utter silence which, as Black Elk said, is "the very voice of the Great Spirit."

The Indians approve of the natural world as it is, they do not try to dominate it, far less change it, nor do they think it matters much to understand it, or not, at least, in the white-man way of analyzing and trying to break down its fleeting parts; rather, they see it, that is, *apprehend* it, by opening themselves to the orenda power in the natural world, to the greater reality that underlies what we think we see. A Yurok holy man says (as a Zen master might say), "To see means to see what is actually there, what actually exists; not what you want to be there, but what is *really* there. It's all *seeing*."

A Mohawk friend sometimes asks me if there isn't a conflict between my interest in Indian religion and my training in Zen. Perhaps it is my ignorance, but I find no important conflict; each teaching illuminates the other. Indians place great emphasis on being attentive to the presence of the Great Mystery in every instant, and in all things; Zen, too, insists before all that we remain mindful of the present moment, the common miracles. *Pay attention! Pay attention! Pay attention!* And what excites me is the instinct that this fundamental teaching derives from the same ancient traditions as the mindfulness of the hunters and warriors of other days, who had to develop and maintain an intense awareness in order to survive.

On many occasions I have seen evidence, among traditional peoples, of what seemed to be extraordinary eyesight. Years ago in New Guinea, I was high on a cliffside with an Ndani warrior. He was gazing a mile or more across a sort of river valley and swamp, toward a dense thicket. Although it was early in the morning, with poor light and dark shadow, he suddenly said, "Enemy!" and sank into the bushes as he pointed. I could see nothing. Even with the binoculars, I could not find the man until he pointed again. Finally I made out a dark naked figure in a tree shadow, absolutely still, gazing up at our hiding place. And I thought, "Damn! That's remarkable eyesight!" I could scarcely believe it.

Years later, at Lake Turkana, in the northern Frontier District of Kenya, I was going along the shore with a Molo tribesman. Ahead of us, off a small point at least a mile away, hundreds of boulders emerged from the shallow water. And this fisherman pointed at the boulders, saying, "Crocodile." All that can be seen of such a crocodile are the two nostrils, sometimes the crown—tiny lumps among hundreds of others. And suddenly I understood the miraculous eyesight of traditional peoples.

That warrior could not afford to miss that dark place in the thicket that was not a shadow. He didn't actually see a man. He saw a darkness that didn't belong. Those people belonged to a war culture; they went to war, with spears and bows and arrows, nearly once a week, and they sent out raiding parties in between. He would not survive long if he ignored details in his home territory. And the fisher on the lake shore saw no crocodile snout, he saw one rock too many in a pattern of rocks that in thousands of days had been imprinted on his brain. A bird establishing its territory memorizes its landscape; it knows where to find food, shelter, water, and how to travel in the dark or in a hurry, and it sees everything that comes and goes; total awareness is the secret of holding the territory and even of survival. In cultures that are still close to the earth, survival may depend on noticing what is menacing or edible, and the people see better not because their visual apparatus is superior but because of an awareness of even the most minute change in their surroundings, the total awareness of a cat at a mousehole, not tense in any way, just empty of everything but readiness, so that when something changes in this field of awareness, it is noticed at once—*bang!*

That awareness born of "emptiness" is the source of a power known to shamans and sages alike: "When your mind is empty like a valley or a canyon, then you shall know the power of the Way."

We all have "power" to one degree or another, but it has withered with disuse, like our appendix, like the ability to run 100 miles in a single day. There are channels of communication, ways of seeing, for which our very limited idea of reality has no vocabulary, and there is nothing "supernatural" about these channels; they are natural attributes of mind that can be reopened through yoga or Zen meditation training, or by the Eskimo technique of carving big circles of soft stone, or by the dances of the Bushman and the Dervish and the Pueblo, which obliterate the structures of the intellect, allowing what an Indian has called "the big heart powers" to rush in. To perceive the true nature of existence was one reason for performing a vision quest: after four days of fasting alone on a high rock, in the great silence and solitude of earth, one is bound to discover that what was thought of as a separate self is not separate from the trees, the rocks, the hawk, the insect peoples, that beyond the senses lies a different plane of consciousness in which all is related, simultaneous, and one.

There are many paths or "ways" to this awareness; one need not be an Indian to arrive there. Indeed one must be careful not to romanticize Indian "powers" or spirituality, especially since most Indians have lost touch with the Old Ways. On the other hand, there seems no doubt that traditional peoples the world over have much to teach a spiritually crippled race which, as Lame Deer said, sees "only with one eye." This half-blindedness has been the curse of the white people as long as the Indians have known us, but we have not always been accursed; at one time, we knew the *mysterium tremendum*. And we must feel awe again if we are to return to a harmonious existence with our own habitat, and survive.

As a first step, we might consider this Great Mystery that is all about us and in every moment; it is the music of the stars, the color of the wind, the dead stillness between tides at dead of night, birds, trees, feet, sea pearls and manure, and it is no less and no more strange or beautiful or scary than our life itself. When modern man has regained his respect for the earth, when science becomes a tool in the service of nature rather than a weapon to dominate it, then the lost Paradise, the Golden Age in the race memories of all people on earth will come again, and all men will be "in Dios," People of God.

Notes:

1. Courtesy of Russell Means.

2. From *Touch the Earth*, ed. T. C. McLuhan (New York: E. P. Dutton, 1971).

3. Chief Sealth, Coastal Salish, in a letter to President Pierce, 1854.

4. From *Ritual of the Wind*, Jamake Highwater (New York: Viking Press, 1977).

5. Chief Luther Standing Bear in *Land of the Spotted Eagle*, ed. May Montoya Jones Warcaziwin (Lincoln, NE: Bison Books, 1978).

6. Howard Norman, *The Wishing Bone Cycle* (Santa Barbara: Ross-Erikson, revised and expanded, 1980).

7. Smoking Star, Blackfoot, in *American Indian Life*, Clark Wissler (originally published by the American Museum of Natural History, New York).

8. From Mary Austen's Introduction to *American Indian Poetry,* ed. George Cronyn (New York: Liveright, 1934).

9. Hyemeyohsts Storm, Cheyenne

10. Alfred Wilson, Cheyenne

11. Washington Matthews, *Navajo Legends* (Millwood, New York: Kraus Reprint of 1897 edition).

12. Chief Sealth, Coastal Salish, in a letter to President Pierce, 1854.

13. Shunryu Suzuki Roshi, *Zen Mind, Beginner's Mind* (New York: Weatherhill, 1970).

14. Jamake Highwater, *Ritual of the Wind* (New York: Viking, 1977).

Acknowledgment: An earlier version of this paper was delivered as the first Belkin Memorial Lecture at the University of California, San Diego in spring 1979.

Parabola
Volume: 24.1
Nature

THE GREAT WITHOUT

Linda Hogan

In European natural histories, human imagination was
most often projected onto the outside world. Pliny's Natural History, for instance, was an errant map of a true world.
There were dog-headed humans who could only bark, men
with heads in their chests, and people with only one foot
but with the ability to leap powerfully and to use the foot
as a shade tree. There were mermaids, springs believed
to grant eternal life, and islands where demons or angels
lived. At one time the Egyptians thought that people on
the other side of the world walked upside down. Bestiaries
included the phoenix, griffins, and unicorns. Unshaped by
fact, knowledge, or even observation, these fantasy worlds
became the world as seen by the human mind.

Even in later times, the relationship between nature
and humanity posed a dilemma. Once it was thought that
the world entered the human eye, and that only through
our seeing of it did it exist. There was much discussion
about how a mountain could fit into the human eye. This
difficulty with perspective pushed humans toward other
conclusions just as erroneous as believing foremost in the
eye of the beholder. Euclid thought the eye was the point
of origin for all things. Plato believed the world emanated from the eye, while others thought that there was
something given off from objects by which we perceived
them. In any case, most of the theories made nature

smaller than it is and made the human larger. Vision was about the seer only, not the seen.

Nothing could be more different from how tribal people on all continents have seen the world. From the perspectives of those who have remained in their own terrain for thousands of years, there were—and are—other points of view. For tribal thinkers, the outside world creates the human: we are alive to processes within and without the self. It is a more humble way to view the world, and far more steady. Nature is the creator, not the created.

There exists, too, a geography of spirit that is tied to and comes from the larger geography of nature. It offers to humans the bounty and richness of the world. Father Berard Haile, a priest traveling among the Navajo in the 1930s, was in awe of the complexity of their knowledge, one that exists within the context of what we now call an ecosystem. In the Upward Moving Way, for example, the ceremony brings in all aspects of the growth of plants: the movement upward as the roots deepen, the insects beneath and above the ground, the species of birds which come to this plant. All aspects of the ceremony reveal a wide knowledge of the world. In order to heal, this outside life and world must be taken in and "seen" by the patient as being part of one working system.

Laurens van der Post, a writer, naturalist, and psychologist who grew up in Africa, wrote in his essay "The Great Uprooter" about how his son's illness was announced by a dream. In the dream, the young man stood on a beach, unable to move, watching a great tidal wave of water bearing down on him. From out of the swell of the wave, a large black elephant walked toward him. It was this dream, van der Post was certain, that announced his son's cancer, the first point of cellular change. Van der Post called the dream something that came from "the great without": such an experience seemed to encompass, he said, all the withouts and withins a human could experience.

Nature is now too often defined by people who are fragmented from the land. Such a world is seldom one that carries and creates the human spirit. Too rarely is it understood that the soul lies at all points of intersection between human consciousness and the rest of nature. Skin is hardly a container. Our boundaries are not solid; we are permeable, and even when we are solitary dreamers we are rooted in the soul outside.

If we are open enough, strong enough to connect with the world, we become something greater than we are.

Turn-of-the-century Lakota writer Zitkala Sa (Gertrude Simmons Bonnin) wrote of the separation between humankind and the natural world as a great loss to her. In her autobiography, she said that nature was what would have helped her to survive her forced removal to Indian boarding school:

> *I was ready to curse men of small capacity for being the dwarfs their God had made them. In the process of my education I had lost all consciousness of the nature world about me. Thus, when a hidden rage took me to the small, white-walled prison which I then called my room, I unknowingly turned away from my own salvation. For the white man's papers I had given up my faith in the Great Spirit. For these same papers I had forgotten the healing in trees and brooks. Like a slender tree, I had been uprooted from my mother, nature, and God.*

Zitkala Sa might have agreed with Pliny that there were dog-headed, barking men, and men with heads, not hearts, in their chests.

Soul loss is what happens as the world around us disappears. In contemporary North American Hispanic communities, soul loss is called *susto*. It is a common condition in the modern world. Susto probably began when the soul was banished from nature, when humanity withdrew from the world, when there became only two things—human and nature, animate and inanimate, sentient and not. This was when the soul first began to slip away and crumble.

In the reversal and healing of soul loss, Brazilian tribal members who tragically lost their land and place in the world visit or re-imagine nature in order to become well again. Anthropologist Michael Harner wrote about healing methods among Indian people relocated to an urban slum of Peru. The healing takes place in the forest at night, as the person is returned for a while to the land he or she once knew. Such people are often cured through their renewed connections, their "visions of the river forest world, including visions of animals, snakes, and plants." Unfortunately, these places are now only ghosts of what they once were.

The cure for susto, soul sickness, is not in books. It is written in the bark of a tree, in the moonlit silence of night, in the bank of a river and the water's motion. The cure is outside ourselves.

In the 1500s, Paracelsus, considered by many to be a father of modern medicine, was greatly disliked by his contemporaries. For a while, though, he almost returned the practice of medicine to its wider place of relationships by emphasizing the importance of harmony between man and nature. His view of healing was in keeping with the one that tribal elders still hold, that a human being is a small model of the world and the universe. Vast spaces stretch inside us, he thought, an inner firmament, large as the outer world.

The world inside the mind is lovely sometimes, and large. Its existence is why a person can recall the mist of morning clouds on a hill, the fern forest, and the black skies of night that the Luiseno call their spirit, acknowledging that the soul of the world is great within the human soul. It is an enlarged and generous sense of self, life, and being, as if not only the body is a creation of the world elements, but air and light and night sky have created an inner vision that some have called a map of the cosmos. In Lakota astronomy, the stars are called the breath of the Great Spirit. It is as if the old Lakota foresaw physics and modern astronomy, sciences that now tell us we are the transformed matter of stars, that the human body is a kind of cosmology.

The inward may have been, all along, the wrong direction to seek. A person seems so little and small, and without is the river, the mountain, the forest of fern and tree, the desert with its lizards, the glacial meltings and freezings and movements of life. The cure for soul loss is in the mist of morning, the grass that grew a little through the night, the first warmth of sunlight, the waking human in a world infused with intelligence and spirit.

Parabola
Volume: 4.4
Storytelling

Doing Your Thinking

Thomas Buckley

> *We look at each other, but we do not see each other any-*
> *more. Our perception of the world has withered away; what*
> *has remained is mere recognition.*
>
> —Viktor Shklovski

The Yurok Indians live where they always have, in north-western California along the lower reaches of the Kla-math River and both above and below its mouth on the Pacific coast near the present-day Oregon border. Num-bering somewhat more than three thousand individuals, the Yurok are but one of several groups indigenous to the area that are at once unique and of similar cultures. Much has changed in the region since 1850, when the Gold Rush brought a massive and devastating influx of non-Indians into the lower Klamath drainage. Yet cul-tural change cannot be simply dealt with as "accultura-tion." Aspects of European-American culture have been adopted, voluntarily and otherwise, by Indians. Usually, however, these have been taken up in a particular, cultur-ally specific way, to be woven into the inclusive fabric of contemporary Indian life. This has been true in education as in every undertaking and expression. It is apparent, at a gross level, in the efforts of college-educated Yurok intel-lectuals towards expressing traditional esoteric values and practices in terms of Jungian and transpersonal psychologies, and in the presence of a young man among the neighboring Hupa who began his training as an Indian doctor, a "shaman," at about the same time that his exceptional facility in mathematics was hitting the local papers. Perhaps the more important and more interesting signs of the persistence of traditional educational ways in contemporary Indian culture are the far more subtle ones; the particular gesture or silence or phrase that a person uses, a specific sort of glance directed at a child or visitor, a certain shared understanding that is present in a group; reactions and recognitions and attitudes that are manifested at the extreme limits of description yet which are distinctly palpable.

I am interpreting aspects of the earlier stages in traditional Yurok education—up through what some Indians consider, today, the old equivalent of a high school diploma; that is, through the acquisition of the necessary tools for higher education. After this point, although studies become increasingly complex and sophisticated, they still rest on the same theories, principles, and techniques. In discussing these aspects of an ever-changing cultural pattern I use the present tense. The "now" thus indicated is to be understood as representing only a part of present Yurok realities—very often and for a great many individuals a submerged, even unconscious part. Nevertheless, the aspects described as occurring in the present are indeed ongoing ones, shifting and entering into new relationships, taking on new guises, as ever throughout the Yurok's long history. Somehow, these things continue to make sense in a context of grammar schools and graduate professional schools, Christian churches and television, home economics and modern hard knocks.

The Universe, *wesonah*, is energy. It moves against itself and creates waves and these waves go through everything. Each person receives and is part of the Universe in this way and, too, each is unique. The energy that enters a human fetus ten weeks after conception is the "life" of that being, its spirit, *wewolocek*. Occasionally this spirit is augmented through the favor and intervention of another human being or a spirit being. In any case, a person's spirit is unique, and to deny this unique life is against the Law.

The Universe incorporates, manifests, is one with, the Law, *tle*, and everything occurring in the world is subject to this Law while expressing it. To guide human beings there are many, many laws—also *tle*—that interpret the (finally unspeakable) Law and apply it to specific situations in the form of rules for conduct. Thus, there is a correct way to behave in every situation, a correct answer to every question; there is truth. Most simply, the truth is what has been known to work, every time. (Some people say that *skuyeni*, "good," really means "successful," *kimoleni*, "bad," "unsuccessful"; but both words have many meanings.)

These things being so, all education and training must move in respect of each unique person's individuality while, at the same time, insuring the success of the results as far as this is possible. That is, the interface between individual and society is specified by culturally defined truth expressed in a legal idiom.

The direct study of the Law itself is advanced study, far beyond the scope of this introduction to "secondary education." One approaches it gradually through study of specific laws as these are encountered in attaining mastery of various sorts of specialized activities. One who has acquired knowledge of many laws and of the Law is *tenohwok*, a "well educated one," a member of an intellectual and spiritual elite minority. One must begin at the beginning and few go that far. To even begin to study the laws pertinent to one's chosen activities one must be able to perceive the "facts" involved in those activities. Thus, before one can learn to think, to define the facts inherent in situations, one must learn to perceive, to "see," *serneryerh, nework*.

Thoughts-and-feelings, being parts of situations, of actions, are simply another sort of *thing*, to be seen and defined. Explanation is largely useless, because a person can only see for himself, and must be both encouraged and allowed to do so.

Thus, a young child is actively taught very little; it learns by watching and copying when it has enough interest. Most things are not explained, since people can only learn by and for themselves, learn to sort out facts, to draw conclusions about what works and what does not. For example, among certain families there is a great emphasis on table manners, a very definite etiquette. Nothing much is said: a young one watches and learns. When it is old enough to know right from wrong but still misbehaves at meals, its meal-basket is turned over, upside down. Hungry or not, no more food. It's up to the child to figure out what's wrong and to fix it, and thus to start learning about the laws concerning food and the respect for both resources and other human beings that underlie them.

To explain too much is to steal a person's opportunity to learn, and stealing is against the Law.

Children grow when they grow, as they learn to see, learn to learn, according to their spirits. A famous man of the last century learned very early to observe the men of his village carefully. After a while, using his toy bow, he killed a bird with valuable feathers. He made a small wooden storage box, as he'd seen done, put the feathers in this, and showed the men. One of them made him a real hunting bow, a small and light one, and from then on he was free to join hunting parties, with all of the rights and responsibilities of a hunter. He had done what a man does and, in this respect, was treated like a man. He was six at the time.

This man was very unusual, leaping to the top of his class in high school, as it were, while most of his age-mates were still in first grade. Most children grow more gradually, spending most of their time with other children, older and younger, helping to take care of the younger ones and learning from the older ones. Usually there is a strong bond with a "grandmother" and, perhaps, a "grandfather"—sources of comfort in a hard world, people who may occasionally explain things. So it goes until puberty. Children are not handled roughly, not scolded severely unless there is really no alternative. They are, after all, only children.

At puberty, when the blood and hair come, things change. The person is an adult now and must act it, or find out about his shortcoming in an emphatic way. Fathers and mothers may occasionally teach their sons and daughters after this point, but it is deemed best to have an "uncle" or an "aunt" do it. Parents and grandparents are considered too emotionally involved to exercise the necessary rigor and objectivity. The leisurely and affectionate learning situation under "grandmothers" and "grandfathers" becomes a thing of the past, although these relatives often remain confidantes. "Uncles" and "aunts" are tougher.

Girls who have been watching their mothers and other older women make baskets and do other household tasks are now expected to do these things well themselves: no more play-baskets. They are helped, taught. A basket is started for the young woman and given to her to finish. The teacher watches, rips out a mistake and hands the workpiece back to be done again. There is very little credit given for "trying"; you can't eat soup out of a good try. If a girl has it in her to be a good basket maker (not all do) she will be one, spending the necessary effort to see how it's done; others are maybe meant to be doing something else.

Once, this was the pattern:

The young man leaves the women's house at puberty (or before if he's ready earlier) and moves into the "sweathouse," the men's house. He no longer plays with the girls and younger children. His education is now largely up to him, and there is a great deal to learn.

Perhaps he decides that it's time to have a real bow, something a man should have—both a weapon and wealth. He finds a man, an "uncle," who is making himself a new bow (maybe not so coincidentally) and he follows this man around, seeing all that he possibly can: where the tree grows, what sort of a tree it is, how it's split and what wood's selected, how this is scraped and fashioned, how the glue is made and the sinew applied. Very little is said. Having seen the whole process, he starts out alone. Maybe he shows his work to this teacher. The older man maybe asks, "Which end of the bow grew towards the top of the tree?" Or, maybe, he just takes the workpiece, scrapes it in the direction opposite to the young man's efforts, hands it back: let him figure it out. He either does or doesn't, and if he doesn't, there's no point in trying to teach him more yet.

I asked an old man canoe maker on the River today if someone had taught him how to build the beautiful old boats. "Naw, nobody taught me nothing. I just watched and picked it up. That's how you used to learn everything; you watched and figured it out and went ahead and did it. Nobody taught you." This man makes fine redwood canoes of a very pure, traditional style. It takes many months, after the tree is felled, and it's a fairly complicated business.

Thoughtful people will tell you that two important things are learned through this process of watching and doing, beyond the actual skill that is acquired. First, one learns to see things as they are, to see the facts. Secondly, seeing the facts, one sees that one must start everything at its beginning and see each necessary step in an action, each constituent part of a situation, clearly, leaving nothing out. If something is left out—like remembering which end of the bow was highest on the tree from which it was cut—one has no choice but to go all the way back to the beginning and start over. The same will be found to be true in thinking through complex problems, in unraveling situations, thinking being an action. One proceeds slowly, in small increments of progress.

If you do leave anything out, if you don't start at the very beginning, or go back to it when you should, your efforts are considered to be out of control. You have reason to doubt yourself and thus, by definition, you are afraid. The process of education is seen as a process of gaining absolute self-confidence, of vanquishing doubt, and thus fear. "Don't you be fearing too much!" are the instructions from the *wogey*, the "Beforetime People." The only way to remove all doubt is to begin at the beginning and follow through, on your own. (An old man to his student who must do something difficult: "Can you do it? Yes or no? Are you doubting? If you have doubts they'll just get in your way when you get out there.")

To see the facts is to see the meaning of the facts: no distinction can be made; a fact *is* a meaning.

I was once sitting with another older man by our fire. When we'd eaten he held up a piece of the wood that we'd gathered. "What's this?" he asked. "Piece of firewood," I answered. He looked sad, disgusted; put down the stick, silent. I thought more. "It's wood, a piece of a tree." He brightened a shade: "That's a little better. What's a tree?"

Later that evening, turning in, he offered a rare bit of direct teaching: "When you can see each leaf as a separate thing, you can see the tree; when you can see the tree, you can see the spirit of the tree; when you can see the spirit of the tree you can talk to it and maybe begin to learn something. Goodnight."

"There are two sides to everything. What a real Man does is to define these and keep them in balance."

A tree is a tree, and it is each of its parts. This is the physical tree, a fact, and there is a spiritual tree as well, another fact, a potential object of perception. This spiritual tree has two sides, a side that can be seen, as the physical is seen, and another side, completely different, as spirit is completely different from matter. These two sides have two sides, too. To know a tree, to be in control of your relationship to trees, is to define all of these sides, these facts, and to act from the totality of this knowledge. But one can only begin at the beginning. Learning to see material things, then, is basic to learning to see nonmaterial things, simply because the former are more obvious, more easily perceivable facts; not because they are, finally, qualitatively different. Seeing the physical is the beginning of a continuum that includes more advanced orders of perception and of definition. One must explore the entire continuum in order to find its middle, the point of balance from which all truly controlled action springs, and at which all fear is rendered irrelevant.

Thoughts, as well as spiritual things, are facts that can be seen. Contemplating, "doing your thinking," *kocpoks, leponol owenkip*, means seeing mental and emotional facts and defining them. Speculation is something quite different, and native-educated Yurok are consistently careful, in conversation, to discriminate between what they've seen to be a fact, and what they think or surmise to be a possibility.

(A simple technique begins to teach one how to define thoughts as facts. One has, let's say, family trouble. He's confused and prey to uncontrolled emotion, to doubt. He should pick up a stone and see it. He shouldn't just look at it, but see it, as though no one were there behind his eye-holes. Now he looks at the situation at home in the same way, defines the facts as they are, as though no "he" were looking at them.)

Every person, again, has a unique spirit or potential. In northwestern California, as elsewhere, "be true to yourself" is, finally, the ultimate expressible law. The question becomes, then, *who* you are, all of you, each aspect clearly defined. Knowing this exactly, doubt vanishes and one becomes capable of living a balanced life. In the Yurok view, only a fool tries to be other than what he potentially is, and only a fool fails to take responsibility for his full potential. Fools are laughed at and usually come to a bad end.

Of course, *who one is* has two sides to it, a personal and a social one, and each of these has two sides, and so on. Education moves to both illuminate and to integrate these aspects and the succession of paired aspects inherent in each. Female puberty offers a succinct example.

Traditionally, when a girl menstruates for the first time she undertakes a ten-day period of seclusion and ritual activity, an amplified version of the routine she'll follow during each of her periods until menopause. One side of menstruation is seen to be polluting and dangerous, even poisonous. The other, balancing side is seen to be that of great, female energy, menstruation marking the time at which a woman is at the peak of her powers, closest to realizing her full potential. It is, thus, a very "pure" and "beautiful" thing, too.

Experienced women instruct the young woman in the laws pertaining to menstruation, socializing her as it were. At the same time, because a young woman is close to her potentials at this time, it is a time for her to "do her thinking," to engage in the most focused sorts of reflection and self-definition. Meditation and contemplation are thus strongly urged by her teachers and supported by various routines and rituals. For example, after a certain period of ritual austerity, the new woman is given an abalone shell to see. (The abalone is identified as both female and as sun-like, or spirit-like.) In the polished whorls and patterns she sees her own life's trail, her direction, unique and individual.

Again, scratching-sticks are used, it being against the law for a woman to touch her own body while menstruating. The standard anthropological explanation of this practice, widespread in native North America, is that one is so highly charged with pollution that, touching oneself, one poisons oneself. The analysis of Yurok women has a more satisfying logic: one makes scratching and touching difficult, keeping it conscious and intentional, they say, so that a woman is encouraged to perceive all of her body exactly as it is, every itch included. Coming to know the body more intimately during this time of heightened access to the truth, the facts, one comes to know oneself more intimately.

Another side of *who one is* is, of course, who one is not. As for the menstruating woman the body is utilized as an organ of perception richly implicated in a process of contemplation, so a young man's body may be used in "doing his thinking" about who he is and who he is not.

A Yurok teacher:

"My nephew was so angry! So mad at the world. I told him, 'Do like they used to do in the old days. You're mad, you think you're pretty tough? Well, go down to the beach in the high surf, you'll find out. You go fight with the waves for a while, kick them and beat them and try to knock them down. Your Father, the ocean, will show you something. Now when you've had enough, when you can't stand up anymore, go lie on the beach, that's your Mother. Kick her and pound her and yell at her too. She'll forgive you. When you're done in, just lie still and cry. She'll tell you something you need to know.'"

Body and mind, then, are both mobilized in "doing one's thinking," in defining facts. To seek perception with the body is to "train," *hohkep*, and the object of "training" is to "make medicine," to experience immediately a direct perception of a certain order of facts which serve to confirm one's potentials, one's particular slice of the Universe's energies, one's area of specialization in life. "Making medicine" equates with what have been called "vision" or "power quests."

In training and in making medicine, exoteric techniques and esoteric experience are interdependent, balanced. To an extent, this is true in all situations and actions: "In the old days everything we did was a prayer. We are the praying people, that's who we are." However, training and medicine making comprise specific educational means, particular categories of action. Because training for medicine making always demands stringent austerity—including continence—young men and women are urged to start out as early as they can, before they get too interested in sex. Most training is an individual matter, involving student and teacher only, although there was once a ceremonial society, a kind of study-club, the *talth*, through which young men and women trained, under a priest, towards participation in the Jump Dance, a major religious event.

Most available descriptions of training and of medicine making and of their equivalents in other Indian cultures have stressed the "supernatural" aspects of such undertakings. These are, indeed, present—but so are other, purely pragmatic elements. Of particular interest here is the role of perception, of "defining the facts," in these undertakings. An old man told me about training for "making ocean medicine" by swimming far out into the sea during a storm on a winter's night:

> *I was afraid of the ocean. I was born that way I guess. When I was about eleven, my uncle made me go sit on a big drift-log that stuck in the beach and hung far out over the surf. I wanted to come in right away, but he made me stay. I sat there all night. Slowly, I began to see the water, to see what the important things about it were. And when I saw this, I started to see the facts about my fear of it. After I came in, for two or three years, I studied the water, and I studied my fear, and I swam a great deal. I defined all of these things for myself. Finally, I was ready to make my medicine. I didn't try to do it; I just did it. Actually, I'd made my medicine while I was training, before I made the swim. If I hadn't my uncle wouldn't have let me do it. The swim itself, going out to that rock at night, swimming*

around it three times, slapping it—that wasn't the medicine. It was
just demonstrating it, a way of making it public, and of recognizing
what I'd become; showing that I could do it any time, on purpose. I
was in control of my fear and of the sea before I started. If I hadn't
been, I would have drowned, and people would have laughed at me
for thinking that I was a Man.

In Yurok, one doesn't speak of "power." One speaks only of "doing," and of "control." Power, as this man's ocean-power, is there, always. But there is no specific Yurok word for it because it is irrelevant without an individual's ability to control it, to *do* with it.

An important part of doing is, then, "doing your thinking," perceiving non-material aspects of situations as objects, facts which may be defined and, hence, controlled. There is truth, and that truth is factual, independent of personal desire; one thus learns, with the teacher's help, to discriminate between "hallucinations"—a fantasy, the product of wishful thinking—and "vision," an objective seeing of spiritual facts manifested in the physical.

All learning is experiential. It follows clearly from the Yurok theory of individuality that knowledge is an object of perceptual experience, and only an individual is capable of experiencing for himself. Here, we find what seems extreme subjectivity being interpreted as pure objectivity. What is thought by a person and what is experienced by him as true are two different things and, in Yurok view, the difference is immediately obvious to the skilled observer, the teacher who has himself experienced the truth at hand. If this teacher does not see for himself the evidence of his student's having experienced, seen, the facts of the matter, the student's solution to the problem at hand is not accepted by the teacher. "Belief," obviously, has no part in the system; an individual either knows the facts, or he is ignorant of them.

The Yurok do, however, have a culture. This is to say that there exist a myriad of ways of directing the individual toward certain experiences, perceptions of specified truths or facts. There is, after all, a correct way to build a canoe, to make a bow, to become brave, to know the world. Individuals must, in a sense, reinvent the culture for themselves; but they must reinvent the culture that has been reinvented by individuals before them, the culture that will work because it is based in a finite series of facts.

Among the modes of directing experience towards specified knowledge is, as in most cultures, discourse and other forms of verbal instruction. Among the Yurok, all discourse must start and end with the individual who wishes to learn. It is the student who defines, through "doing his thinking," what is worth knowing. It is the student who asks the questions not the teacher, and if no questions are asked, no possible clues to answers are offered. When the questions stop, so does education.

Questions may be answered in a variety of ways, none of which seem direct. Perhaps the most common answering device, once, was the exhortatory recitation of myths, historical narratives, and set prayers in which, the teacher felt, were embedded the facts necessary for the student's correct approach to the problem at hand, there for him to see if he chose to and was capable of it. Even answers to questions on simple techniques are often fielded in this apparently obscure way. "I can't learn *for* you, can I?" asks a Yurok teacher. Thus, rare attempts at giving straight instructions usually come out as relatively oblique suggestions: "Well, in the old days, if a fella wanted to do that, maybe he'd get up before dawn and ..."

An interesting variation on the use of narrative and formulas in answering questions is the use of personal songs as *koan*-like problems, sometimes posed by a teacher or counselor in answer to the question of a student or client and sometimes proposed by the student to his teacher in answer to his own question after he'd contemplated further. A modern example, made in English:

The fawn lies quiet
in the grass
The lily
does not sing[1]

(We note, in this example, the tendency to "think in pairs"; it is understood that the adequate "answer" reveals their "balance.")

Having been given such a song by a teacher it is up to the student to show the teacher that he knows what it means; that he is capable of perceiving, of experiencing the facts referred to. Here, the comparison with Zen koan rests on more than form or relative obscurity.

While these songs are of great interest, their use has apparently never been particularly common. Far more common, along with the recitation of myths and other narratives, is the simple technique of returning the question to the student, from a different perspective and, usually, at a higher level.

Back to the bow. If a young man wants to learn, he asks his teacher why he uses wood from the side of the tree that he does. "Use wood from the side that the moon never shines on," the teacher might answer or, "from the side that's away from the water," adding, in either case, "why's that?" (There are two sides, of course, to a correct answer in this case, a physical and a spiritual one.) The young man goes off and "does his homework," as people put it nowadays. When he's answered, proven that he's seen, defined the facts of the matter, he may ask another question and gets it also thrown back at him.

Each step is marked by a clear perception of what is construed to be purely objective, facts as concrete as the manifest world. Teachers tend to be extremely demanding in precisely this regard, and the educational process is accompanied by a good deal of frustration, anxiety, and impatience on the student's part. As Raymond White pointed out to be the case among the Luiseño, far to the south of the Yurok, "No one is permitted information beyond his *demonstrated* capabilities."[2] The only acceptable demonstration is that of having experienced the truth of the matter. "I think that probably ..." will not suffice. Until the student comes up with something better, sees something through and through, he simply hasn't "done his thinking"; having experienced nothing for himself, he has done nothing at all.

From such experience, in the native theory, come self-confidence and freedom from doubt as surely as these things come from a ritual swim in the stormy ocean at night.

As the Yurok *tenohwol* has learned to see two sides to everything while seeing the whole as well, so we must see two sides to the Yurok mode of education. The collective, mystical, "supernatural" and "power-" oriented aspects of indigenous American educational systems have become familiar and popular fare during the past two decades. I have stressed a second side, an objective, pragmatic, and individualistic one that reveals both a consistent and satisfying logic and easily recognizable common sense. It is but one of two sides that have always been intrinsically interrelated, blended into a single cultural mode that might be characterized as pragmatic mysticism.

"To make deer-hunting medicine, first you learn to see the bush that's in front of you, then the bush behind that bush, then the deer behind the bush behind the bush that's in front of you, then the spirit of that deer. Now you can call the deer, his spirit, and he'll walk up to you. The people with the strongest medicine learn to fly out, their spirits, and find the deer that way."

Special thanks to Herquer, expert and unrelenting teacher.

Notes:

1. Harry K. Roberts, "Lonesome trail," *The Windbell*, Vol. 16, No. 1, 1979, 34.

2. Raymond White, "Religion and its role among the Luiseño," in *Native Californians: A Theoretical Retrospective*, ed. by Lowell Bean and Thomas C. Blackburn (Soccoro, NM: Ballena Press, 1976), 356.

Parabola
Volume: 4.4
Storytelling

"It's Where You Put Your Eyes"

Sam Gill

"Attention to the world's art historians!" was the message sent forth in 1885 by the Army physician Washington Matthews upon observing Navajo sandpainting.[1] He was deeply impressed with the beauty and elaboration of these paintings in sand, but that only heightened the shock of the feature he was calling to the attention of the world. A number of people work to make a sandpainting; on the same day they willfully destroy it. Matthews declared these paintings to be the most transient works of art in the world. We know that such short-lived works are not unique to the Navajo, but I don't think that Matthews' cry has been seriously considered. Perhaps that is because it would raise grave questions about the way we see and understand the nature of Native American art. Nearly a century later, I would like to consider some of the questions which echo from Matthews' message.

A description of Navajo sandpainting will give us a place to begin. It is a ritual procedure in Navajo culture which is part of certain religious ceremonials performed to cure an ailing person. The sandpainting is constructed on the floor of a ceremonial hogan and depicts mythic persons who have a connection with the cause of the illness being treated. It must be carefully replicated according to the memory of the officiating singer or medicine man. No visual record is kept by the Navajo people, but hundreds of different patterns are known to exist. The finished picture, like a costume and mask, provides a physical form in which the spiritual beings may manifest their presence. When cornmeal is sprinkled by the singer on the painting and the person for whom the ceremony is being performed, the holy people are present in the sandpainting. The rite identifies the ailing person, who walks onto and sits in the middle of the painting, with each of the holy people present in it. The identification is physically accomplished by a transfer of sands on the medicine-moistened hands of the singer, taken from the feet, legs, body and head of each of the sand painted figures and pressing the sands on the corresponding body parts of the person sitting on the painting. When this identification is complete the sandpainting, badly defaced during the rite, is completely destroyed by the singer who scratches through it with a plumed wand. The mixed sands are removed and return to nature.

In the study of Navajo religion, I have attempted to understand the significance of sandpainting from the Navajo perspective. Each pattern is appropriate to only certain ones of the many Navajo ritual ways. Each has its own stories of origin which in turn are framed by the whole Navajo mythology of creation. I have found that no Navajo sandpainting can be understood very well without placing it in these contexts. Every ritual performance is uniquely appropriate to the specific motivating circumstances which emphasize certain features of a given painting. While attempting to understand any sandpainting is a highly complex affair, I want to present a generalized interpretation.

In the ceremonials in which sandpainting rites play a major role, the cause of the illness being treated is attributed to impaired relationships with specific, life-giving forces in the Navajo cosmos. These life-giving forces are associated with certain holy people whose powers have become directed against the life forces of the ailing person. In the ceremonial cure, rites are enacted to appease the holy people and persuade them to remove their life-threatening influence. But this in itself does not constitute a cure, for the person must be placed again in a state of order modeled upon the creation of the Navajo world. The sandpainting rite is therefore a rite of recreation in which the person is remade in a way corresponding to the conditions of his or her ailment. In this rite of re-creation, the sandpainting is the essential vehicle.

The perspective of the person being re-created is based on his position in the center of the sandpainting facing east, the direction of the road of life. This perspective on the painting is unique and cannot be shared by anyone. It is a view of the sandpainting from within it, being surrounded by it. Only portions of the sandpainting may be seen at any one time and these only from the center outward. To sit upon the sandpainting and to be identified with the many holy people and cosmic dimensions which are alive in it is to experience the complexity and diversity, the dynamics and the tensions of the cosmos as represented in the surrounding painting, but also to experience the one point common to all, and therefore to see and to feel the diversity and tensions.

The illness suffered is an experience of the world at odds with itself, but this experience is cosmicized when the person finds that this is but an incident in the whole drama of the universe. The illness is overcome when the person realizes (in the largest sense of that term) that in some places these tensions and oppositions can be balanced in a unity that signifies good health and beauty.

But how do we understand the destruction of the painting? We must see that it is not the materials of the sandpainting, nor really even the design it takes, that is at the core of its meaning and power. Rather it is the process and use that is made of it that is important. It is a cosmic map. It is a vehicle by which re-creation, health, and beauty in life and the world are achieved. The sufferer finds his or her way to health from within the sandpainting, and by becoming a part of it it disappears and becomes a part of him or her. The picture disappears in the process of a person coming to know the fullness and unity of the reality it represents. The destruction of the picture corresponds to the dissolution of the tensions and imbalances which have given rise to the suffering.

We are now quite used to seeing Navajo sandpaintings reproduced in books and articles on varying subjects. The circle inscribed by a cross is a widely known symbol, but its universal significance seems somehow shallow to me once I have considered Navajo sandpainting, especially when I find that a fully closed border is rare and has very special significance and that double symmetry divided by a cross is but one of many general patterns.

The concerns I have are deepened as I begin to compare how we, as outsiders, view sandpaintings with how Navajos view them, even from a physical perspective. Let me list several points of comparison. We have only representations of sandpaintings drawn or painted on paper or canvas, which we enjoy as objects of art. Navajos strictly forbid making representations of sandpaintings and they are never kept as aesthetic objects. Even the use of sandpainting figures in the sand-glue craft has not met with the approval of most Navajo singers. Sandpaintings must be destroyed by sundown on the day they are made. They are not aesthetic objects; they are instruments of a ritual process. In terms of visual perspective we always view sandpaintings from a position which would be directly above and at such a distance that the whole painting is immediately graspable with each side equidistant from our eyes. This is completely impossible for Navajos. I got a laugh when I asked some Navajos if anyone ever climbed on the roof of a hogan to look at a sandpainting through the smoke hole. When a painting six feet, or even larger, in diameter is constructed on the floor of a hogan only fifteen or twenty feet in diameter, the perspective from the periphery is always at an acute angle to the surface. A sandpainting cannot be easily seen as a whole. The most important point of view is that of the person being cured, and this person sees the painting from the inside out because he or she sits in the middle of it. These differences are basic and cannot be dismissed. The Navajo view is inseparable from the significance which sandpainting has for them.

I think that we can say that for the Navajo the sandpainting is not the intended product of the creative process in which it is constructed. The product is a healthy human being or the re-creation of a well-ordered world. The sandpainting is but an instrument for this creative act, and perhaps it is the wisdom of the Navajo that it be destroyed in its use so that the obvious aesthetic value of the instrument does not supplant the human and cosmic concern which the confinement of our attention to the reproductions of sandpaintings is somewhat analogous to hanging paint-covered artists' palettes on the wall to admire, not acknowledging that these pigment-covered boards are not paintings but the means to create them. There is a certain aesthetic value in artists' palettes, I suppose, but surely most would think of this action as foolishly missing the point.

While I am delighted at the increased interest in viewing artifacts from Native American cultures as objects of art, I cannot dismiss the implications which arise from the Navajo example. Our view of Native American artifacts as aesthetic is a perspective the people themselves do not often take and sometimes explicitly reject. Our way of looking at it is stripped of the complex cultural views unique to each tribe which frame the significance of the artifacts. We often don't know the physical perspective from which the object was intended to be seen. As a result the significance these objects have for us surely has little to do with their meaning for the people who created them.

If this were only a problem with Navajo sandpainting it might ease my concern, but I think it is in a significant measure correct for any artifact not made for sale outside the culture. I will mention some other examples to illustrate the point further.

Dr. Ted Brasser of the Museum of Man in Ontario has for some time been interested in the self-directed aspect of many objects of Native American art in the regions east of the Rocky Mountains.[2] In extensive research he found that such things as moccasins, birchbark dishes, wooden bowls, effigy pipes, drums, woven bags, snowshoes, breechclouts, pipe bags, and other items were commonly designed to be viewed from the perspective of the wearer or user. The intentionality of this he found to be confirmed by many craftsmen. Moccasins have the design on the toe oriented to be seen by the wearer, not by those looking at moccasins worn by others. Dr. Brasser found that effigy pipes were used by the Iroquoian and Algonkian peoples as aides in the concentration of thought; that is, they were instruments of meditation. The pipe bowl bore the effigy of the guardian spirit or the familiar spirit of a shaman. It was so placed on the bowl that only when the smoker put the stem in his mouth did he come face to face with the representation of the spirit. Hence through smoking the pipe, drawing the tobacco smoke through the stem while concentrating on the effigy, the smoker gained power from his guardian spirit.

Among the Sioux peoples, Brasser found that effigy pipes sometimes took the form of a sitting male, with the stem clearly representing the penis. Also among the Sioux he found self-directed effigy pipes of a bear facing the smoker which were used by shamans whose power to cure and benefit war parties was centered on the spirit of the bear. In their ritual performances these shamans personified bears, wearing fur costumes and moccasins with bear paws attached.

Examples from Brasser's research throughout the whole area east of the Rocky Mountains could be multiplied, but our point is that there is ample evidence which indicates that the meaning of the effigy pipe is inseparable from the act of smoking the pipe, from the relationship the smoker had with the spirit represented on the pipe. It is inseparable from the spiritual transfer which took place as a result of long hours of concentrated smoking of strong tobacco. The visual perspective is dictated by the use for which the pipe was intended. When not in use the pipes were not placed on display for aesthetic pleasures, but carefully wrapped in their bags.

To suggest another example, I have long been dissatisfied with our whole framework for attempting to understand Native American ritual drama. I am uneasy especially with our views of masked performances. Our words "mask," "impersonate," and even "perform" suggest that these ritual processes are somehow artificial, illusions, enactments of something else which is being imitated or represented. I have been little comforted that these performances are enactments of the events of the gods in the primal eras. I feel strongly that, rather than enactments or performances, they are the creation of a reality. I have been concerned with some aspects of this process in terms of rites of initiation. I would like to consider another aspect of this related to masks. It is quite common for initiation rites to include having initiates look through the eye-holes of sacred masks. I think we usually interpret this as a means of educating the initiates to the unreality of the mask; that is, we consider it as showing that what the uninitiated think is a real being is actually only a personification. But I think we may be wrong here. Again it is a matter or perspective. I would like to suggest that the perspective from which one gains the fullest meaning of a mask is not finally by looking at it at all, although this is certainly an essential stage in the process. The full meaning is gained by looking through the eye-holes of the mask and seeing the effect it has on the world. That is why it is a privileged view of the initiated.

A couple of Hopi examples might give this some support. The Hopi Don Talayesva told of a time when he portrayed a Giant Kachina in the Soyoko ritual proceedings which are aimed at disciplining uninitiated children. These monstrous-appearing figures come to houses of misbehaving children and demand that the children be given them to eat. This forces the parents to bargain with the kachinas in order to save their children. The children's bad behavior costs the family a great deal, and this along with the fear aroused by the kachinas serves to encourage proper behavior. Talayesva describes a time when he wore the mask of the Giant Kachina and enacted this ritual process. He played his part very well, with great effect on the children. That night Talayesva had a dream which he describes:

> I was tired and restless, and dreamed that I was still a Giant Katchina arguing for the children. I reached out my hand to grab a child and touched him. [Touching a child is strictly warned against for fear of frightening a child to death.] The little one held up his hands to me, crying and begging to be set free. Filled with pity, I urged him to be a good child in order to free himself from the Giant Spirit. I awoke worried, with a lump in my throat, and bells ringing in my ears. Then I spat four times and decided that if I were ever the giant again I would have a better-looking mask and speak in a softer voice.[3]

By looking through the mask from the inside out, its reality was reflected in the faces of the children.

The other example is a comment made by Emory Sekaquaptewa regarding the experience of performing as a kachina. He said:

> I am certain that the use of the mask in the kachina ceremony has more than just one aesthetic purpose. I feel that what happens to a man when he is a performer is that if he understands the essence of the kachina, when he dons the mask he loses his identity and actually becomes what he is representing. ... The spiritual fulfillment of a man depends on how he is able to project himself into the spiritual world as he performs. He really doesn't perform for the third parties who form the audience. Rather the audience becomes his personal self. He tries to express to himself his own conceptions about the spiritual ideals that he sees in the kachina. He is able to do so behind the mask because he has lost his personal identity.[4]

In this description of the experience, Sekaquaptewa expresses the paradox of how one is at once enacting an impersonation and also transformed into what one is impersonating. It is described in terms of perspective. One best "sees" the reality one is oneself manifesting by wearing the mask; while looking through its eye-holes, one gains a view from the vantage of the audience so as to be able to know the reality it presents.

There is an inevitable conclusion which must be drawn from these examples. We can never appreciate some forms of Native American art without also appreciating the contexts in which they are produced. When our understanding of art is so heavily focused on objects, we tend to look in the wrong place for art. We find only the leavings or by-products of a creative process, never even realizing what is transparent to our view. We fail to grasp the inseparability of art and religion. I am reminded here of an essay be LeRoi Jones entitled "Hunting is Not Those Heads on the Wall."[5] In it he criticizes the aspect of Western art which he identifies as a worship of art objects. He feels that the price paid for this is the failure to appreciate the creative processes of art. In his view, art objects are what is left over from the art process and they have no more to do with art than do hunting trophies have to do with the hunt. The Native American examples I have given are related to this, but the case is even stronger because the aesthetic values cannot be separated from religious processes. A point of view commonly found in Native American cultures holds that reverence for objects which we might judge as being of artistic or religious value can become a kind of tyranny which stifles the full expression of ideas and the proper performance of religious acts. These acts themselves are creative in a primary sense: they define and shape reality, they literally make life possible. In light of this we should dissociate ourselves from the notion that for Native Americans art is a noun. We might prefer to adopt the term "arting" coined by LeRoi Jones, so that we can think of the art of Native Americans as a process of creating and maintaining life-giving relationships.[6]

Each year we are dazzled by the publication of beautiful books on Native American art and by stunning museum exhibits. I read the captions to the plates: "Painted Hide, Sioux, Lent by ...," "Mask, Tlingit, from the collection of ..." The more elaborate identifications give a few descriptive notes, but since they are frequently drawn from publications of collectors who have little knowledge of the ethnography, they are often in error or severely inadequate.

When I find a plate depicting an object which is from a cultural context I know something about, I close my eyes and try to picture it in its living setting. Opening my eyes and focusing again on the object propped up with plexiglass or pinned against a completely blank background, I can't help feeling a little sick. While it is true that increasing interest in the aesthetics of what we call "primitive art" has provided an increasing interest in Native American artifacts as objects of art, I think we have done just about everything possible to remove the aesthetic and meaningful elements which they bore in the setting of their creation. And having done this I don't understand how it is possible to appreciate them except in a relatively superficial way.

A few—all too few—publications about the art of Native Americans overcome the sterilization process which strips the cultural contexts from the objects. Outstanding among then is Edmund Carpenter's *Eskimo Realities*. The objects which we consider as art pieces are placed in the milieu of Eskimo world view not simply through verbal description but through the visual effects achieved by this beautifully crafted book (regrettably no longer in print) which leads to the conclusion:

> *The concept "art" is alien to the Eskimo, but the thing itself, the act of art, is certainly there, carefully implemented as a dimension of culture. It is not, however, always easy to recognize. The Eskimo don't put art into their environment: they treat the environment itself as art form.*
>
> *Such art is invisible: it belongs to that all-pervasive environment that eludes perception. It serves as a means of training his perception upon the environment.*[7]

Carpenter's book helps demonstrate this lesson of perspective I have been talking about. The shape of our own reality may blind us to the perspectives of others. Dominant objects from our perspective may, to the makers of those objects, be the leavings of a creative process completely invisible from where we look. What appears to us as an uninteresting background may be to others the ground against which reality gains orientation and human meaning. What we must first realize is that there are many ways of looking; then, that understanding is shaped by where you put your eyes.

Notes:

1. Washington Matthews, "Mythic Dry-Paintings of the Navajos," *American Naturalist*, Volume XIX (1885), 931–939.

2. Ted Brasser, "North American Indian Art for TM," *The Religious Character of Native American Humanities* (Published privately by the Department of Religious Studies, Arizona State University, 1977), 126–143.

3. Don Talayesva, *Sun Chief: An Autobiography of a Hopi Indian* (New Haven: Yale University Press, 1942), 184.

4. Emory Sekaquaptewa, "Hopi Ceremonies," *Seeing With a Native Eye,* ed. Walter H. Capps (New York: Harper & Row, 1976), 39.

5. LeRoi Jones, "Hunting is Not Those Heads on the Wall," *Home: Social Essays* (New York: William Morrow, 1972), 173–178.

6. Robert Thompson in *African Art in Motion* (Berkeley and Los Angeles: University of California Press, 1974), ...others have shown how true this is for African art.

7. Edmund Carpenter, *Eskimo Realities* (New York: Holt, Rinehart and Winston, no longer in print), 202. Another sensitive book introduced by Carpenter is: Bill Holm and Bill Reid, *Indian Art of the Northwest Coast: A Dialogue on Craftsmanship and Aesthetics* (Seattle: University of Washington Press, 1975).

CHAPTER SIX

RELATIONSHIPS: YOU ARE TOGETHER

The aliveness that is all around us is part of a sacred relationship. Nearly all tribes held treaties with the plants and animals and a respect for one another. As these articles show, the connection with all the rest is part of every aspect of life, the love of friends, the love of stones, even respecting the hunted animals. In a healthy society, the correspondences are in place, and we are governed by these in the embodied, enspirited world.

Parabola
Volume: 8.2
Animals

THE BISON AND THE MOTH: LAKOTA CORRESPONDENCES

Joseph Epes Brown

To man as a hunter, the divine became transparent above all in the animals.

—Ivar Paulson

Let a man decide upon his favorite animal and make a study of it—let him learn to understand its sounds and motions. The animals want to communicate with man, but *Wakan-Tanka* does not intend they shall do so directly—man must do the greater part in securing an understanding.

—Brave Buffalo, Standing Rock[1]

One should pay attention to even the smallest crawling creature, for these too may have a valuable lesson to teach us, and even the smallest ant may wish to communicate with a man.

—Black Elk

The bear has a soul like ours, and his soul talks to mine in my sleep and tells me what to do.

—Bear With White Paw[2]

The bear is quick-tempered and is fierce in many ways, and yet he pays attention to herbs which no other animal notices at all. …

We consider the bear as chief of all the animals in regard to herb medicine.

—Two Shields, Standing Rock[3]

Iktomi (the spider) was a man in the early days, just like any person. He was the first who attained maturity in this world. He is more cunning than human beings. He names all people and animals, and he was the first to use human speech.

The most important of all the creatures are the wingeds, for they are nearest to the heavens, and are not bound to the earth as are the four-leggeds, or little crawling people. Their religion is the same as ours. They see everything that happens on the earth, and they never miss their prey.

—Black Elk

You ought to follow the example of *shunktokecha* (wolf). Even when he is surprised and runs for his life, he will pause to take one more look at you before he enters his final retreat. So you must take a second look at everything you see.

—Ohiyesa[4]

Goats are very mysterious, as they walk on cliffs and other high places; and those who dream of goats or have revelations from them imitate their actions. Such men can find their way up and down cliffs, the rocks get soft under their feet, enabling them to maintain a foothold, but they close up behind them, leaving no trace.

—from the Teton Sioux[5]

The rabbit represents humility, because he is quiet and soft and not self-asserting—a quality which we must all possess when we go to the center of the world.

—Black Elk

The turtle is a wise woman. She hears many things and says nothing.

—from the Buffalo Ceremony[6]

The swallow's flying precedes a thunderstorm. This bird is closely related to the thunderbird. The action of a swallow is very agile. The greatest aid to a warrior is a good horse, and what a warrior desires most for his horse is that it may be as swift as the swallow in dodging the enemy or in direct flight.

—Lone Man

Each animal has its own Master Spirit which owns all the animals of its kind … so all the animals are the children of the Master Spirit that owns them. It is just like a large family.

—Raining Bird (Cree)[7]

An intense interaction necessarily takes place between the people of a nomadic hunting culture and the animals of their habitat. This is evidenced in a rich variety of cultural expressions, which projects what could be called the people's total world view. The Oglala Sioux of the North American Plains are a classic example of such a culture. In the words of one of them, Brave Buffalo of Standing Rock, "When I was ten years of age I looked at the land and the rivers, the sky above and the animals around me, and could not fail to realize that they were made by some great Power. I was so anxious to understand this Power that I questioned the trees and the bushes." [8]

What precisely is the Oglala's conception of "power" as manifested through the animals? What is the relationship between the multiplicity of such "powers" and a unitary concept of a "Supreme Being"? Who, or what, is the Indian's acquired "guardian spirit," and what is the relationship between this "spirit power" and the "master" of all the animals?

Basic to the Plains Indians culture was the vision quest, the search for the power and protection of a tutelary spirit. Among the Oglala, for whom it was termed "crying for a vision," the quest was participated in by virtually all the men and, although less frequently and in a somewhat less rigorous form, often also by women. "Every man can cry for a vision, or 'lament,'" Black Elk told me, "and in the old days we all—men and women—lamented all the time." Although the quest which resulted in the attainment of a vision need not necessarily involve formal acquisition of a "guardian-spirit," normally the successful encounter was with a bird or an animal. It was through this agency that the desired goal, or even quality of being, could be achieved if the seeker then carried out properly the specific instructions which were conveyed to him by his mentor.

For the Oglala it seems that distinguishing between dream and vision is of little or no concern, for many of the recorded encounters with animal spirits which took place in the dream state held the same "power" as if the experience had been a waking vision. I remember the emotion and intensity with which Black Elk described a dream to me one morning: "I was taken away from this world into a vast tipi, which seemed to be as large as the world itself, and painted on the inside were every kind of four-legged being, winged-being, and all the crawling peoples. The peoples that were there in that lodge, they talked to me, just as I am talking to you."

Evidently in both dream and vision there is an intensification of the interrelationships with animal forms, and these experiences go beyond and are deeper than the encounters which take place in the waking state. There is a shift to another level of cognition, on which the Oglala is no longer encountering the phenomenal animal, but rather archetypal "essences" appearing in animal forms. Although these could appear in almost any of the forms of the natural world, in an overwhelming majority of documented cases the vision encounter was with representatives of a wide range of animals and birds, any of which could become the seeker's "guardian spirit." After the quest, the "lamenter" returns to his sponsor who interprets the vision, and instructs the man as to actions which must be taken to "actualize" the power he has received.

The component elements of either the dream or vision in which the animals or birds appear may take a number of forms. Among the recurring patterns are association of the animal or bird "spirit-form" with the powers of the four directions, which appear in conjunction with manifestations of the terrifying aspects of these powers, notably the Thunder-Beings. (The vision quests normally take place between early spring and fall when thunderstorms are the most frequent and violent in the Plains.) Or men may turn into animals, and vice versa, or one species of animal may shift into another, or an animal may take on some plant form which is to become the sacred medicinal herb later identified and used in curing. Frequently it is the animal who finally disappears who becomes the seeker's guardian-spirit; or else, "… the animal that appeared … entered his body and became part of his *Wakan* strength. He might fast many times and have many such tutelary spirits within his body."[9]

It is interesting to note that though all men were expected to seek through a vision a "tutelary spirit," certainly not all received such favor, and among those that did there were great variations in its quality. For some, experiences were of such an intense and recurring nature that the recipient might become one of a number of types of "medicine-men"; those who dreamed or had visions of the Thunder-Beings or of dogs were destined to become *hehoka*, or contraries. Although the Oglala rarely express it explicitly, and never systematically, there is a certain ranking of the animals, or of their underlying "spirit-power." Grizzly Bear, for example, was understood to be chief of the underground earth forces, conceived in a negative and terrifying aspect; the bison was chief, in an exclusively positive sense, over all animals of the surface of the earth, and the eagle was seen to have supremacy over all the flying beings. Some animals outranked others in terms of their "attracting" powers, and the spider outranked all in terms of cleverness. So it may be said that the Oglala's conception of his guardian-animal-spirits represents *qualitatively* different manifestations of power, which may be obtained by men under certain conditions.

Success in the vision quest brought with it certain obligations. Among other things (such as the making of a fetish or a medicine bundle) the one who had received a vision was normally obliged, especially in the case of a powerful experience, to extend and share it by enacting it in some way, sometimes by a dance ceremonial, or by singing the songs learned in the vision, or in some other form. By dynamically acting out or dancing the inner, subjective experience, a re-intensification of it results, and the larger social group is able to participate. This helps to influence the young people toward this quality of experience and so to preserve the central values.

An excellent example of what is probably the most complex type of dance ceremonial in enactment of a vision is provided by Black Elk's account of his "Horse Dance." The ceremonial was preceded by fasting and the ritual sweat both for Black Elk himself and for the two medicine-men who were assisting. A tipi was set up in the middle of the camp circle on which were painted images representing aspects of the vision, white geese for the North, and also horses, elk, and bison. In this sacred enclosure an altar was established, and songs received in the vision were taught to the two medicine-men. Sixteen horses were secured, four of which were black for the West, four white for the North, four sorrels for the East and four buckskins for the South. A bay horse was provided for Black Elk similar to the one he had ridden in his vision. The horses were painted with lightening stripes and hail spots. The riders, too, were painted with lightening stripes on their limbs and breasts, and they wore white plumes on their heads to look like geese. On Black Elk's horse a spotted eagle was painted where he would sit, and Black Elk himself was painted red with black lightning, and he wore a black mask with a single eagle feather in his forehead. In the actual dance the vision songs were sung by the four teams of riders, so that the horses pranced to the rhythm as they moved to the four directions of space and circumambulated the camp, finally charging down on the central tipi. All the people in the camp danced along with the horses and all sang the sacred songs. So similar was this enactment to the original vision that Black Elk stated that the vision came to him again, for "…what we then were doing was like a shadow cast upon the earth from yonder vision in the heavens, so bright it was and clear. I knew the real was yonder and the darkened dream of it was here."

Evidence such as this indicates that the gradations of reality which the Oglala attribute to the components of this world represent a type of thinking, an attitude of mind, which is very different from that of the non-Indian. We find here an experienced world which sets less rigid limits than those obtaining for the non-Indian. There is a fluidity and transparency to their apperceptions of the phenomenal world which permits no absolute line to be drawn, for example, between the worlds of animals, men, or spirits. I could cite numerous parallels from Black Elk's own lips to this statement of his quoted by Neihardt: "Crazy Horse dreamed and went into the world where there is nothing but the spirits of all things. That is the real world that is behind this one, and everything we see here is something like a shadow from that world." Sword, another great Oglala medicine man, told James Walker that "the Four Winds is an immaterial god, whose substance is never visible … While he is one god, he is four individuals … The word *Wakan Tanka* means all the *wakan* beings because they are all as if one."[10]

To the non-Indian, the Oglala world structure, modes of classification, and associative processes often appear incomprehensible; but the world of the Lakota is neither unstructured nor chaotic, for underlying the fluidity of appearances there is the binding thread of the wakan concept, and an ultimate coalescence of the multiple into the unifying principle of Wakan Tanka, whose multiplicity of aspects does not compromise an essential unity. Such seemingly disparate companions as the bison, elk, bear, dragonfly, moth, cocoon, and spider have for the Oglala a perfectly "logical" connection. The connecting concept underlying these apparently ill-assorted associates is the wind, or Whirlwind. In Lakota mythology the Whirlwind (*Umi* or *Yum*) is the little brother of the four winds, all five the sons of Tate, the Wind. Whirlwind was born prematurely and never grew up, but remained a playful child, sometimes naughty, but much loved, especially by the beautiful Wohpe, who married his brother the South Wind and who is associated with White Buffalo Woman, bringer of the sacred pipe to the Lakota.

It will be appropriate to begin to examine this strange chain of associations with the cocoon; for it is from the cocoon that there emerges, in a manner undoubtedly as mysterious to the non-Indian as to the Indian, the fluttering butterfly or moth. The moth is thus conceived as similar to the whirlwind due to the "logical" fact that the moth may be no more contained than may the wind. Further evidence of identity of this form with the "formless" wind are the fluttering, wind-producing actions of the wings, a trait possessed by other winged forms, such as the dragonfly, which therefore must also have access to whirlwind power. The cocoon-encapsulated whirlwind power is of obvious value to a warrior; having such power, the man would be as difficult to hit as the butterfly or the dragonfly. Also the Whirlwind's playful, twisting movements have power to produce confusion of the mind—according to Oglala patterns of thought, the minds of the enemy.

Another member to be added to this strange assembly of cocoon, moth, butterfly, and dragonfly is the bison, and even tangentially the bear, said by the Oglala to possess power to confuse the enemy. The buffalo is the chief of all the animals, and represents the earth, the totality of all that is. It is the feminine, creating earth principle which gives rise to all living forms. The bear represents knowledge and use of underground earth forces (roots and herbs) in a "terrifying" and strongly masculine manner. It has no fear of either man or animal, and Black Elk, who was both a medicine-man (*pejuta wicasa*) and a holy-man (*wicasa wakan*) explained that many of his powers to cure were received from the bear.

It has been observed that in winter when a bison cow drops a calf, she is able to blow out from her nose and mouth a red filmy substance which envelops and protects the calf, just as the cocoon protects the developing moth. The imagination of the Oglala has also been stimulated by the trait of the bison bull, who "paws the earth, every now and then deftly scooping up the dust with his hoof and driving it straight up into the air … the buffalo is praying to the power of the whirlwind to give him power over his enemies."[11]

Graphic illustration of this affinity with whirlwind power has been noted on a Gros Ventre ornament where a line is seen connecting the horn of a bison to an insect, explanation being given that this represents "a rapport between the buffalo and the moth … these were two great powers … and they were in sympathy with each other."[12] A double function, from the Oglala's point of view, may be seen in this dust-throwing trait, for it may also be used to lure bison cows away from the herd during the rutting season; this attracting power quality is regarded as especially wakan since among bison it is normally the cow who acts as leader of herds. Similar power over women was sought after by young Oglala males.

The spider is associated with the other beings of our mixed assembly, again through association with the winds. One natural cause of this is the trait, which most certainly has been observed by the Oglala, for the young of certain spiders to send out long filaments which are caught by the wind and which carry them for long distances. Further concrete expression for the Oglala of this wind-relationship is found in the observed fact that at least certain types of spiders lay out their webs on the ground in rectangular shapes with the four corners extended towards the four directions of space. Within the larger context of Oglala mytho-logical belief, the four directions of space are identified with the "homes" of the four winds, and these winds and their appointed directions are under the control of Thunder-Beings.

These conceptions are based on the fact that the spider's web cannot be destroyed by bullets or arrows, which pass through without leaving a hole, and further that as a "friend" of the Thunder, the spider or his web has power to protect from harm. The application of these principles is made specific in the Oglala custom of stringing up a web-like hammock between four trees upon which a young child is placed, which is thought to bring him good fortune. Also, since spider is seen as particularly cunning and industrious—the latter trait being especially desirable in women—and since his nets have the capacity to ensnare, it is conceived that this power may be drawn upon by the men for attracting women to them. It has been recorded that a "courting robe" of bison hide was painted with figures of the spider, along with the whirlwind and elk, and this robe was so manipulated that the desired girl would step upon the design and thereby be ensnared.

The final member to be treated in this assembly of unlikely associates is the elk. The elk plays a dominant role for the Plains peoples gener-ally. There are explicit references to a "hypothetical," supernatural Elk—a "spirit" animal that lacks a heart, or rather, has a space where the heart should be, an animal without a heart being conceived as immortal and supernatural. Such a belief is undoubtedly associated with the rites of the Oglala Elk Festival, where an elk is painted over the door of the ceremonial tipi in such a manner that all who enter must pass through the very body of the animal.

The characteristics of the phenomenal elk are essentially based on the mysterious power of the bull to attract cows to him through his whistling call, or "bugle," which again represents control over the air or Wind principle. The bull elk is therefore considered to be the incarnation of power over the female, which is sought for by the men. The man's further identity with such power is achieved through the simulated call of the bull elk through the use of the flageolet, which is thought to draw irresistibly the young women of the camp to the man playing the instrument. Such Plains "love flutes" frequently have carved upon them the figure of the elk.

In all these interrelationships it is evident that the historical-cultural tradition plays an important role in determining the forms selected, their use, and the nature of the values attached to them. These values are expressed with an extraordinary aptness; the correspondence between levels of reality are as if one were the reflection of the other; they flow into each other in a manner that expresses a total, integrated environment.

Intercepting the horizontal dimension to the world of appearances, there is always, for the Oglala mind, the vertical dimension of the sacred, and in this sacredness there is the sense of "mystery." In sacramentalizing his world of experience, and in recognizing levels of abstraction within and transcendent to this world, the Oglala give place to all components within what for them must be an eminently coherent world view.

Notes:

1. Frances Densmore, *Teton Sioux Music*, Smithsonian Institution, Bureau of American Ethnology Bulletin (Washington, D. C., 1918).

2. *Ibid.*

3. *Ibid.*

4. Charles Eastman, *Indian Boyhood* (New York: Houghton Mifflin, 1902).

5. J. O. Dorsey, *A Study of Siouan Cults*, Smithsonian Institution, Bureau of American Ethnology Annual Report (Washington, D.C., 1894).

6. James Walker, *The Sun Dance and Other Ceremonies of the Oglala Division of the Teton Dakota*, American Museum of Natural History Anthropological Papers, vol. 16, part 2 (New York, 1917).

7. Verne Dusenberry, "The Montana Cree," *Studies in Comparative Religion* (Stockholm, 1962).

8. Frances Densmore, *Teton Sioux Music*, Smithsonian Institution, bulletin of the Bureau of American Ethnology (Washington, D. C., 1918).

9. Edward S. Curtis, "North American Indians," vol. 3 (Cambridge, Mass., 1909).

10. James Walker, *The Sun Dance and Other Ceremonies of the Oglala Division of the Teton Dakota*, American Museum of Natural History Anthropological Papers, vol. 16, part 2 (New York, 1917).

11. Clark Wissler, "The Whirlwind and the Elk in the Mythology of the Dakotas," *Journal of American Folklore*, XVII (1905).

12. *Ibid.*

Parabola
Volume: 10.4
Seven Deadly Sins

GLUSKABE
AND THE FOUR WISHES

Abenaki

Now that Gluskabe had done so many things to make the world a better place for his children and his children's children, he decided it was time for him to rest. He and Grandmother Woodchuck went down to the big water. Gluskabe and his Grandmother climbed into his stone canoe and sailed away to an island. Some say that island is in the great lake the people call Petonbowk, others say that Gluskabe went far to the east, beyond the coast of Maine. They say that the fog which rises out there is actually the smoke from Gluskabe's pipe. But wherever it is that Gluskabe and Grandmother Woodchuck went to, it is said that for a time Gluskabe let it be known to the world that anyone who came to him would be granted one wish.

Once there were four Abenaki men who decided to make the journey to visit Gluskabe. One of them was a man who had almost no possessions. His wish was that Gluskabe would make it so that he owned many fine things. The second man was a man who was very vain. He was already quite tall, but he wore his hair piled up high on his head and stuffed moss in his moccasins so that he would be even greater in height. His wish was to be taller than all men. A third man was very afraid of dying. His wish was that he would live longer than any man. The fourth man was a man who spent much time hunting to provide food for his family and his village. But he was not a very good hunter, even though he tried very hard. His wish was that he would become a good enough hunter to always give his people enough to eat.

The four of them set out in a canoe to find the island of Gluskabe. Their trip was not an easy one. The currents were strong and they had to paddle hard against them. The man who owned nothing knew a song to calm the waters and when he sang it the currents ceased and they were able to go on their way. Now a wind began to blow very hard, pushing them back towards shore. But the second man took out some tobacco and offered it to the wind and it became calm enough for them to continue on their way. Soon great whales began to come up near the boat and it seemed as if they would tip the boat over. But the man who was afraid of dying had brought with him a small stone figure shaped like a whale. He dropped it into the water as an offering and the whales dove beneath the surface and were gone. Now the island of Gluskabe was very close, but they could not see it because a fog came up over the ocean and covered everything. The fourth man, who wanted to be a good hunter, took out his pipe and began to smoke it, making an offering of his smoke so that Gluskabe would stop smoking his own pipe and let the fog lift. Soon the fog rolled away and they saw the Island of Gluskabe was there before them.

They left their boat on the shore and made their way to the place where Gluskabe sat.

"Kuai!" Gluskabe said. "You have had to work hard to come here to see me. You have earned the right to each make one wish."

"I wish to own many fine possessions," said the first man.

"My wish is to be taller than any other man," said the second.

"I want to live longer than any man," said the third.

"My desire is not so much for myself," said the fourth man. "I want to be a good enough hunter to provide food for my family and my people."

Gluskabe looked at the fourth man and smiled. Then he took out four pouches and gave one to each of the men. "In these you will find what you want. But do not open them before you get home and in your own lodge."

The men all agreed and went back to their canoe. They crossed the waters and reached the land. Then each of them started on his own way home. The first man, who wanted many possessions, took the canoe which had belonged to the one who wanted to live longer than any man.

"Take this to go home in," said the man who wanted to live long, "I am going to live forever, so it will be easy for me to get another canoe."

As the man who wanted many possessions paddled along he thought about all that he would have. He would have fine clothing of buckskin, he would have ornaments made of shells and bright stones, he would have stone axes and finely made weapons, he would have a beautiful lodge to live in. As he thought of all the things he would have he grew more and more anxious to see them. Finally, he could wait no longer.

"It will not hurt anything if I just peek inside this pouch," he said. Then he opened it just a crack to look inside. As soon as he did so all kinds of things began to pour out of the pouch. Moccasins and shirts, necklaces and wampum belts, axes and spears and bows and arrows. The man tried to close the pouch but he could not do so. The things came pouring out and filled the canoe, covering the man. They were so heavy that the canoe sank and the man, tangled in all his possessions, sank with them and drowned.

The second man, who wanted to be taller than all others, had walked along for only a short time before he, too, became curious. He stopped on top of a high ridge and took out the pouch. "How can this make me taller?" he said. "Perhaps there is some kind of magic ointment in here that I can rub on myself to make me grow. There would be nothing wrong with trying out just a little of it before I get home." Then he opened the pouch. As soon as he did so he was transformed into a pine, the tallest of the trees. To this day the pines stand taller than all others, growing on the high ridges, and in the wind you may hear them whispering, bragging about their height, taller than all men.

The third man, too, did not go far before he became curious. "If I am going to live forever," he said, "then nothing will be able to hurt me. Thus there is no reason why I should not open this pouch." He opened it up. As soon as he did so he turned into a great boulder, one which would stand unchanged for thousands of seasons, longer than the life of any man.

The fourth man, though, did not think of himself as he traveled home. He had further to go than all the others, but he did not stop. "Soon," he said to himself, "I will be able to feed my people." He went straight to his lodge and when he got inside he opened the pouch. But there was nothing inside it. Yet as he sat there, holding the open pouch, there came into his mind a great understanding. He realized the ways he must proceed to hunt animals. He began to understand how to prepare himself for a hunt and how to show the animals respect so that they would always allow him to hunt. It seemed he could hear someone speaking to him, more than one person. Then he realized what he was hearing. He was hearing the voices of the animals themselves, telling him about their ways. From that day on he was the best hunter among the people. He never took more game than was needed, yet he always provided enough to feed his people. His was truly the best of the gifts given by Gluskabe.

Retold by Joseph Bruchac.

Parabola
Volume: 16.2
The Hunter

EXPLORING THE NEAR AT HAND

An Interview with Richard Nelson

Richard Nelson spent twenty years as an anthropologist working with Native peoples in Northern Alaska and studying with Koyukon elders there. His most recent book, The Island Within, *examines their life experiences, focusing especially on the reciprocal relationship between human beings and nature.*

Parabola: *In your book,* The Island Within, *you speak of "becoming fully involved with the near at hand." All too often, most of us seem to ignore the ordinary, everyday aspects of life, failing to see their relationship to a greater whole, to the laws that govern the universe. The metaphor you use is your own search for meaning within the confines of a small, uninhabited North Pacific island. Can you say how this "becoming fully involved with the near at hand" on that particular island relates to a respect for the universe at large and a continuing search to understand and relate to it in a deeper way?*

Richard Nelson: I think in the Koyukon way—or at least what I understand about it—the moral and ethical principles that guide and restrain you in your relationship to the world extend beyond the enclave of humanity. In our western tradition, law is pretty much restricted to our fellow human beings—to our family and the members of our community. But for Koyukon people, and I think for traditional people all over the world, this web of legal and moral obligations extends all the way out, to everything that exists in the world around. And so my teacher, a Koyukon woman named Catherine Attla, said, "There's a really big law that we have to obey." She compared it to the Supreme Court for non-Native people. And she said, "That law is respect. We have to treat everything with respect. The earth, the animals, the plants, the sky. Everything." What enforces that law is the world itself, not other humans. So for a Koyukon person, if you mistreat a part of the natural world—if you're disrespectful toward it, if you don't approach it with humility and restraint—you suffer, you pay consequences. That can be through personal suffering or illness, or you can lose your luck, or something bad can happen to you. So in the Koyukon way of seeing the world, the enforcement is always around you. As one old Koyukon man said, "There's always something in the air that watches us," meaning that everything we do, no matter where we are, whether there are people around or not, we are always subject to these rules, because everything around us is aware of what we're doing.

P: *Let's take one concrete example from the first chapter of your book, about hunting a deer. What laws are involved there?*

RN: For me—the way I understand the teachings of Koyukon people and the way these rules impinge on me when I'm hunting—first of all, it means to speak and think respectfully of this animal. Even here, in New York City, far away from my home, I wouldn't say something disrespectful about any animal back where I live. I would try not to behave in a way that was arrogant, or that in some way set myself up as superior to anything in the world where I live. And in hunting, there's a sense of approaching the animal with right-mindedness: that what you're doing is something delicate and powerful and profound, that you come to this place asking an animal for its life, and in a sense, asking it to grant you yours, or to become a part of yours. That's the most important gift you could ever ask of anything—to be a part of your life. When I'm hunting, if I kill an animal, that's when I feel the most powerfully obligated to that animal: to use all of it that I can possibly use. There are parts that you leave behind, parts of the insides, and the head. I always say something when I do that, that that is left for the other animals; it's sort of a sharing. When you remove the animal's body, and you're doing things with it, when you take it home and hang it up and work on it, for example, you always need to be very careful where you do that.

Mostly I hunt alone, but sometimes I hunt with other people. And I never hunt with someone who I think might be disrespectful in some way. I'm very, very careful. There are very few people I would hunt with. I have to know a lot about a person before I would go, because I think it wouldn't be right for me to hunt with someone who in his own way didn't show respect. I don't care if it has anything to do with my way, as long as there is respect.

I don't know what kind of spirit and power and awareness might exist in the natural world, but I feel I should behave as if it's there. So the matter of knowing is less important to me than the matter of respect. Making some kind of daily gestures of respect towards your source of life keeps you mindful of where you come from. By doing all these little gestures, saying "thank you" to people, saying "excuse me," treating friends and community members with respect, we remind ourselves that we belong to a community and we need each other. We make these gestures to keep the bonds between us strong.

P: *Why is that relationship based on respect so necessary?*

RN: Because there is this constant reciprocity. We are inclined to treat people kindly because we are in direct, reciprocal relationship with them at all times. If I mistreat you, I'll find out about it right now. But as a culture we have created a kind of distance between ourselves—a physical distance, of space—between ourselves and what keeps us alive. And so we forget, we become a really forgetful people. We've forgotten that we are just as dependent on the environment as a pygmy or a Bushman or an Australian aborigine, or an Eskimo or an Indian living in a traditional way. We are as much a part of nature as they are. The only difference is, we have forgotten.

P: *What about that moment of confrontation between the hunter and the prey? At one point in the book, you are about to shoot a deer. Then you realize that she has a fawn with her, so at the last moment, you don't shoot. That moment seems very much the same as the moment when you do finally shoot another deer; only your action is different. Can you describe those two moments?*

RN: One of the really important focal points of my life is to find moments of intensity and intimacy and closeness with animals. I don't know why that is. For me there is very little difference between moments when I only watch an animal and moments when I am hunting—they are part of the same thing, in the sense of a complete focus of mind. There are a few times when I'm out in the woods walking all day long hunting, and it's as if no time had passed. If my mind is really focused that way, it's like a walking meditation. But then when I'm hunting and I meet an animal, there are decisions to be made on both sides. The animal may stay there or the animal may leave; that's something you take as it comes. But then there are other moments, when the decision is yours. Probably ninety-five or ninety-nine percent of the time, I make the decision not to hunt an animal. I don't know exactly what the reasons are. But when I make the decision to hunt an animal, it's usually really early, when I've first seen it. At that time, it's almost as if another mind clicks in. As I expressed it in the book, the mind that loves to watch animals shuts off, and the mind that hunts animals—and loves them in the hunter's way—turns on. From that point onward, it's just like a whole different way of thinking. It's incredibly elemental. That emotional part of me, the bird-watcher, isn't there any more. Once I've made that decision, I don't engage in ambivalence.

P: *You talked about the focus. Is the focus absolutely narrow and direct, on the animal, or is it a kind of wider focus, so that, for example, you did notice the fawn that time, out of the corner of your eye?*

RN: The thing I remember, especially from living with Innuit people, is that they never completely focus their attention on one thing, because to do that is dangerous. You have to remind yourself, if you're approaching an animal as a hunter, to always look around for something else that might be going on. On the island, that something else is most likely to be a brown bear. You could find out that you're not the only person who's interested in that deer, or that the deer is not the only person who's interested in you.

Also, as one of the stories in the book emphasizes, when it's a doe, you have to be extremely careful not to kill an animal who has a young one. Young ones very quickly become independent of the mothers, in the sense that they only take milk for a short time, six weeks or so, but they follow them around until the next spring. I don't want to interfere with that.

P: *There must be a great difference between hunting for sport, and hunting for survival, for food, the way Native people do, and the way you do when you're living on the island.*

RN: For me, the number one thing that's in my mind in hunting an animal is that this is for my food, and that I'm doing a very difficult thing in order to stay alive—that it's not a game, and I am not the person who has the power out here. I've heard some sport hunters talking back and forth, and they speak in ways that I won't even repeat, because of the arrogance and the disrespect for animals. There's a big power thing going on. One of the deep teachings in the Native American tradition is always to try to rid yourself of the impulse to feel powerful: to remember that the power is out there, the power is not in you.

P: *You referred before to how we all have a certain relationship with the world. Even people who live in New York City have a relationship with nature, without knowing what that is, exactly, or on what level. How could a person, living in this city made of concrete, learn the kind of lessons that you've been able to learn because you were so immersed in nature itself?*

RN: As I was saying earlier, it's a matter of becoming mindful that we all live from the earth, and that we are all a part of the earth. And that's not some sort of a hazy saying: that's the truth. Every time we eat some- thing, we're engaged in a direct, one hundred percent dependency and reciprocity with the earth. The problem is that it is so easy for us to forget where the Granola and the hamburger and the bean sprouts and the pancakes and the eggs and the corn chips, all the rest of that stuff came from. It's like saying grace. Gary Snyder talks about how we need a grace, like a little reminder. That's what I'm talking about with gestures of respect towards things. If people would think each time they sat down to a meal, if they would consciously remember where that food came from, I think it would be a significantly different world that we live in. If people at least once a day were aware when they drew air into their lungs that that air was a gift to them from everything around them, that that came from trees, and had gone through all sorts of other animals and all sorts of other people—if people would think of that once a day, we could be moving in the direction of a different world. That to me is the really deep wisdom of the Native American tradition—and probably of traditional cultures all over the world: that mindfulness of where it all comes from.

P: *To take another example from the book, you speak about the way Native people go and choose a tree and make sure that it's the right tree, and take a long time to cut it down. How does that attitude differ from the way logging is done commercially?*

RN: Among Native American people whom I've lived with, a person cuts down a tree individually. One tree. Among Koyukon people, when you do that, you've created a reciprocal relationship to that tree and you have to treat the tree in a certain way. If it's a birch tree, and you cut it in the winter, you wouldn't just strip the bark off of that tree and leave it out in the open overnight. You're supposed to cover it with snow. People say that after you use the wood from the tree, if there are shavings, you should take those shavings and put them out in the woods somewhere, not just leave them, as if they don't matter. You should put them out in the woods in a place away from a lot of human activity. There are all these gestures of respect towards that tree; each tree is treated as an individual.

When you start to cut down trees for commercial purposes, then they become a resource, they become a product. Loggers cut down thousands and thousands and thousands of trees, and not for their own use. When we do things commercially, the person who actually harvests our food for us, does it *en masse*—huge quantities every day. The fishermen kill thousands of fish, so the fish or the trees are no longer individuals, they're resources. And somehow I think that that mass engagement with things must numb us to the need to be sensitive to their life. We take whole mountainsides and wipe them completely bare of trees, and whole valleys, and take away all the trees, and the ones we can't use, we leave there, lying on the ground.

P: *But isn't it a bit too easy to say that we all need to go back to a simpler way of life? It seems to me that now we have a new situation. We now have these large-scale demands on the food supply, pollution exists, there's a new hole in the ozone layer. We can't just say that it shouldn't be, because it is. Perhaps everything that is going on now is not really unnatural. Maybe it is lawful.*

RN: You're right. We struggle with this idea of restoring some sort of natural condition. But what is that? One in which there are no humans? I think this is the real flaw in the whole environmental movement, and in a lot of our nature writing, our nature photography—this attitude that there's something wrong if there's a human being in the picture. To me that's not the point at all. It's not a matter of eliminating humans from the situation; it's a question of having humans integrated into a situation in a way that's healthy. You can't live in a place without changing the environment. All animals change their environment in some way.

There's another issue related to hunting. People think of a natural condition as a place in which there's no hunting. How can you say that? Human beings were here hunting for thousands of years. The whole environmental community of the entire continent was one in which hunting was integrated.

People talk about our culture as if it's unnatural and other cultures are natural. But wait a minute. That's too easy.

P: *Native people don't see bad guys and good guys in nature either, do they, in such a simplistic way? The brown bear, which is dangerous, is still treated with respect.*

RN: In our own tradition, not so much today as in the past, we took it upon ourselves, as part of creating a "right" community, to get rid of grizzly bears, to get rid of wolves, to get rid of mountain lions. We didn't want any predator there but us. But the Koyukon people compete directly with wolves for food, so some of the elders have said to me: "We don't think there should be too many wolves. We should hunt wolves, or we should trap wolves. But we would never want to get rid of them. Because they belong here. That would be like eliminating something that is your kin." They believe, for example, that wolves leave food for people. Wolves will sometimes kill an animal, and people come along and there it is, and they interpret that as food left for them, by the wolves.

That's a very different way of looking at things. If everything is there because it belongs there, you may change something, but you shouldn't eliminate anything. That would be a pretty big transgression. Also, that would be too much of an exertion of power.

Once I was living in Huslia, a Koyukon village, where each spring the ice on the river breaks up and moves out in a great chaos of churning spans of ice, grinding against the banks. Sometimes the ice jams up, and when it does it creates a dam and the river rises up and floods villages. So what people do when the ice is moving is go out and talk to it. They thank the ice for giving them a road to travel on all winter, and they say, "Now I hope you'll go on away easy." They're thankful, and they're sort of humble in asking the ice to take it easy with them. Then they pray in Christian ways, too, to the ice—they hold a church service next to the river.

Once when the ice jammed up down river, white men had a different way to deal with it: they brought in jet airplanes and bombed it. The people thought that was deeply wrong, because it was an assertion of power: you're not doing what we want, so we are going to make you do what we want. People didn't like that at all.

And then, for the next couple of years there were these terrible floods. People say that was because of the offense, the affront to the ice that was done by bombing it.

I thought that was a really nice juxtaposition of the two ways. One, you pray to it, you ask it to do right, and the other was, you bomb it and make it do what you want.

P: *How does the central image of your book fit in with these ideas? What do you actually mean by "the island within"? And how do you use the symbol of the island itself, and its mirror image: that which surrounds it?*

RN: It makes a nice metaphor because we all live on an island in one way or another. After we moved to where we live, because the island is nearby, I spent more and more time there. I became increasingly curious about my relationship to the island, especially about the way it was coming inside me in different sorts of dimensions. First, the island was so much in my mind, the way someone you love is in your mind all the time. That was one way. And in whatever nebulous way I have a sense of a spiritual relationship to the world, this island became the focus for that, for my sense of spiritual relationship to a place. And third—and this came as a real surprise to me—was the recognition that, physically, I was coming to be made out of this island. I made this conscious decision to get as much of my food as possible from the island. Venison. Fish from the waters around it. Berries. I was taking the island inside myself, as food, and so there was a sense that the boundaries between myself and this place had become less and less distinct. I know that my body is made partly out of that island and that something from the island flows through my body. I think that's where "the island within" idea came from.

P: *In a sense, each of us has an "island within" that we can explore?*

RN: Anyone can have this sense of moral and spiritual engagement with a place. One of the deep sources of that is to choose a place and focus on it in some way or another. It doesn't matter if it's your backyard in the city, or Central Park, or a farm field. It's to find a place in which you can feel deeply engaged, and then go back to it over a long period of time. Make that your place. I think there's something very very important about that engagement.

Coming back to the question of urban life, that engagement is something that's available to all of us. We can say, "This is going to be my place, and I'm going to take care of this place, and I'm going to try to understand my engagement with it."

Another way to express it is—and I'm not sure I'll say this exactly the same way I did in the book—but what I wrote was something like, "There may be as much to learn by climbing the same mountain a hundred times as by climbing a hundred different mountains."

P: *Are you going to stay where you are, near the island?*

RN: I don't know.

P: *Is there another island to move on to?*

RN: It would break my heart to leave.

P: *Are there more books on this island?*

RN: I hope so. I've started a book about deer. I'm sort of at the beginning stages of that right now. It basically will be an excuse to be involved with these two things that I love: the island and the deer. I hope to spend a year or so following deer around, at the same time studying the western scientific way of knowing this animal and the Native American way of knowing this animal, and then to try to integrate it all into a book. But the real reason I want to do this is because I want to know more about deer: by my own personal experience, and by learning from scientists and from Native American traditions.

I think it's very important to understand what hunting truly is. We really need to understand better, as a society, what it means to be a hunter, and what the various permutations of hunting are.

P: *This intense research seems to be a kind of hunt in itself. That need for careful preparation and study—it's as if the laws of nature, or writing, or any real search or effort we're involved in, require something from us in response. We have to meet them to a certain extent. We can't just glamorize going out to climb a mountain in our sneakers, for example, with no equipment or planning: it's too dangerous. There has to be a certain amount of daring and exploration, but also a certain amount of sensibleness.*

RN: Knowledge is so much the key to living in a wild place. I first encountered this living with Innuit people in northern Alaska, and then with the Athabaskan Indians. As you live in a place longer and longer, your knowledge just seems to become deeper and more and more detailed. For me it's one of the most exciting things about being on the island: learning a little bit more all the time. And the more you learn, the more you realize your ignorance. My teacher, Catherine Attla, who is one of the most knowledgeable people I've ever known, points out constantly what little we know of this, what little we know of that. There is a deep humility in the tradition, an idea that we can't pretend we know a lot. Part of it is that if you do pretend that, once again you're being disrespectful. But part of it is that you really recognize that the world is vastly more complex, and vastly more detailed than you could ever comprehend.

That's one of the reasons why I've taken pains in my work as an anthropologist to always say as an opener that I know very little about this. And the same thing goes for the island. When I began the island book, I said, I'm going to write this book, and that implies some sort of completeness and some sort of knowledge. But I said the only way I can feel comfortable with this is to write the book as a kind of progress report: this is where I am now, recognizing that there will always be farther to go.

P: *"Becoming fully involved with the near at hand." Perhaps that's the most interesting thing of all: to want to stay and explore further, when most people would be on the next plane, to the next adventure.*

RN: Wendell Berry has a book called *Traveling at Home.* That idea fascinates me. For me, I know that I could spend the rest of my life in an area that's within a twenty-mile diameter of my home and have plenty more to explore.

Right now, I can't wait to get home.

Parabola
Volume: 16.2
The Hunter

Mukushan

Benjamin Baynham

Among the Cree tribes of Canada, there is a group who call themselves *Innuts*, which simply means "people" in their own Cree dialect. Davis Inlet is an Innu village on the south shore of a small island on the coast of Labrador, and the Innuts there, like others of the Cree nation, have a ceremony which they call "Mukushan."

The details of Mukushan vary from tribe to tribe. Among the people of Davis Inlet, it is intimately linked to their relationship with the caribou, with the spirit of the animal, and with the Great Spirit of all life. The Innuts, or the Naskapi or Nascopi, as they are sometimes called, are a traditionally nomadic people whose life for centuries was wholly dependent on the migrations of the George River caribou herd of Labrador. They are sometimes called the Mushuau Innuts, meaning the People of the Barrens, for they follow and hunt the caribou into the barren lands north of the tree line, though they prefer to live south where there is shelter and wood.

Though their way of life has altered drastically since an influenza epidemic in the 1930s killed many of the elders of the tribe, it is still the goal of every man in the village to go out and hunt caribou. Many families still live in the village only in the summer when travel in the bush is difficult. But once the myriad lakes are firmly frozen in the fall, family after family slowly disappear into the wilderness, hunting and fishing, setting up their white canvas tents, moving when the need or mood arises, living very close to the way their people have lived for centuries.

The caribou was, and spiritually still is, the heart of the life of these Mushuau Innuts of Labrador. Over countless centuries the animal has sustained their life in country much harsher than the southern lands. This is "the land God gave to Cain" in the words of the early European explorers, and in the harshness of such a life, the caribou have been a source of almost everything needed to survive. Such a source of life was and is not taken lightly. The caribou is an animal to be respected, a true gift of life from that Spirit from which comes all life.

This idea of the "Great Spirit" was certainly not new with the Christian missionaries. Mukushan, sometimes translated "peace," is a ritual meal, ritual communion, ritual communication, ritual "thanksgiving," with all that these words connote in any spiritual tradition.

In May 1985, three of the families who made up the core of the *kauauastats* (literally "those who arrange things," a kind of parish council for the tribe)—the Nuis, the Piwas and the Gregoires—invited me and Sister Joan, a teaching sister from Newfoundland who taught at the school in the village, to their camp, which was located about six miles from the village. They were going to celebrate Mukushan.

In early May the thick sea ice is beginning to crack to make way for the spring break-up, so the way was long and rough, over humped ice and thin pools of water. They were camped on a high bluff on the north shore of Shango Bay, a long inlet which penetrates from the Atlantic Ocean into the mainland of Labrador at this point and provides a quick access route to the interior in winter by snowmobile and in summer by boat. In this in-between time of spring, travel is difficult.

We followed Bob Piwas, George and Agathe's son, along the shore ice and pools of early melt, snowmobiles rattling and banging on the ice, watching out for holes or widening cracks down to freezing salt water. A minute in that water could mean death.

As our part of the celebration we brought the consecrated bread of Catholic communion; we would celebrate together our story as Christians and share this communion, together with song and ritual.

We arrived shortly before noon and gathered in the central tent of the three which had been set up on the bluff, flaps open to the slowly warming breeze blowing over the still frozen water of the bay. In the distance across the bay to the south rise mountains which spread as far as one can see. Earlier this month I had been here ice-fishing for trout, drinking tea with George Gregoire, and trying to learn more words for mountains and ice and land, watching the light fade on those mountains across the bay as we lay in the mouth of his tent at sunset.

Following our communion and song and some brief talk we moved to the easternmost tent, that of the Nui family, Joachim and Mani-Shan. Joachim had led the two caribou hunts I had taken part in previously. The night before each hunt, seated in the tent as if in meditation, without any ceremony, Joachim "talked" to the caribou we hoped to kill, explaining our purpose and good will.

In their tent a sheet had been placed over the fresh spruce boughs in the body of the tent behind the wood stove, boughs which make up the "floor" and keep away the cold of the snow below. Seated in a circle around this sheet, each adult received a portion from Joachim, a little of the *pimin*, or fat skimmed from the boiled long bones of the caribou mixed with the marrow—pure white and fine as lard, almost buttery in taste, with the pink of the marrow standing out—and some dried and crushed caribou meat along with a little freshly boiled caribou meat. This was eaten with fresh *pakueshikan*, or soda bread made in a frying pan on the wood stove, and plenty of strong tea.

When the pimin is just made, the liquid in which the bones have been boiled for hours, along with remnants of the fat congealed by the addition of snow floating in it, is passed around and everyone drinks until it is gone. This liquid, too, is sacred and must not fall to the ground or be mishandled. Even the utensils, spoon and cup, are made special by contact with this liquid.

This is a ritual meal. Little is spoken, but the food is consumed with great respect and with a clear consciousness of its sacredness. Nothing must touch the ground (thus the sheet). Children eat their portion after the adults are finished and are watched closely so their food, also, is not dropped. Anything left over is carefully put away for later use.

Every caribou which is killed and eaten in the village contributes its long bones to the preparation of Mukushan. The bones are pounded and crushed, every splinter saved and boiled, nothing discarded. It was not unusual in winter to see these bones placed on the roofs of the village houses where the dogs could not get at them, safely stored for later use in the ceremony. There is a "hierarchy" of animals in this culture, to do with actual family relations told in the myths in which certain animals intermarry with humans and become part of the "chain" of relationships. Certain bones are always burned, certain ones buried, some meat must never be salted and so on.

The ritual has its origins in the mists of antiquity, but clearly it arises out of a profound sense of thanksgiving and respect for the animal which provides so much for the life of this people. Its affinity with the Catholic experience and understanding of eucharist is striking. I could not help thinking, also, of the early Hebrew desert experience, where sheep and lamb take on the significance of source of life and nourishment, and expiatory sacrifice. Jesus thus comes to be called the "Lamb of God"; perhaps it would be most understandable, in this case, to call him the "Caribou of God" as a way to appreciate the significance of this ritual meal for the Innuts and their relationship to *Tschishe Manitu*, the Great Spirit.

This relation to animals hunted, lands lived upon, and communal life is in crisis. But it is not yet lost, as the liturgy of Mukushan reveals. What it also reveals is the paradox of primal relations, hunter and hunted, in which the hunted can suddenly reveal transcendence, to the extent of becoming divine, and the hunter becomes the hunted, the one sought by the Great Spirit, the true Hunter. One walks with great care in the course of such a hunt.

Parabola
Volume: 17.1
Solitude and
Community

ALL MY RELATIONS

Linda Hogan

It is a sunny, clear day outside, almost hot, and a slight breeze comes through the room from the front door. We sit at the table and talk. As is usual in an Indian household, food preparation began as soon as we arrived and now there is the snap of potatoes frying in the black skillet, the sweet smell of white bread overwhelming even the grease, and the welcome black coffee. A ringer washer stands against the wall of the kitchen, and the counter space is taken up with dishes, pans, and boxes of food.

I am asked if I still read books and I admit that I do. Reading is not "traditional" and education has long been suspect in communities that were broken, in part, by that system, but we laugh at my confession because a television set plays in the next room.

In the living room there are two single beds. People from reservations, travelers needing help, are frequent guests here. The man who will put together the ceremony I have come to request sits on one, dozing. A girl takes him a plate of food. He eats. He is a man I have respected for many years, for his commitment to the people, for his intelligence, for his spiritual and political involvement in concerns vital to Indian people and nations. Next to him sits a girl eating potato chips, and from this room we hear the sounds of the freeway.

After eating and sitting, it is time for me to talk to him, to tell him why we have come here. I have brought him tobacco and he nods and listens as I tell him about the help we need.

I know this telling is the first part of the ceremony, my part in it. It is a story, really, that finds its way into language, and story is at the very crux of healing, at the heart of every ceremony and ritual in the older America.

The ceremony itself includes not just our own prayers and stories of what brought us to it, but includes the unspoken records of history, the mythic past, and all the other lives connected to ours, our family, nations, and all other creatures.

I am sent home to prepare. I tie fifty tobacco ties, green. This I do with Bull Durham tobacco, squares of cotton which are tied with twine and left strung together. These are called prayer ties. I spend the time preparing in silence and alone. Each tie has a prayer in it. I will also need wood for the fire, meat and bread for food.

On the day of the ceremony, we meet in the next town and leave my car in public parking. My daughters and I climb into the back seat. The man who will help us is drumming and singing in front of us. His wife drives and chats. He doesn't speak. He is moving between the worlds, beginning already to step over the boundaries of what we think, in daily and ordinary terms, is real and present. He is already feeling, hearing, knowing what else is there, that which is around us daily but too often unacknowledged, a larger life than our own small ones. We pass billboards and little towns and gas stations. An eagle flies overhead. It is "a good sign," we all agree. We stop to watch it.

We stop again, later, at a convenience store to fill the gas tank and to buy soda. The leader still drums and is silent. He is going into the drum, going into the center, even here as we drive west on the highway, even with our conversations about other people, family.

It is a hot balmy day, and by the time we reach the site where the ceremony is to take place, we are slow and sleepy with the brightness and warmth of the sun. In some tribes, men and women participate in separate sweat lodge ceremonies, but here, men, women, and children all come together to sweat. The children are cooling off in the creek. A woman stirs the fire that lives inside a circle of black rocks, pots beside her, a jar of oil, a kettle, a can of coffee. The leaves of the trees are thick and green.

In the background, the sweat lodge structure stands. Birds are on it. It is still skeletal. A woman and man are beginning to place old rugs and blankets over the bent cottonwood frame. A great fire is already burning, and the lava stones that will be the source of heat for the sweat are being fired in it.

A few people sit outside on the lawn chairs and cast-off couches that have the stuffing coming out. We sip coffee and talk about the food, about recent events. A man tells us that a friend gave him money for a new car. The creek sounds restful. Another man falls asleep. My young daughter splashes in the water. Heat waves rise up behind us from the fire that is preparing the stones. My tobacco ties are placed inside, on the framework of the lodge.

By late afternoon we are ready, one at a time, to enter the enclosure. The hot lava stones are placed inside. They remind us of earth's red and fiery core, and of the spark inside all life. After the flap, which serves as a door, is closed, water is poured over the stones and the hot steam rises around us. In a sweat lodge ceremony, the entire world is brought inside the enclosure. The soft odor of smoking cedar accompanies this arrival of everything. It is all called in. The animals come from the warm and sunny distances. Water from dark lakes is there. Wind. Young, lithe willow branches bent overhead remember their lives rooted in ground, the sun their leaves took in. They remember that minerals and water rose up their trunks, and birds nested in their leaves, and that planets turned above their brief, slender lives. The thunder clouds travel in from far regions of earth. Wind arrives from the four directions. It has moved through caves and breathed through our bodies. It is the same air elk have inhaled, air that passed through the lungs of a grizzly bear. The sky is there, with all the stars whose lights we see long after the stars themselves have gone back to nothing. It is a place grown intense and holy. It is a place of immense community and of humbled solitude; we sit together in our aloneness and speak, one at a time, our deepest language of need, hope, loss, and survival. We remember that all things are connected.

Remembering this is the purpose of the ceremony. It is part of a healing and restoration. It is the mending of a broken connection between us and the rest. The participants in a ceremony say the words, "All my relations," before and after we pray; those words create a relationship with other people, with animals, with the land. To have health it is necessary to keep all these relations in mind.

The intention of a ceremony is to put a person back together by restructuring the human mind. This reorganization is accomplished by a kind of inner map, a geography of the human spirit and the rest of the world. We make whole our broken off pieces of self and world. Within ourselves, we bring together the fragments of our lives in a sacred act of renewal, and we reestablish our connections with others. The ceremony is a point of return. It takes us toward the place of balance, our place in the community of all things. It is an event that sets us back upright. But it is not a finished thing. The real ceremony begins where the formal one ends, when we take up a new way, our minds and hearts filled with the vision of earth that holds us within it, in compassionate relationship to and with our world.

We speak. We sing. We swallow water and breathe smoke. By the end of the ceremony, it is as if skin contains land and birds. The places within us have become filled. As inside the enclosure of the lodge, the animals and ancestors move into the human body, into skin and blood. The land merges with us. The stones come to dwell inside the person. Gold rolling hills take up residence, their tall grasses blowing. The red light of canyons is there. The black skies of night that wheel above our heads come to live inside the skull. We who easily grow apart from the world are returned to the great store of life all around us and there is the deepest sense of being at home here in this intimate kinship. There is no real aloneness. There is solitude and the nurturing silence that is relationship with ourselves, but even then we are part of something larger.

After a sweat lodge ceremony, the enclosure is abandoned. Quieter now, we prepare to drive home. We pack up the kettles, the coffee pot. The prayer ties are placed in nearby trees. Some of the other people prepare to go to work, go home, or cook a dinner. We drive home. Everything returns to ordinary use. A spider weaves a web from one of the cottonwood poles to another. Crows sit inside the framework. It's evening. The crickets are singing. All my relations.

Parabola
Volume: 2.4
Relationships

An Appreciation of Navajo Relations

Barre Toelken

Literary critics are fond of observing that each work of great literature treats at least one of three relationships: Man and other Men, Man and Nature, Man and God. And students are fond of asking, "What else *is* there to talk about, after all?" While the students are accurate in pointing out the obviousness of these sets, we may still use them profitably as coordinates of our own cultural way of abstracting things: we recognize these as separate kinds of relationships which will bear scrutiny, which will allow for recognition and response.

These categories are especially helpful, I think, in providing us with a temporary "place to stand" when we inquire into the nature of important relationships in other cultures. The concept of *relation* itself is of course very broad until it is focused by some particularized inquiry. In the case of the Navajo, what relationships are considered central in these arenas of Man and Man, Man and Nature, Man and God? The answers—even those which can be brought forth in so superficial an essay—are illuminating. Of course, I suspect the matriarchal Navajo might like first of all to rephrase the sets as: Woman to Woman, Woman to Nature, and Woman to Holy Spirits. But in practice they would be sexually more fair; at the same time, they would reveal a basic set of Navajo relationships: The People, The People's relations among themselves; The People and Nature; The People and the Holy People. In this hypothetical renaming of the categories we begin to see our own familiar designations crumble, but in the erosion itself we begin to see more clearly those details of culture-specific attitude which characterize a people's way of looking at the world and which often sets them sharply apart from other peoples—in spite of the well-intentioned liberal view that after all "we are all alike under the skin." The tripartite framework of these relation-ships, that favorite device of Western logic and conversation, will also begin to disappear; for the time being, however, precisely because it is a meaningful frame for our own perceptions, we may as well keep it artificially patched together.

The People and The People

My first direct experience with the formalities of Navajo inter-personal relations came in the mid-1950s when I had to cope with learning Navajo names. I found out through making a number of mis-takes that each person had several names, some more important than others. First of all, each person had a "war name," which was known only to close members of the immediate family and was not to be divulged to others. This was thought of as a person's real name, but it was never used in direct address, nor was it used among friends in reference to the person in his absence. For purposes of conversation about others, each person had what I would call a "descriptive name" which called his atten-tion to some feature of his past history, or his looks, or his situation in life, or his geographical region. The old man who eventually adopted me was called by other Navajos (but never to his face) Little Wagon. In the Navajo, Wagon translates literally "a piece of wood rolling, wheel-like," and the adjective "little," placed after the noun, can mean small or it can mean offspring of. I was never able to determine if this old man was the son of someone called Wagon, but I could see that he was rather small in stature, and I had heard reference to the fact that when wagons first became available in that area, he had bought one of the smaller models. I found it was not an uncommon custom for Navajos to apply descriptive names to people that might have a number of possible meanings. Such names could be humorous as well as serious delineations; names ranged from Son of the Late Singer Blind in One Eye, to names like Old Man by Chinle Wash Where the Goats Sleep on the Rocks, to a name for a local woman of prodigious sexual appetites: Woman Whose Genitals Are Always Hungry. These names were used only by others, and were never used in direct address to the persons so described.

For direct conversation to take place in Navajo, some kind of relationship must be established which becomes the basis for personal terms used. One refers to his mother as *shima*, literally "my mother," and to all other people directly addressed the speaker must use the formula *shi-X*. Thus one can refer to another as "my friend," "my maternal grandfather," "my little mother," (the word usually employed for maternal aunt) "my older sister," "my granddaughter," "my close companion" (*shilna'ash*, literally "my one who travels with me").

This is certainly as much a matter of Navajo grammar as it is custom, but in daily practice it insures that conversations seldom take place unless there is first some kind of amiable relationship established. These relationships are almost invariably matters of family alignment or of function, and they testify to the basic assumption of the Navajo that conversation itself is an enactment of relationships existing between people. In other words, conversation is not seen simply as a matter of passing information objectively between total strangers, but it is seen as a form of close relational intercourse in and of itself.

In addition to a "war name," a "descriptive name" and constantly shifting terms of personal address, most Navajos have an "Anglo" name which relates them to the non-Navajo world. Someone whose father was called "John" by the Anglos becomes John Begay (John's son): the schoolteacher or government employee takes Begay to be the "last name" and sets it down so; since there are twenty or so John Begays in the vicinity each is awarded, gratis, a middle initial (John A. Begay, John B. Begay and so on) or number (John Six Begay). Far from protesting, the Navajos find this a useful custom, for their formal relations with the Anglos require them to have a name; they cannot say their war name, usually will not say their descriptive name, and have no reason to use a relational appellation. Of course the local whites think that the Begays and the Bennallys (grandson of) are huge families.

The family relationship for a Navajo is more extensive than the recognition of immediate relationships with parents and siblings. First, each

Navajo belongs to two clans; primarily, he or she belongs to the mother's clan, but one is described as being born "for" the father's clan. His relationships with anyone in the clan of his mother are viewed as if they are the relationships of an immediate family: a young man from the Bitter Water clan, for example, cannot marry—or for that matter engage in amorous actions—with a young woman of that same clan, even if their actual genetic ties are distant. At government boarding schools, it is common for young people attending a dance to ask a stranger initially what clan he or she belongs to before engaging in a public embrace on the dance floor which would be interpretable as incest. Family relationships are thus ritualized, and each Navajo's attention to these details helps to underscore and maintain the deep personal involvement with relational matters in everyday life which may extend far beyond the individual; these responsibilities are thought of not simply as onerous obligations, but as positive aspects of belonging to a large and strong group. On the reservation, this set of relationships has much to do with the maintenance of personal stability.

One of the harshest things I ever heard said of another person while I lived among the Navajos was "he acts like he doesn't have a family." This accusation, heard a number of times, seemed to be the epitome of personal degradation and lack of responsibility. For a person to act as if he had only himself or herself to care for or be concerned about was tantamount to an admission of interest in, or practice of, witchcraft. This brief essay does not allow an excursion into that fascinating and frightening subject, but it should be at least mentioned here as an adjunct to the topic. If close family and clan relationships are basic to a sense of normalcy in life, if one's reciprocal relationships with others are thought of as a basic premise on which stability stands, then the lack of those relationships is seen as essentially evil. Those who are thought to be witches are usually characterized by selfishness, acquisitiveness, lack of concern for other family members and for clan relationships. This would seem to be another vivid example of the Navajo insistence on one's attention to the details of relation with other People. It is interesting to note in this regard that many Navajos do not consider the same relationship a necessity with non-Navajos. For example, one friend of mine who makes moccasins in the traditional way uses only "sacred deerskin" when he makes moccasins for his family (sacred deerskin is obtained by a special manner of hunting, a special ritual skinning of the deer, and a ritual disposal of the carcass); on the other hand, he feels that moccasins made for sale to tourists do not need to be made of sacred deerskin because "whites don't care about that kind of thing." In this we see a distinct difference from the ordinances carried out by various of the Pueblo tribes for the benefit of all of mankind. The Navajo concern for relationship tends to be directed inward among The People themselves, rather than outward towards the whole world. Nonetheless, as I found out in my own experience there, the Navajos find it rather easy to accept an outsider who is willing to move in with them and live life on their terms. So it is not that they do not care about other people, but that one must move into and within their system for the relationship to "work."

An example of this is the customary way of receiving visitors at a Navajo hogan. If the members of the family are outside, they all run in and shut the door; and each takes his right place in the circle and starts doing whatever is appropriate there. Everyone is occupied. The visitors sit outside for a while, perhaps ten or fifteen minutes, as if to say "we're here"; then one of them knocks or pushes on the door, and if it opens he goes in. Someone inside may call out a Navajo word that means "Straight ahead" or "Come in," and the guest enters and makes the circle sunwise, from left to right, shaking hands quietly with each person. Nowadays there is a good deal of variation, but the old custom was that the women sat on the south—the first person to the left of the door, which is on the east, being the mother or owner of the hogan. This is because the south is represented by the color green of the turquoise, which stands for fertility and the female generative power. So the first person to be greeted is the owner, and then the other women, and then the men who generally are on the west. The other visitors come in, one or two at a time, and shake hands around the circle and each one squats or sits down without talking, or with very few words. It is a very delicate way of sharing the living space. The coming together is quiet and low-key, not joyous or noisy; there is a lot of smiling but not much eye-contact. It may be half an hour before a conversation begins to take place, but somehow in the middle of all this a communication is established about the visitors' needs and whether they will stay to eat or sleep. The guests are absorbed into the family circle without disturbing or interrupting it, in the gentlest way possible.

The People and "Nature"

In discussing Navajo attitudes toward relationships with what Westerners call Nature, we find rapidly that the category is inadequate. First of all, Navajos tend to group and categorize things in Nature according to various kinds of ritual usage as well as in terms of shape and movement. For this reason, the word Nature is not as usable for us here as are some clear subdivisions. For example, there is a large frame of reference among the Navajo for what might be called sacred geography and geology. There are the four sacred mountains which relate to the cardinal directions; Navajos feel most stable and secure when they are living within the precincts suggested by these ritual points. Indeed, many Navajo families of my acquaintance carry along with them in their suitcase of ritual materials and items four bags of soil wrapped in sacred deerskin, one from the top of each sacred mountain. In this way, each family has its own particular physical reference point to those geographical places which bound the Navajo world. One could also mention the volcanic plug called Shiprock which some Navajos believe represents the spot where mankind first entered into this present world. As well, there are many other areas of geologic importance which may be referred to as mythic monuments for the Navajos. Their shape, their form, their structure, their color, all lead to certain details in Navajo mythology in such a specific way that the places themselves are not seen primarily as objects or results of natural phenomena but holy spots bearing continual testimony to the validity of Navajo myth, ritual, and religion.

Indeed, the terrain of the Navajo world is actually viewed as the latest scene in the development of mankind and as such is directly related to those other worlds inside this one through which people and animals passed in order to come here. To put it more simply, this world is a visual confirmation of the previous world, seen in ritual terms, and it physically relates us to the mythic past, not to geologic "fact."

Another aspect of Nature as it is registered by the Navajos could be called sacred astronomy. Again, rather than the sky being seen as the arena of free flowing natural phenomena, it is referred to as a compendium of patterns which relate directly to mythic and ritual events. A good number of star constellations appear in the sand paintings which are made to cure people of various sicknesses, and several of the more complex string figures done as "games" during the winter are representations of ritually important constellations.

Relationships with animals are in many ways central to Navajo thought, but the relationships differ according to whether the animal is wild or domesticated. For example, relationships with the coyote, the bear, and the spider are all ritualized and heavily ordered by myths and tales. One is not supposed to mention the word for bear, especially while traveling alone in the mountains or forest, for surely it will bring forth a bear on the spot. Coyote tales are not told except in the wintertime. String figures are to be done only in the wintertime, otherwise Spider Woman will become annoyed and will perhaps capture young people in her snare. Whatever one makes of these beliefs, it is clear that they represent among other things a subordination of human activity, even in areas such as storytelling and game playing, to religious assumptions about the proprieties of actions during certain times of the year. These concepts bear witness to the fact that nature is not seen as something outside the people which must be related to in any kind of practical approach to survival within it, but, rather, it represents a ritual circumstance in which man moves as carefully as in any other ritual occurrence. The principal parts are always related to each other.

The Navajos' connection with sheep, although it is historically quite recent, is perhaps their best known feature to outsiders. How the Navajos turned from nomadic hunters and raiders into such avid herders of sheep may never be fully appreciated; certainly it is due in large part to the "encouragement" of the U.S. Government, but the sheep have assumed such an important position in Navajo life that there must be other philosophical and cultural reasons beyond the economic and political dilemmas of the 1860s. The sheep do not show up prominently in any particular ritual that I know of, but they have become basic to the Navajo concept of relationship between people and fertility of the land. The woman of any family, since she is not only the matriarch but because it is from women that fertility proceeds, is usually the owner of the family's flocks. Thus women and sheep are central images in today's Navajo concept of stability and process in Nature. If something goes wrong with the grass or the rainfall, if sheep are getting sick, it is blamed on something unnatural and infertile in the world (in most conversations I heard, the blame was usually laid on the proximity of white people or attributed to intrusions of the U.S. Government). So central are sheep to the Navajos' relationship with the occurrences of everyday life that when anthropologist John Adair and filmmaker Sol Worth wanted to do some research on Navajo filmmaking, they were asked by a local medicine man if the filming would hurt the sheep. When they replied in the negative, they were asked if the filming would *help* the sheep. When they were forced to admit that filmmaking would not help the sheep either, they were asked by singer Sam Yazzie, "then why make films?" When I showed my adopted Navajo father a news photo of the Empire State Building, his first question was, "How many sheep will it hold?" I first took his query to be related to the perception of space, then I assumed it was sarcastic in nature, and finally I realized that what it meant was "what is that thing good for, in terms of anything that relates to my way of life?"—obviously a complex cultural question to ask, and askable only in terms of those relationships which the asker recognized as valid.

Other ritual categories cause items from different parts of nature (as the Western eye would see them) to be grouped together; for example, in one category of medicine we will see stone arrowheads, corn pollen, lizards, and lightning, all in the same category because they are all used medicinally in a particular curing ritual. Even though these items come from "different" parts of nature, and would therefore be discussed under different headings by a scientific-minded person in Western culture, a Navajo would assert that just as naturally they go in the *same* category because they are ritually connected. It is for reasons like this that the consideration of the relationship between "Man and Nature" must be reexamined, at least from the Navajo point of view. As one sees these various natural phenomena appearing in Navajo conversation and custom, one realizes that they actually fall into our third category, relationships that exist between People and the Sacred; indeed, there seems to be no Navajo basis for separating these sets of relationships from each other to begin with. If it has been worthwhile for me to do so here, it is primarily because it has led to a demonstration of the culture-specific basis for the category itself.

The People and the Sacred

The *yei* are hard to define using English words. They are very much in the nature of *kachinas*, the sacred embodiments of cosmic forces made manifest in physical form when humans dedicated to the task assume their clothing and song for the purpose of ritual. The *yei* whose figures appear on the floor of a hogan in the complex sandpaintings used for healing are no less real than the *yei* who appear in the dances using a human being for locomotion. Dealing with the *yei*, in other words, is not a matter of make-believe; rather, it is an attempt to align the people with the actual forces which surround them by making manifest the close relationship, practically the identity, between the two spheres of interest. During a healing ritual, for example, the patient is caused to walk around on the delicate sandpainting of the *yei*, and through ritual is closely identified with each one and with the world of reality they live in. Psychologically, the patient is taken from his own context, the interior of his own hogan usually, and is described as standing on patterns, ledges, floating through the air with jewels, and other kinds of suggestive actions which bring the person simultaneously into two dimensions: this world and the "other world" interpenetrate and reciprocate at the point of the ritual. The patient is made whole, it is hoped, partly by the application of medicines, and partly by the forced realization of a deeper relationship between the person and sacred forces than might be evident in everyday life.

On another level, relationships play an equally important role in healing ceremonies (perhaps it is well to mention in passing that *all* Navajo ceremonies have to do with healing). In addition to the ritual itself, which relates the patient to the *yei*, there is the gathering of relatives and friends who share in the healing ceremony and who usually are administered the same medicines taken by the patient. It is as if one's relations are potentially ill, or perhaps likely to become ill, if one among them is sick. In any case, the participants in the healing ceremony are not present in the role of onlookers, but as actively involved components of the ceremony: they may sing and chant along with the singer when requested to do so, they spend a good deal of time concentrating on the health of the patient (especially the restoring of stability and health to particular affected parts of his or her body), and in sharing the medicine with the patient they proclaim a close relational tie both with his sickness and his cure.

It would be possible, on the basis of such sketchy evidence, to make one of those grand, romantic summations showing that for the Navajos, all parts of nature are related; animals, plants, and people exist as brothers and sisters in a stable world; mankind has close relatives in the other world with whom he may share his sicknesses and woes and from whom he may expect succor. But I think the evidence does not allow us to entertain such dreamy conclusions. It is indeed true that the Navajo home life, in the immediate family, is extremely warm and supportive. There, relationships are at their most informal and deep interactions are expressed with an emotional power that would surprise most outsiders. However, beyond the immediate family, it seems to be that the relational ideas are applied as ritual metaphors, not as loving extensions of the family circle. At least I have never heard a Navajo speak of being a brother to his sheep, a sister to the *yei*, a cousin of the bear. Rather, the relationships seem to be part of the tremendously complex system of ritual enactments the aim of which is to maintain stability in a world which inclines toward instability. Most of the serious relationships are invoked at times of ritual enactments, when the illness of a patient is central to everyone's concern. It is an extension of the belief that one can always call upon relatives to help out in a dilemma, and it is based on the assumption that relatives must help if they are indeed part of the system. But it is ritual enactment and mythic system and religious belief which compel the relationships to work beyond the immediate family. These obligations a Navajo feels as he moves through a world which is ordered more by ritual order and by its opposite—the disorder of sickness—than by broad natural forces.

The system is impressive to us because of its assumption that all phenomena are integrated and interdependent, not extractable and abstractable from each other. Similarly, individuals are integrated and interdependent with other individuals in the culture, and are not encouraged or expected to be totally independent agents. While individuality is allowed, and expected, it is always tailored to the larger ritual expectations of the group. Rather than viewing the Navajos as some kind of primitive desert "flower children," moving easily through a harmonious world because of their recognition of the relationship among all things in nature, we need to recognize that the Navajos are participants in an extremely rigorous philosophical and ritual system which places demands on individuals that most non-Navajos would find it difficult to cope with.

One can only begin to imagine the terrible impact on the Navajo and on other tribes of a system in which realities are always separable, discussable, abstractable; in which people are expected to be in competition with each other in order to be thought of as healthy individuals; in which animals are objects of scrutiny or quarries in the hunt rather than ritual counterparts in a complex and delicate environment; in which the stars are in random order and the gods are not partly ourselves; in which all multiform and delicate relationships necessary for stability in the world can be subdivided into three main parts and discussed in an essay.

Parabola
Volume: 29.1
Marriage

You Are Together

Linda G. Johnston

In the early 1920s my mother and her grandmother, Kay Bay Way, walked through the Chippewa National Forest, gathering plants for medicines. Kay Bay Way was a midwife and healer in her small northern Minnesota Ojibwe community. The first teachings that came to the Anishinabe, who are more commonly known as the Ojibwe, were the *Mide wi win*, and Kay Bay Way lived according to those teachings. Mide wi win is the Anishinabe spiritual way of life that promotes walking in balance, respecting all living things, and healing with native plants. My mother often talks of this time spent with her grandmother as being her happiest. Her mother, Emma Bear, was baptized Catholic as an adult; my mother was raised Catholic, and she raised her family the same way. Every summer the Benedictine nuns came to teach catechism. My mother said she was afraid to tell them that her grandmother had already taught her the Ten Commandments as a small child while walking through the woods, though neither of them spoke English at the time or had ever been in a Catholic church, or any church. My mother's faith and love for God was strong, but I noticed a subtle irreverence toward some of the Catholic doctrine. Observing this, I decided at the age of twelve not to be Catholic, although I was required to go to church every Sunday and to follow the precepts until I was eighteen and left my parents' home to go to college.

My husband Joe was brought up differently, never entering a church, but learning some of the Mide wi win teachings and other traditional ceremonies from his parents and their parents, all of whom are Anishinabe. He was in his late thirties when he was given the invitation by his father's uncle to go through the Mide lodge. This lodge is the physical structure for a healing ceremony that initiates one deeper into the spiritual life of the Anishinabe. He has been an *Osh ca bewis*, or helper, to those going through the Mide lodge ever since. One does not choose to be Mide wi win. One receives a message from a third party, or has a vision or a dream, or perhaps as a child your parents feel you need the Mide lodge for an illness or to help with special problems. The Mide lodge ceremony is helpful for all afflictions of the mind, body, and spirit.

When Joe asked me to marry him, I hesitated for months as I couldn't think of how we would marry. We don't attend any church, though we pray every day by putting down our *asama*, or tobacco, and expressing our gratitude to *Gitchie Manidoo*, which is the great spirit and creator, for another day of life. I certainly didn't want to sanctify our loving commitment before a justice of the peace, and I wanted very much for our life together to have a spiritual focus. Our only real alternative was to offer tobacco to our elder and good friend, Amig go ga bo wi qwe, to marry us. We were told that choosing to marry in this way was to embrace our identity. Our spirits are identified as Anishinabe, and to follow the original teachings would be to nurture ourselves. Our natural law by birth is Anishinabe, and recognizing those teachings would bring peace to our lives. We would be role models for a good Anishinabe life, planting seeds of pride and empowering our native community. An Anishinabe ceremony such as we were choosing would pave the way for us to add that spiritual focus to our lives, to not be sidetracked by materialistic values, and to appreciate the aging process together.

The importance of tobacco is always in the forefront of Anishinabe rituals. The tobacco symbolizes the acknowledgment of the *Manidoog*, the spirits, in everything we do. We put down our tobacco when a child is born, when we move into a home, when we take any living thing— including berries, wild rice, deer, fish, and even the rocks, *misho-misag*, that are used in a sweat lodge—or when we pick cedar, sweet grass, or sage to burn for purification and healing purposes.

What can I tell you of our traditional Anishinabe wedding ceremony? That it was an intimate ritual shared with family and very close friends? That feelings were good all around and prayer was profuse? That we picked cedar boughs to sit on and had blankets made for ourselves and as gifts for our mothers and siblings? That an offering of our native foods—blueberry sauce, bread, wild rice, fish, and venison—was prepared for Gitchie Manidoo? That we spoke openly of why we wanted to be together, both of us with tears?

When we gave tobacco to Amig go ga bo wi qwe to marry us, she said there was no word in the Ojibwe language for marriage. Translated, the name of the ceremony means, "You are together." We met with her several times while she decided whether to do the ceremony and determined if we were ready for this commitment. The ceremony she planned to do hadn't been done for eighty or ninety years, as far as she knew. Traditionally, the fathers were given gifts, smoked their pipes, and then decided if their two children—in our case, middle-aged—should be together. Both our fathers had passed on, so Amig improvised by having our mothers be the key to the ceremony. At least twice in the beginning of the ceremony she leaned over to us and said quietly, "If they say no, we'll all just get up and go home. There'll be no ceremony. It's over."

Parental involvement is good because a parent's tendency is to look at the overall picture. They have standards for their son- or daughter-in-law. Are they industrious and knowledgeable in many skills in order to be a good provider and caretaker to each other? Are they at peace? What are their spirits like? Calm? Soothing? And of course the parents use their intuition, their gut feeling about that person. They look at all these qualities, as opposed to the children who may be influenced by physical appearance or lust.

Amig's helper smoked the pipe on behalf of our mothers since neither uses tobacco. A little nervous at being the center of attention, our mothers accepted our gifts and our simple words of request to be together. Their ensuing discussion in Ojibwe ended with agreement as they placed our hands together.

Amig, unexpectedly, asked Joe first why he wanted to live with me, and then asked me why I wanted to live with him. Joe responded that before he had met me his life had seemed incomplete and he had felt lost. With my presence in his life, gifts had come to him that gave him direction, such as the sweat lodge, teachings, a pipe, eagle feathers, a drum, and going through the Mide lodge. He said his purpose in life is to help people and that doing that has been easier with me, since I believe in him. Most importantly, he added, he loves me. In turn, I spoke of my dream for a partner in life who was Indian and believed in our traditional ways, who would support me in all I needed to do in my life, and I said that I loved him also. I could have said more, but I was overcome with tears.

We alternately filled Amig's black pipe with our tobacco. Before lighting her pipe her helper covered us with a blue-and-white blanket with a purple bear-paw design made by Joe's aunt. We watched as the smoke from our individual tobacco offerings rose together. Speaking Ojibwe, Amig offered all our gifts, first to *Ni gan ni Manidoo* (the leading Spirit or Creator) and to the leading creators' helpers along with those Manidoog that sit with them. They went to the Manidoo that sits in the center of the earth and her Manidoog that sits with her; to the Manidoo and corresponding helpers that sit in the East, South, West, and North; and to the layers of Manidoog in the sky and to the layers of the earth and the Manidoog that sit with them. She offered our gifts to the animals, to the Manidoog that exist in the lakes and rivers, and to the Mide Manidoog, since those doing the ceremony and Joe are Mide. She prayed to the Manidoo that lives in the East Lake area where she resides, who asked to be remembered each time the Anishinabe put forth tobacco and has agreed to assist always. There was prayer to the Manidoo within the trees as Amig pointed out the beauty of the tall red pines standing around us. She also prayed to the *Bines si wag* (thunder beings) and to *Wena bosho* and his grandmother; to the big helper, the sun, and finally to *Gii gaa nan* ("night sun," or moon).

As Amig extended the tobacco and other offerings to the Manidoog, she made the following requests, using the Ojibwe words "*ni bagosendan/damin*" or "I/we wish for." These words reflect humility as a people, as opposed to a harsh approach where one might attempt to direct the Manidoog. This humble approach recognizes that it is their will that we live by. In addressing the success of our marriage, Amig stated, "*Ni bagosendamin* [We wish that] *da ii ne nim goo wad* [it is decided by] *iin giiw Manidoog* [the spirits] *da nii wii chii yan di wad* [that they are to live together] *Oo sha wash go gishig go qwe* [Linda] *minawa* [and] *Be shig go ga bo* [Joe]. She expressed the wish that we not run into obstacles, that we work together in harmony and have good health, that we not be lacking on a spiritual level, and that we always know where to go when difficulties arise. She prayed that we help each other to accomplish our purpose in life as decided by the Manidoog; and that we have an ample supply of the foods that we have been given by the creator. She prayed that the Manidoog assist our close relatives and look upon us favorably for showing our appreciation for what we have been given by doing the ceremony in this way.

Every living thing has a mate, Amig said—even the earth. She talked about all the spirits to which she prayed, and said that all these mighty powers work together. The four corners of the earth put their hands together to take care of the wind. The pipe is the joining of rock and tree. The rock and water work together in the sweat lodge to create steam, *bimadaziiwin*, which means life. We were told to work together to accomplish our purpose for living. We were told of our spiritual identification with our mate, that everyone's spirit is pure, and that we are related to the animals on a spiritual level. Some say that in the earliest of times animals and humans spoke the same language. She said that if you're mean to one another or any living thing it's an indirect attack on Manidoog because of our connection to the spirits. She emphasized that there is no clear definition of Gitchie Manidoo as male or female— that each Manidoo or spirit is both male and female, unless specifically named, such as the spirit that sits in the center of the earth. She told us that gentleness, caring, and loving are qualities of strength in both male and female, and that we are not to be influenced by society's superficial values or by surface thinking but approach all things spiritually and make our home a comfortable home with love in the air.

She requested that we put out a tobacco and food offering at least once a year and meet with her periodically. She ended by imploring that if she had forgotten anything, the Manidoog would please correct it.

Through all this we sat patiently on the fresh cedar boughs, both of us wearing black velvet vests with colorful floral beadwork meticulously sewn by my mother, who also made the brain-tanned buckskin moccasins we wore. I felt beautiful, and Joe looked very handsome with his long dark hair braided neatly by his mother.

There was a long moment, immediately following the ceremony—one of those moments that takes your breath away and makes you wish time could stand still. I stood with the warm sun on my back, surrounded by family, children swimming and laughing nearby. I glanced over at Joe, who was hugging one of his sisters and talking. He had a relaxed, pleasing smile. He looked better than chocolate cherry cake. I wanted to go over and lick his face, right up his cheek, just as a mother lion licks her cub, eyelids half closed, filled with the most unconditional love.

A few weeks later I was enjoying dinner with several close women friends. One of them casually asked if I felt different now that I was married. Instead of responding glibly, I hesitated and then said, "I do feel different toward Joe. I feel more tenderness and understanding toward him." When I was telling Joe about this he said, "I feel different too. I see in you an inner beauty I didn't see before."

On our long walks we are inevitably greeted by wild animals, most often deer or squirrels and chipmunks, sometimes a bear; and once, while we were forging a path through the thick brush along a lake's edge, an eagle flew up unexpectedly, directly above us, its six-foot golden wingspread causing us to open our mouths in awe. We grabbed each other's hand, laughing.

It's calming to burn sage, cedar, tobacco, and sweet grass sprinkled with *mino mush ki kii*, medicine, that was given to me by my namesake. It's a treasure to cuddle each newborn baby in our family and wonder at the continuation of life. I'm enjoying many good things in life, and I thank Gitchie Manidoo each day with full knowledge that feeling gratitude is incompatible with anger or despair.

Many times I have marveled at the depth and vitality of Amig's prayers for our life together. Or is what we experience a result of our faith? I think it's both. This fall we had harvested wild rice and were hand-parching it in the old way in our back yard: cooking it slowly over an open jack pine fire in a heavy black kettle, turning it with a canoe paddle just as you stir gravy, continuously, stopping only long enough to hand the paddle off to another. I took the paddle, and as I turned the rice round and round I silently praised every Manidoo in the cosmos for this good life. *Mii gwetch, mii gwetch,* a million *mii gwetch.*

Translations:

Ojibwe: one of the Algonquin-speaking tribes of North Eastern America

Anishinabe: What the Ojibwe call themselves meaning "the good people" or, as some interpret, "spontaneous people"

Gitchie Manidoo: great spirit

Manidoo(g): spirit(s)

Mide wi win: spiritual way of life of the Anishinabe that promotes healing and walking in balance

Mide Lodge: medicine or healing ceremony of the Anishinabe

Wena bosho/Nana boozhoo: a spirit who often represents the archetypal human being

Mii gwetch: thank you

Parabola
Volume: 29.4
Friendship

A Telling of the Love of Winnedumah for Pahwanike

Shoshone

In my father's time there were two men of our camp who had mingled their blood after the custom of our people, swearing that they would love one another more than brothers. Out of the keeping of that vow there arose a saying, "Like the love of Winnedumah for Pahwanike."

Winnedumah was a Shoshone who had married into our tribe, and he dealt with every evil under the Six Quarters, not, as our fathers did, by the use of roots and herbs and the sweathouse, but by singing and dancing. He would dance and sing, and by singing his soul would ascend to the Friend of the Soul of Man, and he would have power beyond the strength of roots and herbs to reach. How this was I do not know, but it was so. When he had made the sick to lie straight and warm, he would dance and sing until the sick had fallen asleep with the sound of it and the earth was beaten to a fine dust under him. Then his soul would climb and climb—how do I know where the Friend is?—and from that height he would stoop and snatch the sick from his sickness. So it seemed; for when the sick would awake, his evil would be gone from him. Moreover, Winnedumah, passing to and fro between the Friend of the Soul of Man and his client, as the shuttle is passed by the blanket-maker, could weave such strong medicine that no harm could get through to the man for whom he had made it. This I have heard my father say of Winnedumah, who had mingled his blood with Pahwanike's, so that they loved more than brothers.

I do not know how long it was after the vow before Winnedumah began to fear that his friend might fall ill or come to some hurt in battle, and for the sake of his friend he made a singing medicine. Often at night, for the night is the best time to give the heart to singing, in a cleared space between the creek and the house of Pahwanike, at such times as his love for his friend moved him, you could hear the sound of Winnedumah's feet and the voice of his song and the sound of his gourd rattling. In this fashion for many years Winnedumah kept his friend from hurt and sickness. And all this time there was nothing said about it, for being true friends, they got on without much talking. But toward the end of his life, Winnedumah felt his power go from him and he was sad in his heart, wondering if his friend would love him as well when he had nothing more to give him.

And at last Pahwanike said to him: "Why are you troubled?"

"Because," said Winnedumah, "I fear that a time may come when you will no longer love me."

"How can you fear that," Pahwanike reproached him, "when you know that for all these years I have had no other friend besides you?"

"Nevertheless," said Winnedumah, "I wish that I had a sign that whatever happens there will be no lessening of your love for me."

Then Pahwanike considered how he could give his friend a sign. At last he said:

> *"You know all that noise you make every night by my house, singing and dancing—when I could endure that all these years and say nothing, what other sign do you need of my great love for you?"*

CHAPTER SEVEN

STRUNG MEMORIES: THE CALL TO REMEMBER

Memory is one of the ways in which we keep tradition intact. Remembering has been a significant part of tribal history, mythology, and even ceremony. Without it our people would have ceased to be under the fire of time and assimilation. It is happiness. It is the foretold birth of a white buffalo calf that will change color. It is a sacred feather that stirs the heart of the surrounded and imprisoned. Through memory the vital seed of wisdom is held until it is ready to sprout and grow.

Parabola
Volume: 5.1
The Old Ones

Legacy

Native American Elders

> *The stories that are told can be repeated ... to make them last. If we keep them to ourselves, in about fifteen or twenty more years we will not have them. It will all be gone. There will not be any songs or prayers because the legends go along with all this. One cannot exist without the other.*
>
> —Tom Ration, Navajo[1]

> *My maternal grandfather and my father used to speak their prayers on top of the Navajo Mountain many years ago. It was at a level spot, where the home of Monster Slayer was. That is where they sat, Monster Slayer and Born-for-Water; they sat there, it is said. That is the place where they placed precious stone offerings, these old men. They used to carry these offerings there, calling on the name of Naatsis'áán (Head of the Earth), it is said. They also made an offering at the place where the Spring is. That is what the old men were saying and doing. But nowadays the White people do all kinds of things up there. The old men's ceremonies made life good for the men and women of long ago.*
>
> —Long Salt, Navajo[2]

And it is said, that below the Rainbow Bridge one cannot live for the purpose of aging. Because of the prayers, the place is made strong. And this place where the Spring is had a name, and today it still has a name. And it was designed by the gods, for as long as it is there, for the purpose that the People will be blessed with an abundance of children. So it was decreed. It cannot be revoked. That is the way it is. And then from the Rainbow Bridge area human prayers and offerings are talked about on the four sacred mountains. And the way it is with the mountains—the prayers proceed from the feet of the mountains on up. That is the way the elders, who do these sacred things, do in the Mountainway chants and in other sacred ceremonies. They obtain their power from each of the four mountains.

—Buck Navajo, Navajo[3]

... men can better their existence and soften the harshness of fate. Now I no longer feel alone, and my old age is a restful time. But when I chance to think of my childhood and recall all the memories from those days, then youth seems a time when all meat was juicy and tender, and no game too swift for a hunter. When I was young, every day was as a beginning of some new thing, and every evening ended with the glow of the next day's dawn. Now, I have only the stories and songs that I sang myself in the days when I was delighted to challenge my comrades to a song-contest in the feasting house.

—Ivaluarjuk, Iglulik Eskimo[4]

When I was young, my grandfather and I, almost every evening we would sit on the west side of the summer house and watch the sun set or we would sit on the east side and watch the colors cover the mountains. My grandmother would join us. Then they would tell me about the mountain, about evening sounds, my grandfather would sing a particular song and tell me "remember it." I would try. Sometimes I would ask my grandmother to help me remember. She would only tell me that that was between my grandfather and me. She would not interfere and it was the same with what my grandmother was teaching—my grandfather did not interfere. And these things they were advising me, their thoughts were the same.

—Soge Track, Taos[5]

The sweat bath had prepared me for my vision-seeking. Even now, an hour later, my skin still tingled. But it seemed to have made my brains empty. Maybe that was good, plenty of room for new insights.

Darkness had fallen upon the hill. I knew that hanhepi-wi *had risen, the night sun, which is what we call the moon. Huddled in my narrow cave, I did not see it. Blackness was wrapped around me like a velvet cloth. It seemed to cut me off from the outside world, even from my own body. It made me listen to the voices within me. I thought of my forefathers who had crouched on this hill before me, because the medicine men in my family had chosen this spot for a place of meditation and vision-seeking ever since the day they had crossed the Missouri to hunt for buffalo in the White River country some two hundred years ago. I thought that I could sense their presence right through the earth I was leaning against. I could feel them entering my body, feel them stirring in my mind and heart.*

We Sioux haven't got your generation gap. We believe in bringing the young along to take our place because this is nature's way. It's maybe this, our willingness to share power with the young, which makes our old people loved and respected, which makes talk easy between the generations.

—Lame Deer, Minneconjou[6]

Gently traced,
  this hand of bark-dry grooves
  lies on fels naptha sheets
  not a sacred relic
  but a legacy of strength.

its last will and testament reads:

that when she delivered him
into the gentle hands of the shaman
she asked for his moccasins
so he couldn't leave without her.

they laughed together

but he left and walked
the cold journey alone,
and she bore the weight
of the family tree.

now as i sit in haunched acceptance
i feel my share of the future
descend from those hands so,
gently traced.

—Dr. Lois Bissell Jircitano[7]

Notes:

1. Quoted by Peggy V. Beck and A. L. Walters, *The Sacred* (Tsaile, Arizona, Navajo Nation: Navajo Community College, 1977).

2. Quoted by Karl W. Luckert, *Navajo Mountain and Rainbow Bridge Religion* (Flagstaff, Arizona: Museum of Northern Arizona, 1977).

3. Quoted, *ibid.*

4. Beck and Walters, *op. cit.*

5. *Ibid.*

6. Reprinted with the permission of Pocket Books, a division of Simon & Schuster Adult Publishing Group, from *Lame Deer Seeker of Visions*, by John (Fire) Lame Deer and Richard Erodes. Copyright © 1972 by John (Fire) Lame Deer and Richard Erodes. All rights reserved.

7. Published in *Akwesasne Notes* [a newspaper], Summer 1975. Reprinted by permission of the author.

Parabola
Volume: 4.4
Storytelling

Strung Memories

Sister Maria José Hobday

When I was small, I used to stand with my mother and look across the land to the Sleeping Ute Mountain. The sun set often between his folded arms. His feathered headdress lay in quiet dignity across the plain, and the moccasined feet, so distinctly Indian, pulled the eyes upward along the sleeping form. We would be very quiet, my mother and I, looking at the legendary Indian asleep on the land. The promise was that one day he would rise up and lead his people, the Utes, to new power and life. And my mother would tell me, "Take this beauty into your heart; learn it. Some day you will be far from here, and you will only be able to see this with the eyes of your heart. Then it will be important for you to have the beauty inside you. Memorize the land." I did not completely understand what she was saying, but I did remember those land pictures. When we walked along a dusty country road, she would say, "Feel the earth. Your feet are trying to teach you about the land. Some day your toes will not be walking in this warm dirt, but your feet will remember the road, and this will make you happy."

My mother was right. Because of her manner with me, her quiet and ranging look, I came to know that it was important to think with the senses. It was important to smell with more than the nose, feel with more than the feet, touch with more than the fingers, see with more than the eyes. My mother said that people who are not homesick for the land, the weeds and grass and flowers and trees that helped them grow up, probably would not hurt too much, either, from homesickness for those they love. As I have grown older, I have found myself fingering the memories of such moments. They are like a necklace of experiences. Each story, each teaching, is a bead, having its own space, but also creating a string of beauty for remembering. Together, these have influenced my attitudes, my values, and how I share with others.

My mother, of Seneca Iroquois descent, was truly a woman of the earth. She walked tall in her own ideals and search for good living. She was five feet five inches tall—but people always judged her to be taller. She and my father were always reminding us to stand high, to keep our backs straight, to walk firmly, to lift our feet with spring and set them down softly. My friends were told, "Throw back your shoulders!" but my brothers and I were told, "Lift up your heart bone." Later I learned that my parents were quite accurate in their anatomy. The heart bone is the place to lift so that the shoulders rest without strain. Mother said that the soul had to teach the body, had to help it know how to stand and sit.

So many of the best lessons I learned were stories from everyday happenings. As a sister in a religious community, I have taken a vow of poverty. But what that freedom is all about first came to me through my parents. I learned the heart of this vow from a strawberry-ice-cream evening.

We were rather poor during the 1930s; not desperately so, but poor enough to feel the lacks and to live on the edge of insecurity. One Saturday evening I was working late on my homework. I was in the living room, my brothers were outside with their friends, and my parents were in the kitchen, discussing our financial situation. It was very quiet, and I found myself more and more following the kitchen conversation, rather than attending to my homework. Mama and Daddy were talking about what had to be paid for during the week, and there was very little money—a few dollars. As I listened, I became more and more anxious, realizing that there was not enough to go around. They spoke of school needs, of fuel bills, of food. Suddenly, the conversation stopped, and my mother came into the room where I was studying. She put the money—a couple of bills and a handful of change—on the desk. "Here," she said, "go find two or three of your brothers and run to the drugstore before it closes. Use this money to buy strawberry ice cream."

I was astonished! I was a smart little girl, and I knew we needed this money for essentials. So I objected. "What? We have to use this to pay bills, Mama, to buy school things. We can't spend this for ice cream!" Then I added, "I'm going to ask Daddy." So I went to my father, telling him what Mother had asked me to do. Daddy looked at me a moment, then threw back his head and laughed. "Your mother is right, honey," he said. "When we get this worried and upset about a few dollars, we are better off having nothing at all. We can't solve all the problems, so maybe we should celebrate instead. Do as your mother says."

So I collected my brothers and we went to the drugstore. In those days you could get a lot of ice cream for a few dollars, and we came home with our arms full of packages. My mother had set the table, made fresh coffee, put out what cookies we had, and invited in the neighbors. It was a great party! I do not remember what happened concerning the other needs, but I remember the freedom and fun of that evening. I thought about that evening many times, and came to realize that spending a little money at that time for pleasure was not irresponsible. It was a matter of survival of the spirit. The bills must have been paid; we made it through the weeks and months that followed. I learned that my parents were not going to allow money to dominate them. I learned something of the value of money, of its use. I saw that of itself it was not important but that my attitude toward it affected my own spirit, could reduce me to powerlessness or give me power of soul.

Not money, only, but solitude, too, had to be learned in relation to power—the power to be truly free and responsive to life. One summer Saturday morning when I was twelve, I was waiting for my friend Juanita to come over. We had planned a morning together, and she was quite late. I was fretting and complaining, and generally making a nuisance of myself. In fact, I was becoming rather obnoxious to everyone else in the house. Finally, my father said to me, "Get a book, a blanket, and an apple, and get into the car!" I wanted to know why, but he only repeated the order. So I obeyed. My father drove me about eight miles from home to a canyon area, and said, "Now, get out. We cannot stand you any longer at home! You aren't fit to live with. Just stay out here by yourself today until you understand better how to act. I'll come back for you this evening."

I got out, angry, frustrated, and defiant. The nerve of him! I thought immediately of walking home; eight miles was no distance at all for me. Then the thought of meeting my father when I got there took hold, and I changed my mind. I cried and threw the book, apple, and blanket over the canyon ledge. I had been duped and I was furious. But it is hard to keep up a good, rebellious cry with no audience, so finally there was nothing to do but face up to the day alone. I sat on the rim, kicking the dirt and trying to get control of myself. After a couple of hours, as noon approached, I began to get hungry. I located the apple and climbed down to retrieve it—as well as the book and the blanket. I climbed back up, and as I came over the top I noticed the piñon tree. It was lovely and full. I spread the blanket in the shade, put the book under my head, and began to eat the apple.

I was aware of a change of attitude. As I looked through the branches into the sky, a great sense of peace and beauty came to me. The clouds sat in still puffs, the blue was endless, and I began to take in their spaciousness. I thought about the way I had acted and why Daddy had treated me so harshly. Understanding began to come, and I became more objective about my behavior. I found myself getting in touch with my feelings, with the world around me. Nature was my mother, holding me for comfort and healing. I became aware of being part of it all, and I found myself thinking of God. I wanted harmony, I wanted to hold the feeling of mystery, I wanted to be a better person. It was a prayerful time, a time of deep silence. I felt in communion with much that I could not know, but to which I was drawn. I had a great sense of discovering myself as great, of seeing the world as great, of touching the holy. This sense lasted a long time, perhaps a couple of hours. I found I liked being alone, enjoyed the rich emptiness, held the stillness. It was as if I had met another person—me—who was not so bad, after all.

By the time my father came to get me, I was restored. Daddy did not press me about the day. He asked no questions, and I gave him no answers. But I was different, and we both knew it. My father had dumped me into solitude and had challenged me to grow. Before I got out of the car, I thanked him. And from then on, especially during the summers, I would take a day to go off alone. I loved those times of solitude, of contemplation, of prayer. I loved the person, the world, the God I had met that day. This habit of seeking solitude has stayed with me all these years.

Another time that I loved was Tuesdays—late afternoon during school days, and all day during the summers. This was the time when my mother and I ironed together. From the time I was very small, I had my little ironing board set up next to hers. I was ironing before I even had an iron that was hot! I graduated from handkerchiefs to flat pieces, then to white shirts and frilly curtains. I had many brothers but no sisters, so time alone with my mother was a great treat. But Tuesdays were a long line of the best days, for those were close times of sharing. Ironing was no drudgery for me, and never has been; I think this work was too pleasant to be infected with weariness. It was a day when I walked around in my mother's adult world of thoughts and experiences, and prepared quite directly for my own grown-up life. My mother taught me songs from her girlhood, and I taught her the contemporary songs. She told me about her problems when she was my age, and about her parents and home. After two or three hours of ironing, we always stopped to look through part of her album, and every picture was a story. I came to know her school friends, the boys she dated, the people who made a difference in her life. My mother was a great storyteller, and over the years had memorized long poems of love and courage and heartache.

The album was very selective, not crammed full of the same picture with different poses. Mother said it was better to have a few good story pictures than to have so many crowding the album that you never looked at them all. Sometimes we laughed, sometimes we cried; as old as the stories were, each time they held something new for me.

But ironing days were serious, too. My entire education on sex came over the ironing board. My mother was at ease with her body, liked being a woman, and read a great deal. Her explanations were always accurate, direct, and generous. I was always prepared a year or two in advance for what was happening to me as well as to boys of my age. I became the chief source of information for most of my friends—I had the knowledge and vocabulary. Changes that frightened my friends or burdened them with discomfort never bothered me; Mother kept the point of view that what was natural had to be understood, appreciated, and accepted as healthy.

One ironing board discussion centered around my reading. In junior high someone had given me a couple of pulp romances, and I had hidden them in my room for late-night reading. Mother found them, and the next Tuesday we talked about them. She did not scold me for my trashy selections, but said it might be good if I read a great deal of such stories so that I could find out for myself if they were worth my time. I was surprised, but quite happy. The next day while I was at school my mother went to the drugstore and bought me a whole quantity of real love, true romance and glamorous experience. I found the stack in my room, and attacked the magazines with zest and freedom. After a couple of dozen of these in a row, it occurred to me how very much alike they were. They were good for setting off the imagination, but I knew every story before I read it. At one point, I stopped midway through the story, decided they were all a waste of my time, and the next morning I burned the whole pile. It was a clear but easy lesson of evaluation.

It was at the ironing board, too, that Mama asked me some of the most important questions. One she asked for a number of years was this: "What are the five most important things, do you think, in the man you would want to marry?" I can remember the change from early answers such as "rich, handsome, a car" to "intelligent, a good sense of humor, loves life." My mother would comment on my choices, not so much by judging as by wondering or questioning. One day it occurred to me to ask my mother what *she* felt were the five most important qualities in the man she married. That day I grew up quite a bit. I also saw my father differently and appreciated him more.

It was not only my mother who could ask one question for ten years. My father also had a few favorites which he repeated at regular, well-spaced intervals. One was, "Are you thinking about what you want to do with your life when you grow up?" It was a good question, and the way he asked it was larger than thinking of a job or career. He had asked me that question when I was a mere second-grader. I knew the answer then, too, but I did not tell him that early. How I came to know so soon has always been a shining memory for me.

There were about eighty of us second-graders in one classroom. We had a wonderful teacher named Miss James. She had never married, was in her sixties when she taught me, and was a remarkable woman—full of life and fun. For all of us, she made the classroom an experience of discovery and pleasure. She treated us as if we were important, and took us seriously. There were many chances to grow individually. She told us many stories and taught us how to tell stories on ourselves, to make dramatic the little things that happened to us. My mother and father did this, too, and I still consider it one of the strongest forces of my education.

One area that we all liked was the contests. She ran so many that everybody came off a winner during the course of the year. Two big ones pitted girls against boys and the subjects were mathematics and spelling. The boys could pick the ONE they wanted to represent them in these two contests; the girls could do the same. We were always having to pick the good ones in this or that, which in itself was a great education. It got us off the superficial level of seeing each other.

The two chosen for the grand finale in math and spelling were a boy named George and I. The final tests were in writing and all in the class took the tests with us—but our scores decided whether boys or girls were the champions. George had won the math; only spelling was left for us girls. We were given a few minutes to review the long list of words from our homemade, dittoed books. Then we took the test, and I had a perfect paper. George missed one. As Miss James was recording the girls as winners, one boy looked back at me and then said, "She cheated. Her book is still on her desk." I had forgotten to put the book inside the desk and there it was, bold and accusing on the corner of the large double desks we shared. I had not cheated, but the evidence was clearly against me, and I knew it. My eyes filled with tears, and when Miss James came back to my desk, I could not look at her. I had lost for the girls. It meant a lot to us. She stood by me for what seemed ages. Then she put her hand on my shoulder and asked softly, "Did you look at any of the words during the test?" I couldn't speak. I shook my head "No" as tears ran down my cheeks. Then she said, "I believe you. That could happen to anyone. You and the girls are the winners of the spelling contest." I will never forget the feeling of relief and gratitude that flooded me. She had accepted my word in the face of what looked like guilt. Shortly afterward, the dismissal bell rang to end the school day, but I just sat where I was. It was a thing about power. She had had the power to make all the difference, and by believing me, she had given me a certain power. I felt as if I had been saved from death. By her faith in me she had handed me back to myself. Sitting there in that desk, I decided that what she did was a great thing, and that I too wanted to be able to make such a difference with people. Right there I decided to become a teacher, and a really good one. I went to the drugstore after school and bought a notebook, and it became my journal of what makes for a really good teacher. Miss James was my first entry. I split the first two pages into four columns, writing her name at the top of the page. The column headings were : 1) What I like; 2) What I don't like; 3) What the other kids like; 4) What the other kids don't like. I kept that book for eleven years, evaluating every teacher I had, trying to learn how to be the kind of person that would make important differences in people's lives. I never showed the notebook to anyone, but I studied it and kept it up-to-date.

During those eleven years, I had only two teachers that I thought were great, but that was enough. Miss James, in the second grade, and Grace, in the eighth grade. Grace took us into a wonderful world of drama and poetry and literature. She treated us with dignity and responsibility. She helped us search out and find and treasure our individual gifts. When my father asked me during my eighth-grade year, "Are you thinking about what you want to do with your life when you grow up?" I answered, "Yes." With a twinkle in his eye, he followed with the questions, "Does it include talking?" Again I said "Yes." My work, interests, lifestyle, and successes and failures have been varied, but the thread of those meaningful experiences held. I find myself in the world of education, no matter what form it takes. It was a great gift to be awakened by women who were truly educators.

Other stories from my life that stay close to me come from my father's way of teaching. Daddy wanted us to be self-reliant and courageous. He did not live in fear, and did not want us to be afraid of challenge, of life, of people. So, he took risks with us; he can't have always known what would happen, and I am sure he lived with some misgivings about his decisions regarding us. But mostly, they were good decisions. None of us grew up afraid to try, afraid to reach out, afraid to venture. During the 1930s, many traveling men stopped at our home. Some of my friends were afraid of hoboes and warned me never to let them into the house. Others told wild stories about them. But I had a different experience of the depression hoboes. My father always welcomed them, included them in the family meals, and instructed us children: "Listen to these men. They have been getting a different kind of education from what people get in school. They travel, and meet many people, and have to make their way in hard times. They can teach you a great deal. So, when we have these men as guests at the table, be sure you ask them questions and get them to tell you about their adventures. They have a different view of life from people who never go anywhere or try to get along without much of anything." So, for a few years, hoboes were part of our life. They were not just different and exciting. They were living geography lessons. We were not afraid of them, were not put off by their rumpled clothing and sometime smudgy faces. A few were ordinary, but mostly, they were great teachers, hungry for more than a hot meal and a place to clean up.

Speaking of fear reminds me of an evening when I was nearly ten years old. I was coming home rather late from a movie, and I was alone. We lived only six blocks from the theater, and I was never afraid to come and go by myself, except on Halloween. This particular evening I was walking along the dimly lit main street when out from behind the courthouse bushes jumped a man, waving what looked like a knife. I recognized him at once as Crazy Tom. Crazy Tom was a good enough man when he was sober, but if he got hold of too much whisky, he went wild. Those wild escapades had earned him the name of Crazy Tom. Well, he was yelling and looked wild, and whatever he had in his hand wasn't to be examined! He yelled at me, and I started running, he was running right behind. My heart was pounding, and it seemed as if he was getting closer and closer. My imagination was no help. Finally, I was running down the last block, and I saw our house lighted up, the door open, with only the screen door between safety and me. I jumped onto the porch, pulled open the door, and ran inside, panting heavily. My father was sitting in the rocking chair, reading. "Daddy, Daddy," I cried, "Crazy Tom's chasing me with a knife!" My father lowered the paper slowly and then said quietly, "Well, he didn't catch you, did he? I always said you were a good runner." I was dumbfounded. Here I was, bursting in after a run for my life, and my father defused the entire chase with a simple question and a sincere compliment. I stood there looking at him, and then I laughed. What he said was true. Crazy Tom had *not* caught me. I had outrun him. There was nothing to be afraid of, nothing to worry about. I suddenly felt it was a great experience, worth telling everyone as soon as I could. What could have become a crippling experience was a victory, a show of courage. I knew Daddy approved of my fast sprint. He never even mentioned Crazy Tom.

Daddy had a way of making us philosophize about what happened to us. In fact, "philosophy of life" was one of his favorite phrases. My mother surely had a clear philosophy that she lived, but she did not talk about it as much as Daddy. The joke in the house was that Daddy had the philosophy and Mother lived it. Mother taught us out of what happened, but Daddy reflected on experience more verbally. He made us articulate, while Mother tried to keep moving us gently toward understanding.

An incident that happened when I was in junior high would be to the point. We were having a poster contest in art class, and I had what seemed to me a great idea. I shared it with one of my friends. Well, she used my idea, turned it in first, and won the prize. I was furious—not even so much at the betrayal as at not getting credit for an original idea. I went home fuming, and several hours later, when my father came home from work, I was still complaining. Daddy asked what was the matter and I told him how my friend had stolen my idea. She hadn't even said that it was mine, but just claimed it as if it were her own. Daddy listened, and then he sat down and took me on his lap. "Honey," he said, "let me give you a lesson that you might need for the rest of your life. It is very hard in this world to have a good idea and also get credit for it. Not very much that we have is ours alone. We pick things up from books and people without even knowing it. But even if it comes together in a new way in us, we might not get credit for it. Which do you think is really better—to be the kind of person who really has good ideas, even if you don't get credit for them ... or, to be the kind of person who is willing to take credit for what isn't hers? Which do you think would make you happier, make your life more exciting?" It was not hard for me to see. Again, it was a question of where real power was, in reality or appearance. Dad taught me that being creative was more important than being acclaimed as creative. It is pleasant to have our gifts acknowledged, but it is a shame to let the joy of the gift hinge on such recognition. What matters is what is in the heart: that is how we keep from getting blood poisoning—by keeping a heart that makes all the actions healthy.

Stories, symbols, were always important in my life. Mother taught so much that mattered through actions. She taught me many ways to pray, and often these were connected with nature, with the land, with the sky. She took dirt from the place where I was born and kept it for me. When I was born she saved a little piece of the umbilical cord, dried it, crumbled it, and mixed it with the earth. Such gifts, held for years until a child can understand, make deep impressions on the subconscious. My brothers and I have spoken of these mystery gifts, which have been good medicine for the mind and body and spirit.

My mother did not speak, when I was very young, of death. But she taught me death. One of the best ways she taught me was through prayer, and my favorite prayer was the Sacrifice Flower. My favorite flower was the dandelion. It was so happy, and fun, and changed its petals for wings. When I brought great gatherings of dandelions home to decorate every table and window sill, my brothers sometimes laughed. They said I was picking weeds. But my mother said to ignore them—they had learned from non-Indians to call dandelions weeds. Calling any plant or blossom a weed, my mother would say, was just human bias. Each had its place and use, as well as its own beauty.

Now and then, when I had something heavy on my heart, or a special favor I wanted very much to receive, Mama would say, "Maybe this would be a good time for the Sacrifice Flower." At first she went with me to help me find a special flower. But after awhile, I went alone. This prayer started with a search for just the right flower to put your heart and thoughts and dreams in. You had to wander around and look at many, then select the ONE you wanted to hold your prayer. You picked the flower, took it home, but you did not give it a drink of water. This flower was going to offer its life to help you receive your favor. So, you went apart to your room with the flower, and held it in your hand. You looked at it with love and admiration, thankful for its beauty and dignity. When you knew the flower and had taken time to love it, then you gave into its keeping your request or dreams. This was like an intense meditation and trust. You placed your spirit into beauty in the fragile flower. Then you placed the flower in a safe place (safe from brothers!), but where you could see it. Often you looked at the flower and remembered it was giving its life for you, bit by bit offering your prayer to God. The flower did not get tired or distracted; your prayer was in its perfume and color, and in its dying. It was a holy offering, and its presence kept you remembering what you yearned for, what you prayed for. Finally, the flower had offered all the life it had—this may have been days after you first chose it. Your prayer was almost complete.

When I felt the flower had died, I took it from its safe place and showed it to my mother. Then she taught me. Look at the flower again. See, it has given all its own juices to help you, to keep you remembering the things of your spirit. Now, you must hold it with reverence and gratitude. Take it outside and dig a small place for it to rest and mingle with the earth. It has died as a flower, but there is still life power in it. After a while, it will be new energy for the earth, and more flowers can grow. Unless you can learn death, my mother would say, you cannot learn life. Dying and living are part of the same way. The day dies to be born again. The harvest is picked to make way for a new planting. Your flower sacrifices itself for holy thoughts and prayers. Learn from it, so you may know what in you has to die if you are to live more nobly. Then, what looks like death becomes part of the greater life you live.

I thank my parents and all my teachers; they have strung many beads on the necklace of my memories.

Parabola
Volume: 4.3
The Child

TWINS TWISTED INTO ONE

Don Talayesva

In 1890 Don Talayesva was born at Oraibi, Arizona ...

When we were within our mother's womb, we happened to hurt her. She has told me how she went to a medicine man in her pain. He worked on her, felt her breasts and belly, and told her that we were twins. She was surprised and afraid. She said, "But I want only one baby." "Then I will put them together," replied the doctor. He took some corn meal outside the door and sprinkled it to the sun. Then he spun some black and white wool, twisted the threads into a string, and tied it around my mother's left wrist. It is a powerful way to unite babies. We twins began, likewise, to twist ourselves into one child. My mother also helped to bring us together by her strong wish for only one baby.

My mother has described how carefully she carried me. She slept with my father right along, so that he could have intercourse with her and make me grow. It is like irrigating a crop: if a man starts to make a baby and then stops, his wife has a hard time. She had intercourse only with my father so that I could have an easy birth and resemble him.

She refused to hold another woman's child on her lap and took care not to breathe into the face of small children and cause them to waste away. She had nothing to do with the tanning of skins or the dyeing of anything lest she spoil the goods and also injure me. When she grew big, she was careful to sit in such a way that other people would not walk in front of her and thus make my birth difficult. She would not look at the serpent images displayed in the ceremonies, lest I turn myself into a water snake while still in her womb and raise up my head at the time of birth, instead of flying with head down seeking a way out.

My father has related how he took care to injure no animal and thus damage my body. If he had cut off the foot of any living creature, I might have been born without a hand or with a clubfoot. Any cruel treatment of a dumb beast would have endangered my life. If he had drawn a rope too tightly around the neck of a sheep or burro, it might have caused my navel cord to loop itself about my neck and strangle me in birth. Even if I had been able to free myself from the cord, I might have remained half choked and short of breath for a long time.

Whenever I made movements in the womb, my mother was encouraged to expect an early and easy birth. She worked hard at cooking, grinding corn, and bringing water, so that her body would be in trim for labor. My father fed her the raw flesh of a weasel and rubbed the skin on her body so that I could be active and come out swiftly, in the way that sly little animal slips through a hole.

I have heard that I had a hard birth. It began in the early evening of a day in March, 1890. Since the exact date was not remembered, I could never have a birthday. When my mother's face darkened and she felt the expected pains, she settled down on the earthen floor in the third-story room of her Sun Clan house. She had sent my five-year-old sister Tuvamainim with my little brother Namostewa to a neighbor's house. Namostewa was about two years old and still nursing.

My grandfather (mother's father, Homikniwa of the Lizard Clan), who lived in the same house with my mother and father, has told me how he climbed the ladder to the third floor where my mother lay. There he rubbed her belly and turned me straight to come out. The power in his hands helped her womb. His presence encouraged her, too, because he was the best medicine man in Oraibi. My father, Tuvanimptewa of the Sand Clan, also came in to help, which was rather unusual for a Hopi husband. He soon sent for Nuvaiumsie, an experienced old midwife and a member of his father's linked Water-Coyote Clan. As soon as she came, she heated water in a clay pot over coals in an old-fashioned fireplace in the southwest corner of the room.

In labor, according to all reports, my mother moved over on a pile of sand which was especially prepared for my birth, rested herself on hands and knees, raised her head a little, and began to strain downward. My father and her father took turns standing over her with their arms around her belly, pressing down gently and trying to force and shake me out. If I had refused to come, more and more pressure would have been applied, but no Hopi doctor would have opened her body to get me.

I was a big baby. I caused a lot of trouble and took a long time coming out—head first. Old Nuvaiumsie is said to have taken me fresh and crying from my mother. She cut my navel cord on an arrow to make me a good hunter, folded back my end of the cord, and tied it about a finger's length from the navel to keep out any fresh air. She used a piece of string from my mother's hair, which was the proper thing to do. If she had not tied the cord securely, fresh air would have entered my belly and killed me. My mother was given some small twigs of juniper to chew and some juniper tea, in order to strengthen her and to hasten the discharge of my afterbirth.

My grandfather, my father, and Nuvaiumsie examined me closely. Sure enough, I was twins twisted into one. They could see that I was an over-sized baby, that my hair curled itself in two little whorls instead of one at the back of my head, and that in front of my body I was a boy but at the back there was the sure trace of a girl—the imprint of a little vulva that slowly disappeared. They have told me time after time that I was twice lucky—lucky to be born twins and lucky to just miss becoming a girl.

Wrapping me in a cloth, they laid me near the fire and waited for my mother to free herself from the afterbirth. Nuvaiumsie is reported to have taken hold of the free end of the placenta cord and pulled gently, while my father stood behind my mother, held her around the waist, and shook her. She was told to stick her fingers down her throat and gag until she expelled the afterbirth. Finally it came out. Then my mother was placed near the fire in a squatting position on a low stool—perhaps the Hopi birth stool—so that the blood could drip upon the sand. She was given a drink of warm juniper tea to clear out the womb. A little later Nuvaiumsie bathed her in warm yucca suds, wrapped her in a blanket, fed her some warm corn mush, and had her lie on her side before the fire so that the bones could fit back into place. The old lady carefully swept up the sand and blood from the floor with a little broom, placed them with the placenta, the dirty rags, and the broom in an old basket, sprinkled the whole with corn meal, and gave them to my father to throw on the placenta pile. This he did at a special place near the southeast edge of the village, so that no person would step upon them and cause his feet to become sore and chapped, his eyes yellow, and his urine thick.

When all bloody traces of the earth were removed, my father hastened to the house of his mother's sister, Masenimka. He would have fetched his own mother, had she been alive. Masenimka came quickly, bringing a bowl of water, some corn meal, a piece of yucca root, two white corn ears, and some baby wrappings. She came with a smiling face and a happy heart, hoping thereby to bring me good luck and to insure my having a cheerful spirit.

Masenimka has related how she greeted me with tender words, washed my head in warm yucca suds, rinsed it with clear water, and bathed me from head to foot. She rubbed the ashes of juniper or sage bush over my skin to make it smooth and to cause hair to grow only in the right places. Then she pulled up her black dress (*manta*) to her thighs, rested me on her naked knees, and announced that I was her boy and a child of her clan. Chewing some juniper twigs, she spat upon my ear lobes and rubbed them to numbness. Then she pierced them with a sharp instrument and passed a thread through the holes to keep them open. She placed my arms by my sides, wrapped me in a warm baby blanket, and laid me on a wicker cradle made of a frame of bent juniper branches which was filled in with a network of small lemonberry stems and other twigs. There was a face guard of the same material. The cradle was padded with cedar bark or old clothes. A larger blanket was wrapped about me and the cradle and bound tightly with a string. Masenimka sat before the fire with me in the cradle upon her knees for a long time. Then she placed me on the floor near my mother and put an ear of corn on either side, one to represent me and the other my mother.

In the early morning hours when the cocks began to crow, Masenimka took a little finely ground corn meal and rubbed four horizontal lines, one inch wide and six or seven inches long, one above the other, on the four walls of the room. Then she resumed her seat by my mother and me and said, "Now, thus I have made a house for you. You shall stay here while we wait for you twenty days." Soon after she went to her own home and brought over some corn which she cooked with a few small twigs of juniper. This food was to make my mother's milk flow freely. Masenimka might have given her some unsalted gravy and some milkweed for the same purpose, since when that weed is broken the milk runs out.

Before the eastern sky had turned gray, the Sun Clan women propped two poles against the door that faced the rising sun and draped a blanket over them. This was to keep out the sun's rays from the birth chamber, for they were considered harmful until I had been properly presented to the Sun god. By breakfast many neighbors are said to have dropped in, taken a little food, looked me over, congratulated my mother, and expressed best wishes for my life.

I was bathed again by my godmother, Masenimka, who rubbed me anew with juniper ashes or the powder of a special clay found near the village. After my bath I was fastened back in my cradle and given the breast. My brother may have thought that I was stealing his milk, but he could do nothing about it. If my mother had been dry, I would have received the breast of a relative, fed upon finely ground sweet corn mixed with the juice of stewed peaches, been given a little gravy without salt, or perhaps some milk from the cows of the missionaries. If I had taken the breast of another woman, her own nursing baby might have discovered the theft of milk, worried, and even become nervous or sick. Babies are pretty wise about these things and quickly learn what is going on. I could not have taken the breast of another pregnant woman, for that might have caused my death.

For twenty days my mother was not allowed to eat or drink anything cold or salty, lest blood clot in her womb. All her food was cooked with juniper leaves. The fire in our room was kept going. No one was permitted to kindle other fires from it, for this fire belonged to me and such a theft would have made me unhappy. If it had become extinguished through accident, it would have been rekindled immediately, and that day would have gone uncounted. No food could be cooked on the coals themselves, although it might be cooked in a vessel over the fire. Neglect of this rule would have made me a "fire meddler" and caused me to play with fire carelessly in childhood. My father could not have intercourse with my mother during those twenty days, nor for twenty days thereafter. If he had done so before all the blood had drained from my mother's womb, a new baby would have been started which would have worried me, brought on sickness and nervous spells, and perhaps spoiled me for life. Had he attempted intercourse, the sisters and clan sisters of my mother would have interfered. If he had had intercourse with some other woman and then had an argument with my mother over it, that would have been almost as hard on me, for I would have sensed that something was wrong.

A routine was set up for me. Every morning I was unbound, bathed, rubbed with "baby ashes," and put back on the cradle. A little pad of cloth was placed at the back of my neck to keep me from becoming bull-necked and soft cedar bark was placed under my buttocks to drain off the urine. Someone probably cleaned me three or four times a day. I was always fed in the cradle and could move only my head a little in nursing. I do not know that anyone took saliva from my mouth and rubbed it on the nape of my neck to conceal my crying from the evil spirits, as is done with many Hopi babies.

When my navel cord dried and dropped off, it was tied to an arrow and stuck beside a beam overhead in the room. This was to make me a good hunter and to provide a "house" for my infant spirit in case I died, for my soul could then stay by the arrow in the ceiling and quickly slip back into my mother's womb for an early rebirth.

On the fifth morning I was bathed as usual, but with a special application of yucca suds to my head. My mother's head also was washed with the suds, and her body bathed with warm water in which juniper leaves had been boiled. Her clothes were changed and the soiled ones were taken to a near-by rock cistern and washed. After our bath my mother scraped off the lowermost of the four lines of meal from the walls of the room. She took the scrapings in her hand, and going to the edge of the mesa, held them to her lips, prayed for my long life, and sprinkled the meal to the rising sun. On the tenth and fifteenth days the same ceremony of bathing and prayers to the sun was repeated. If I had been the first baby, my mother could not have gone out before the sun on the fifth day and thereafter. Had she been too sick or weak to go, my godmother would have gone for her. The water with which our bodies had been bathed was carried to the placenta pile and emptied there.

On the twentieth day of my life I was named according to strict custom. About four o'clock in the morning Masenimka and her sisters, Kewanmainim and Iswuhti, and many other clan aunts—any woman of my father's clan and linked clans—came to our house to wash our heads again. Masenimka first washed the two "mother corn" ears in the yucca suds, rinsing them with fresh water. These were the ears that had been by my side since the night of my birth. Then she washed my mother's head, as did all her sisters in turn. Fresh water was poured over it, after which her hair was wrung out dry. They also bathed her arms and shoulder with warm water which had a few sprigs of juniper in it. Sweeping a little sand from the corner into the center of the room, they heated a stone, set it upon the sand, and laid yucca roots and juniper leaves on top of it. My mother stood with her right foot and then her left foot resting upon this heap of sand, stones, roots, and leaves while Masenimka bathed them. The entire heap was then placed in a tray along with the broom that was used to sweep the floor. The last of the corn meal lines from each wall was scraped off and the dust thrown on the tray. A live ember from the fireplace was put on top and the fire permitted to go out. One of the women took the tray and its contents and some of the bath water and carried them to the placenta pile.

Within a few minutes the customary naming ceremony began. Masenimka unfastened the wrappings that bound me to the cradle, stripped me bare, and washed my head in a bowl of yucca suds. Then she bathed me from head to foot, rubbing on "baby ashes." My head was rinsed in fresh water and each of my many aunts bathed me in the same manner, one after the other. The last one handed me back to Masenimka, who wrapped me in a blanket that had been warmed by the fire. My bath water—like my mother's—was handled with care and carried out to the placenta pile. During so many baths I probably cried a little, but no one has reported it.

Masenimka took me again on her left arm, picked up my "mother corn" ears with her right hand, waved them forward over my chest, and said, "May you live always without sickness, travel along the Sun Trail to old age, and pass away in sleep without pain. And your name shall be Chuka." Chuka means mud, a mixture of sand and clay. Masenimka and my father are of the Sand Clan, which made my name appropriate. This name was a sign to everyone that although I was born into the Sun Clan of my mother I was also a "child of the Sand Clan" and that my father and all his clan relatives had a claim on me. Each aunt repeated the ceremony and each gave me another Sand, Lizard, Earth, or Snake Clan name, but they have been forgotten. Even if I had never been told these things about myself I could be sure that they happened, for there is no other way for a new child to get a good name among the Hopi.

After the naming ceremony most of the women went back to their houses. But just before sunrise Masenimka placed me in a blanket upon her back and started with my mother to the edge of the mesa where they were to present me to the Sun god. Each took along a pinch of corn meal, and my mother carried my pair of mother-corn ears. They stopped with me southeast of the village where the trail leaves the mesa. This is a kind of "highway" of the Sun god, the main Sun Trail for the Oraibi people.

My mother took me with the cradle and blanket from Masenimka's back and placed me on the right arm of my godmother. Masenimka, thus holding me before the Sun god, breathed a silent prayer on a pinch of meal which she held in her right hand. Then she uncovered my face to the early dawn with her left hand in the proper way, rubbed some of the sacred corn meal between my lips, and threw the rest to the rising sun. She then sucked the meal from my lips with her mouth and blew it toward the east four times. Taking the ears of corn from my mother, she extended them toward the east with a circular motion from right to left and brought them close up to my chest four times. As she concluded she prayed again for my long life and called out to the Sun god the different names I had received, in order that he might hear them and recognize me. It was my mother's privilege to take me in her arms and repeat the same ceremony, but it is not required by Hopi rules, and I have never learned whether she did it or not.

When we returned to the house where my father had just washed his own head in yucca suds, a big breakfast feast was served to relatives and friends. They were invited to eat *piki* (native wafer bread), boiled meat mixed with hominy, puddings, and other choice foods. Masenimka received a big load of food in payment for her services as my godmother and carried it home on her back. Many of my mother's sisters and clan sisters were present and were all called my "mothers," while the sisters and clan sisters of my father were called my "aunts." The Sun Clan men who came and ate were called my "uncles," while my father's brothers and clan brothers were all called my "fathers." Almost everyone praised my mother, made hopeful remarks about me, and predicted that I would become a good hunter, a fine herder, and perhaps a powerful healer, for I was a special baby—twins twisted into one. There was no doubt about this, for they could see the two whorls of hair on the back of my head, and those present at my birth told others how large and double-sexed I looked when fresh from the womb. All knew that such babies are called antelopes because these animals are usually born twins. It was anticipated, therefore, that I would have a special power to protect myself, do many strange things before the people, and be able to heal certain diseases, even as a boy. My mother, father, and grandfather made careful note of these signs and sayings and were prepared to fill my mind with them as soon as I could know anything.

Adapted from *Sun Chief: The Autobiography of a Hopi Indian*, edited by Leo W. Simmons, Yale University Press, Copyright © 1942. Reprinted with permission.

Parabola
Volume: 22.4
Miracles

With Visible Breath: Miracles in Native American Traditions

Joseph Bruchac

> *With visible breath I walk,*
> *Toward the nation I walk,*
> *With visible breath I walk,*
> *Something holy, something ancient*
> *Something red I bring... .*
> —The Song of the White Buffalo Calf Woman

On August 24, 1994, a female buffalo calf was born in Janesville, Wisconsin. Word of the birth spread quickly along what has long been called the "moccasin tele-graph," the word-of-mouth network that links together the million and a half Native Americans in the United States, and the story was picked up in the dozens of American Indian newspapers around the continent. Soon pilgrimages were being made to the forty-three-acre farm where the calf, now known as "Miracle," was being respectfully cared for by the white farmer and his family who seemed both honored and slightly bemused by the event. Hundreds of Lakotas and other Indians, including Arvol Looking Horse, the contemporary guardian of the sacred pipe of the Lakota Nation, trav-eled to see Miracle. The gate and the fences of the corral where the young buffalo was kept were soon covered with eagle feathers, prayer fans, and other sacred objects left in homage and in prayer.

What was it about the birth of one female buffalo calf that was so special, an event that some Lakotas have described as an Indian equivalent to the second coming of Christ? It was simply this. Miracle, the female buffalo calf, was white. Even in the times when millions of buffalo thundered across the Great Plains, a white buffalo was an extreme rarity. That a white buffalo should be born now, when only thousands of the great animals once so central to the lives and cultures of the Plains Indians remain, was miraculous enough. But that the white buffalo was female was regarded by many Native Americans to mean only one thing. The Lakota people had not been forgotten by Wakan Tanka, the Great Mystery. A miracle had been sent to them: White Buffalo Calf Woman had returned. The coming of White Buffalo Calf Woman is one of the oldest and arguably the holiest of all the stories of the Lakota Sioux. This is that tale.

Long ago, there was little food and the people were starving. Two men were sent out as scouts to look for buffalo. They climbed to the top of a tall hill and saw something coming toward them. They first thought it was a buffalo, but as the figure came closer they saw it was a beautiful young woman. She wore white buckskin and carried something in her hands.

One of the scouts had bad thoughts about that young woman while the other one saw that she was a sacred being. The one whose thoughts were bad reached out to grab the young woman. As he did so, a white cloud covered him. When it blew away he was a skeleton, and worms crawled over his bones.

Then the woman spoke to the man whose thoughts were good. "Go home and tell your people that I am coming. Prepare a tepee in the center of your nation for me. I am bringing something holy to your people from the Buffalo Nation."

The young man did as she said. His people prepared a tepee for her, and she came into their camp, singing as she walked. She gave them the gift of the Sacred Pipe; she taught them how to use it and gave them seven sacred ceremonies.

"I am going to leave," she said. "But you will see me again."

Then she walked away. As she went, she stopped and lay down on the earth and rolled, and when she stood up she was a black buffalo calf. She went a little further and lay down and rolled again, and stood up as a yellow buffalo calf. Again she went further and lay down and rolled, and stood up as a red buffalo calf. The fourth time she lay down and rolled, she became a white buffalo calf and walked away until she was out of sight.

As soon as she had vanished, great herds of buffalo came all around the camp.

One of the oldest and most common themes in Native American sacred stories is the coming—or the return to earth—of sacred beings who are messengers from the Creator. That they should come to earth at all is a great miracle, a sign that the powers of creation truly care for human beings. Such caring in itself is a mysterious thing, especially when it seems universally true that such appearances are occasioned by great human need and prayer on the one hand, or human failures and misdeeds on the other.

In every Native American language, there is a word which refers to the mysterious, unknowable power of the universe: a power which, even when it manifests itself in ways that affect human beings, still remains a great mystery. Among the Lakota, that word is *wakan*, while among Algonquin-speakers, such as my own Abenaki people, it is *manitou* or *manido*. When great and powerful things occur which are beyond ordinary human power or understanding, when there are miracles such as the coming of the White Buffalo Woman, they are wakan.

Among the Cheyenne of the western plains, the tale of the man named Sweet Medicine or Sweet Root Standing is their most sacred story of such a manifestation in flesh of the mysterious power of the Creator, the one they call Maheo, "The Great Mysterious One." As Fire Wolf, a Sun Dance Priest of the Cheyenne, carefully explains, "There is only one god, but one man was used to bring all good things to the Cheyenne. That man was Sweet Root Standing. He is not Maheo himself. He is the Prophet, not the one true God."[1]

Maheo also created four Sacred Persons, known as the Maheyuno, who dwell in the four directions, as well as the Maiyun, the sacred powers which live above and below the earth. The Maheyuno guard creation and are friendly toward human beings. When a human fasts, prays, and sacrifices to show veneration, the Maheyuno may send help to that person in a number of different ways. Wisdom, supernatural protection, and miraculous power may be given to the person who is favored by the Maheyuno.

Clearly, Sweet Medicine was greatly favored by the sacred powers, although his life did not begin in a promising way. His parents died when he was a baby. Raised by a poor old woman, he had only a torn piece of a buffalo robe for clothing. Yet he grew to be a strong, good-looking young man known as Nivhevoss, which means "Eagle's Nest."

One day, Nivhevoss killed a buffalo. A great chief saw that buffalo and told the boy to give him the buffalo's skin. Nivhevoss refused, and the two fought. Using the buffalo's leg bone as a weapon, the boy killed the chief.

The Dog Soldiers and the Kit Foxes, the Red Shields and the Elk Society, those men whose job it is to make sure that things are done properly, then tried to catch the boy. They vowed to beat him to death for killing the chief. But Nivhevoss was impossible to catch. Each time they surrounded him, he turned into a bird or an animal and escaped, first as a coyote, then as a magpie, a crow, a blackbird, and an owl. He came back to the camp and stood where the people could see him. One day he did so dressed as a Dog Soldier, the next as a member of the Red Shields, then an Elk and a Kit Fox, as a Contrary and a Chief. And, as before, each time the men tried but could not catch him. Then the people noticed that each time he disappeared, the buffalo disappeared with him, and they had nothing to eat. Each time he returned, the buffalo herds came back, too. They realized that his power was helpful to the people. So he was welcomed back to live among them.

The next thing that Sweet Medicine did was to make a pilgrimage to the Sacred Mountain. There he was welcomed by many people who were actually the animals and birds and all things on the earth showing themselves in human form. Four principal men sat around the lodge, and Sweet Medicine was asked to choose which of them he wanted to resemble. He chose the best-looking one. Had he chosen one of the others, he would have lived forever, but because he chose the one who was the best-looking, it meant that some day he would have to die.

When Sweet Medicine returned from the Sacred Mountain he brought back with him Four Medicine Arrows. Those arrows are still kept by the Cheyenne people to this day. He taught the people all the things they needed to know to live well. He lived for as long as the lives of four ordinary people. Each summer he looked like a young man, but he grew older with the fall and looked like an old man each winter. But when spring came, he became young and strong again. At last, after four lifetimes, it was time for him to die. Then he told the people about the things that would happen in the future. He told them not to forget his name. He told them that people would come to fight with them. He told them a new animal would come with a round hoof and that they would ride upon its back. The buffalo would disappear and white people would come and be all over the land.

Then, in the summer, when he was a young man, Sweet Medicine died. And the things that he predicted have come true.

In the Northeastern woodlands, perhaps the most powerful of such stories about miracle-workers sent by the Creator is the Iroquois tale of the Peacemaker. Like the Cheyenne, the Iroquois say that the Creator, Shonkwaiatison, has four sacred messengers who dwell in the four directions and come to earth in human form to assist the people.

Long ago, they say, one such messenger was sent to tell the people the proper way to live by always giving thanks. For a time the people followed that path. They remembered to give thanks for everything. To this day, saying the Thanksgiving Address is still the first thing that people must do at the start of any gathering or any ceremony. But as generations passed, the human beings began to forget to be thankful. So a second time a messenger was sent. This messenger taught the people the ceremonies that would help them remember to be thankful. Once again, many generations passed and the people became forgetful of the message given them by Shonkwaiatison and his Sacred Messengers. This time, in fact, the people strayed very far away from the Creator's ways. The times were violent and bloody, dark and hopeless. The Five Nations of the Iroquois people—the Seneca, the Cayuga, the Onondaga, the Oneida and especially the Mohawk—seemed to live for nothing other than war and revenge. Even women and children and old people were not safe. The trails were covered with blood.

So, a third time, one of the Messengers came to earth. He was born in the shape of a baby to a woman who had never been with a man. He was the Peacemaker. As Sakokwenionkwas/Tom Porter, a Bear Clan elder of the Mohawk Nation, explained it to me recently, the Peacemaker's job was to go among the worst of all the people on the earth—the Iroquois—and bring peace to them. Such an undertaking was, in itself, a miracle, but there were various events in the Peacemaker's life which can be seen as miraculous by any definition, beginning with his birth. There are so many events which occur in the Peacemaker's story that it would take days to tell them. So I will recount, briefly, the first of the stories about the Peacemaker.

His mother was not a person of the Five Nations. She was a Huron woman, an enemy of the Iroquois. To escape the fighting which was happening everywhere, her mother had taken her to live in a little lodge near the northwestern shore of Lake Ontario, far removed from all people. When that baby was born in the midst of winter it was a great shock to the older woman.

"Who is the father?" she asked.

"I have not been with any man," the daughter answered.

The new grandmother became angry at her daughter for lying. She did not want anyone to know that her daughter had given birth in such a shameful way. So she took the child, went to the lake, and chopped a hole in the thick ice. Then, with a long pole, she shoved the baby into the hole and far under the ice. But when she returned to the lodge, she found her daughter holding the baby in her arms.

A second time the grandmother took the child. She dug a deep hole in the earth and buried him. But, just as before, when she returned to the lodge she found the baby in his mother's arms. The third time, she made a big fire. She thrust the child into it and watched him burn until only ashes remained. She was certain that was the end of it. But when she came back to the lodge, she found the baby there again, unharmed and whole. Then the grandmother realized that the baby was a sacred being sent by the Creator. She would no longer attempt to harm him. He was the Peacemaker and his mission would be to restore health and balance to his people.

For whatever reason they occur, miracles are so common in Native American traditions that they are more readily accepted—or even expected—among American Indian nations than perhaps any other peoples in the world. Seeing the world as a place alive with miracles means being aware of the miraculous nature of life itself. The breath, which carries words, stories, songs, and prayers, is also life itself. When the sacred tobacco is smoked, the breath becomes visible. As the stories I have just told indicate, when miracles happen, divine favor becomes visible to the people. It is visible and accepted, but not understood. Like the great gift of life itself, miracles remain a part of that which is wakan, the visible breath of the Great Mystery.

Notes:

1. Peter J. Powell, *Sweet Medicine* (Norman, Okla: University of Oklahoma Press, 1969).

Parabola
Volume: 17.3
Oral Tradition

The Call to Remember

Arthur Amiotte

When I was six years old, I killed my first bird. My grandmother and step-grandfather made a feast for me. They invited people from White Horse Creek: Henry Weasel and his wife Lucy; John and Mary Bear Shield; Alex Pablo, one of my own grandfather's good friends; the Red Elks; and Frank and Mary Black Tail Deer.

My grandmother cooked the little bird all by itself in a tiny little pan, the same one in which the first kill of my uncles had been cooked. In addition to this she also cooked much more than the guest could ever eat at one sitting.

Once the people had gathered, Frank Black Tail Deer stood up and made a long speech in place of my own grandfather, who had died when my mother was five years old, many years before I was born. Frank Black Tail Deer had also been one of my grandfather's good friends. He told the people that I was now a little man and that life was going to change because I now had to go to school. His wife Mary then handed him a muslin bundle which had been made from many Bull Durham tobacco sacks ripped open and sewn together to form a larger bag.

From this bundle he took out a furry little something which turned out to be a cap made of beaver fur. It had small beaded ears and two shiny beads on the front for eyes. He told me this cap had belonged to my grandfather.

Then he gave me good advice, reminding me to always be kind to the old and hungry people, to remember the *Tunkasilas* (the Lakota Gods), to do what my parents told me to do, and not to be stingy.

He said that since I was going to school, I would need some special help. Giving me the cap, he said, "Remember it is the beaver who can make a whole world. Now that you are going to school you will be making the world all over again and you should do it in a good way so your relatives will be proud of you."

Mary Black Tail Deer then opened her shawl and pulled out another bundle from which she took a little patchwork pillow. She said it was filled with goose down. "*Takoja* (grandchild)," she told me, "you will use this for a long time to rest your head because learning will make you tired sometime. Some of what you learn will be stored here, like a dream sack."

Everyone then ate a little pinch of the cooked bird I had killed. I was embarrassed but my grandmother made me pass it around to all of them. As each took a little portion, he or she thanked me politely in Lakota; some of them even passed their hand downwards in front of my face, an ancient and most sincere sign of gratitude. The larger meal was then served to them, and the extra food was packed away in metal lard buckets and little bundles which had been brought especially for this occasion.

My grandmother then opened one of her trunks and pulled forth shawls, patchwork quilt tops, yardages of calico, silk scarves, and pieces of new tanned and beaded deerskin cut in the shape of moccasin tops before they are sewn to the rawhide sole. These she handed out to the ladies. My step-grandfather, who by biological kinship was the uncle of my own grandfather, gave the men cartons of Bull Durham tobacco, silver dollars, black silk neck scarves; to Frank Black Tail Deer, for his part in the event, he promised a half of the beef which we were going to butcher in about two weeks.

Frank Black Tail Deer then stood and, without a drum, sang an honoring song for me in which he used my childhood Lakota name, *Wahpa Tanka Kuciyela*, Low Flying Blackbird. It had formerly belonged to my grandfather, his grandfather, and the grandfather before him. It was given to me at birth and was part of my inheritance. Everyone arose and one by one came and shook my hand while he sang. Then everyone left and I hauled water in buckets from the spring so my grandmother could wash the dishes and pots. My step-grandfather went back to work in the field with his horse-drawn hayrake.

I still have that pillow today and it is very hard and flat because it is now so very old. I know for certain it also has a few nightmares stored in it.

I quickly learned the lesson of the cap when, several days later, much against my wishes, my grandfather and grandmother took me in the wagon to school. There I was given over to a very scary-looking, red-haired, freckled white woman teacher who nevertheless treated me well. At storytelling time she would say, "Okay children, let's put on our thinking caps." I knew precisely what she meant because I owned such a cap, even though I did not actually have it there with me. In my imagination, I would reach inside the white sack, take out the cap, and put it on my head. I just knew I was learning much faster by wearing that imaginary beaver cap.

At home in the evenings, Grandfather and Grandmother would tell *Iktomi* stories, the Lakota trickster tales. Into late autumn, sometimes even after the first frost, we continued to sleep in a large green army tent in which there were numerous beds, including those of my grandparents. Other adults and the very young cousins slept inside the house. Once tucked in our beds under heavy patchwork quilts, the kerosene lantern was turned down low, and the stories began.

I would reach under my pillow and put on my beaver cap and pull it over my eyes so I could not see anything. As the Iktomi stories were told and also other stories of long ago, the scenes would come alive inside my head. Sometimes my grandparents would orally take the roles of the various characters and with their voices bring to life the mythic and historical dramas they were reliving for the benefit of their grandchildren. Many times the stories wove themselves into my dreams until someone, usually my grandmother, removed my beaver cap before she went to bed so that I would not smother in my sleep.

Native American stories are not mere random tales from some eclectic collection that old people remember. They are not consciously memorized as in a classroom, but are part of a larger body of lore incorporated into the psyches of generations of listeners through repeated listenings and tellings in settings where the very rhythm or cadence of the telling is an actual ingredient in the process.

Natives take into account the various dimensions of the mythic tradition: the sacredness inherent in certain tellings, the readiness of the listener, and tribal or family ownership rights to certain telling. Even though someone may know a part of the sacred lore, he is not necessarily the right person to tell it if someone else more qualified is present, such as a shaman or other holy man. Certain telling of a historical nature should also not be told by an inappropriate person, since the person might be accused of taking credit for somebody else's accomplishment or story.

The story of my beaver cap represents the first level of acquiring some facility in the oral tradition. The actual event was a ritual taking place at a significant moment in my life as a contemporary Lakota person. Though it took place several hundred years after the time when the practice of such a rite was common and fifteen years after the last time the same pan had been used to cook the first kills of my uncles, the elders present still attempted to impress upon me the significance of what it meant to me as a human being and as a Lakota male. I had passed through one of the first stages of becoming a responsible person on the way to acquiring tribal cultural ideals. This was put into perspective by the act I had just performed: to kill for food is a reality of life and is necessary if others are to live—it is a most important skill for survival. As my first kill, it was a significant moment which needed to be impressed upon my mind so that I would *remember* it.

The other implications arising from the incident are that the ritual was sponsored by my grandparents, which says something important about the role of the elderly in the lives of contemporary native cultures. During the last years of World War II, many Lakota men and women had left the reservation to work in military installations. My mother, because of her dexterity, served as a fork-lift hoist operator, one hundred miles from the reservation, loading bombs onto railroad boxcars for transport to East and West Coast ports during the war years and afterwards. My father had served during the war but the couple had divorced shortly thereafter, and so I lived with my grandparents.

Though the ritual took place in 1948, the moment was timeless, in that a young person was being taught the fundamentals of the wisdom of his culture which emanated from an ancient place and time, and now extended into, and ultimately accommodated, a very different time and place.

Ritual on this level serves to focus the minds and memories of the participants upon a specific significant event and its implications for becoming what the culture prescribes as a "good person." The attending actions, songs, and orations, done with extraordinary feeling and sincerity, make a profound impression on the being of the central person. He in turn is admonished to *remember* the all-important condition for retention of *Lakol Wicoha* (the Lakota traditions), and incorporation of his own life story into that of his people, their history, and ideals.

Native storytellers often preface a narration with the proper linguistic device to make it perfectly clear which dimension of time, mythological or actual, and which level of significance they are about to reveal. In doing so they give the audience the necessary clues to adjust their "thinking caps."

Among the Lakota of North and South Dakota, to preface a delivery with "*Mitakuyepi*" (my relatives, my people, or my everything) immediately signifies that something very grave, serious, profound, or sacred is about to be said. Following this would be one of several terms to designate which mythological time or level is about to be narrated. The rough English equivalents are phrases like "once upon a time" or "long, long ago." For the Lakota, *Ehanni* spoken with long, reverent duration—"Ehaaaaaaaaaaaaaaanni"—is equivalent to saying "long, long, long, long ago" and properly identifies that body of myth relating to a mythological time even before the world was created: it has to do with the creation of the gods and then the creation of the world and all its plants, creatures, and mankind.

Stories from this era would appropriately be told as instruction by a shaman or holy man to those apprentices who were about to undergo some sacred rite, such as their first purification, their first vision quest, or, in the case of younger people and their parents, as a part of the Youth Sanctification or the Young Woman's Ceremony. Sometimes a portion of the ancient mythology might be told to explain the significance of a particularly troubling dream as a means of reconciling for the dreamer the disparity between the dream and the reality of the tribal beliefs, between the sacred realms and the everyday world.

The next category of telling are identified as *Ehanni Ohunkakan*. Ehanni in this case may be stated with less duration—"Ehaaaanni"—long ago, but not as long ago or as deep or as sacred as "Ehaaaaaaaaaaaaaanni." Stories from this era, while still about the interaction of the gods and the ongoing creation, focus of the gradual differentiation among the gods and the gradual retreat of the pure gods, who now speak through their messengers and appointees. Mankind now appears upon the newly created face of the earth, having migrated from the immortal underworld through the aid of or intervention of certain god-associates, and these men must learn the new order of things and what powers are necessary for their new roles in a state of quasi- and semi-immortality.

Trickster stories proliferate in this category and help describe the ongoing creation and differentiation of man and his activities in relation to the primal gods and their wills. Humans are punished in this period for disobeying, or forgetting, the wills of the gods, or for being led astray by lowly human or Trickster ways. It is also at this time when the definition and role of the intercessor is established and sanctioned as an institution to be nourished and remembered. Through ceremonial means, the people are able to periodically retrieve something of their diminished sacred heritage.

A third category of telling, referred to as *Ehanni Wicowoyake*, are those events which have taken place within the living memory of the people as *Lakota Oyate*, or the people as a distinct tribe. These telling come close to an approximate living history of human events, and include specific references to actual landmarks and approximate dates as recorded in the mnemonic devices such as winter-counts and skin paintings. Most crucially, these are personal accounts of life events, passed down through successive tellings from generation to generation, and they account for much of the content of Native ethno-history.

The mythic is never totally removed from these more contemporary tellings, however, as the stories themselves often recount how a particular event was altered by the intervention of the sacred in some form or another, including ceremonies, visions, dreams, near-miraculous healings, and the fulfilling of vows made to the gods in exchange for favors granted.

The continuing persistence of the oral history tradition is evident today, not only in those households where the stories are still told as a matter of course in daily or nightly family affairs, but also in public, during formal periods of the ongoing ceremonial life. For example, an important aspect of the vision quest among the contemporary Lakota is still the *Hanbloglaka*, the actual telling of visions and the vision experience. This telling is done before the shamans, and then before the collective body of relatives and guests who gather specifically for that reason following a formal fasting with the pipe; in some cases, it is also told following participation in a Sun Dance.

Today, our concerns are of a new order: Can what was originally communicated through the oral tradition be converted to the printed word, without losing the nuances and vitality of the spoken word, in light of the gradual passing of the older generation? Can succeeding generations continue the oral tradition in spite of having been greatly affected by the printed word and electronic media? What will be the impact of the fact that educated natives must read about their own traditions from the academic perspectives of anthropology, sociology, literature, and religion?

Perhaps we need not be concerned about all this, but instead should be grateful for the phenomena taking place on most Northern Plains reservations. Here, we see a cultural renaissance of native languages, music and dance, traditional and contemporary visual arts, ethno-history projects from the point of view of natives as researched and written by natives, and the growing participation on all levels of native society in the sacred traditions.

Perhaps these concerns about preserving the qualitative aspects of the living traditions come from a very non-native perspective, one which perceives only the outward appearances of a beaver cap, without pulling it down over one's eyes in the dark so one can finally see.

Parabola
Volume: 28.2
Prison

THE HAWK IN THE PRISON

Joseph Bruchac

> *They are taking us beyond Miami*
> *They are taking us beyond the Caloose River*
> *They are taking us to the end of our tribe ... .*
> —from a Seminole song

> *I am of the Icse Wicasa—the Common People,*
> *the Original People. Our sacred land is under*
> *   occupation*
> *and we are now all prisoners, not just me.*
> —Leonard Peltier, from *Prison Writings*

Incarceration has been a much more common experience
for Native Americans than for the European-American
populace of the United States. The list of famous Native
Americans, past and present, who have been imprisoned
is one indication of that. Geronimo of the Apaches, Qua-
nah Parker and Kicking Bear of the Comanches, Chief
Joseph of the Nez Perce, Chief John Ross of the Cherokees—these are only a few of the well-known Indian
leaders of the nineteenth century who spent time behind
bars. There were also those who died—either in prison
or while being taken there. Osceola, of the Seminoles,
perished while in prison. Crazy Horse of the Lakotas
rode in to what he thought was to be a peace council.
When they tried to throw him into a guardhouse, he was

fatally stabbed with a bayonet as he struggled to escape. Virtually all of the leaders of the contemporary American Indian Movement in the last few decades of the twentieth century were imprisoned for several years, including Dennis Banks, Leonard Crow Dog, and Russell Means, who has now gone on to an even more visible and successful career in Hollywood. Some of them, most notably Leonard Peltier, are still in prison.

Prison, to the American Indian, means something different from what it does to most other Americans. Both the reasons for imprisonment and the response to it are different among Native Americans. To understand this, we need to look at American history and Native traditional beliefs.

While forced imprisonment has never involved more than a small percentage of the overall American populace, there have been times within the last two centuries when the majority of Native Americans were kept in some form of incarceration. Usually the issue was land: Indians had it, whites wanted it. The clearest example of this may be the early nineteenth-century experience of the so-called Five Civilized Tribes of the American South, the Cherokees, Chickasaws, Choctaws, Creeks, and Seminoles. Forced against their will from their ancestral homelands in such states as Alabama, Georgia, Tennessee, and North Carolina, they were sent to Indian Territory in the west.

The Cherokees, despite their successful appeals to the United States Supreme Court, were the last to be removed. In May and June of 1838, fifteen thousand Cherokees were rounded up by United States troops. They were first crowded into thirty-one stockades and then concentrated into eleven camps in Alabama and Tennessee. During their three months in those concentration camps, even before being sent onto the now-infamous Trail of Tears, thousands of Cherokees died. Some of the stories and songs that came about as a result of those years of loss and removal survive to this day among the Five Tribes. The Seminole song, collected in the early twentieth century by the ethnologist Frances Densmore, is only one example.

Later in the nineteenth century, most of the Indian nations of the West also found themselves either totally removed from their homelands or kept by force within an extremely small part of the land that was once theirs. The entire Navajo nation spent four years on a barren reservation in New Mexico called Fort Sumter before finally being allowed to return home. To the Navajo, Fort Sumter was Hweeldi, the "place of the wind," for only the wind could live on the salty soil of that forsaken landscape.

If anyone doubts that these reservations were anything less than outdoor prisons, they need only consider what happened to those Indians who left those designated lands. They were hunted down by the Army to be killed or returned to the reservation. Their status—often by definition, as far as the United States was concerned—was that of prisoners of war.

But Indian captivity goes back more than two hundred years. Sadly, the experience of bondage has been a far too common part of the American Indian history since the arrival of Europeans on the shores of the New World. That bondage first took the shape of slavery. Among the first things Columbus did on the island of Hispaniola was to take Taino captives back to Europe with him. His return to the Caribbean brought the development of large-scale Indian slavery, as the Native population was decimated while being forced to work in Spanish mines on the island.

Today, American Indians in prison are still living out a history begun with the coming of the whites. Some, like the men and women of the American Indian Movement (AIM), have been widely viewed as political prisoners. Others have clearly ended up in prison because they broke the law in less romantic ways—murder, robbery, rape. But when we consider the why of their breaking those laws, when we place their lives within a much larger story that is still being told, we often see that their lives, too, fall within that pattern set so long ago.

I believe that prisons do not work. I do not say this out of some abstract liberal humanitarianism, but from much thought and many years of personal experience. Although I've never been a prisoner, I've been in prisons in almost every state in the Union over the last thirty years. I've been there as a writer, as a storyteller, and—for eight years—as the head of a college program inside a maximum-security prison. I have grown to know hundreds of incarcerated men and women not as convicts, but as human beings. Granted, there are a few individuals who are so dangerous to themselves and others that they need to be kept away from the general population. But the vast majority of people who are in prison should not be there. The costs to the individual and society, costs that are social, financial, and spiritual, are far too great. In general, whatever long-term problem prison is meant to solve, it can be simply said that prison just makes it worse. It is especially so for American Indians.

Among the many different native nations of both North and South America, there appears to have been no tradition of incarceration among American Indians. What was done to those who broke the rules of the culture? In a society without jails or police, how was order kept? It was done through a combination of individual conscience and the desire to be true to one's family and one's homeland. One of the most common punishments was the requirement of restitution. If someone was incapacitated or killed as a result of your actions, in many American Indian cultures it then became your responsibility to provide for that person's family as that person would have done. There were also cases where someone might be condemned to death. After the coming of Europeans, selling land to the whites was made a capital offense among several Indian nations, including the Cherokees.

The idea of taking away a person's liberty by jailing them and, as a result, limiting the liberty of others by requiring them to be jailors, seems to have been foreign to the Americas. Ironically, considering how many American Indian nations were sent away from their homelands through no fault of their own, the most serious punishment among pre-contact Native Americans appears to have been either temporary or permanent banishment. It was a punishment still commonly practiced among the northeastern tribes well into the nineteenth century. That for many Native Americans death itself was preferable to being separated forever from one's home and family is illustrated by the following story.

A Shawnee man sold some of his land to a white man. Even though he did so because the white man got him drunk and tricked him into signing the papers, he knew that he had broken the law of his people and that his life might be forfeit. When he confessed what he had done, he was told that he could choose between death and being banished for his punishment.

"I choose death," he said, "but I ask a favor. Allow me to go home for as long as it takes to do the planting and then bring in the harvest. That way my family will not go hungry over the winter."

"You may go," he was told. "But you must return as soon as you have brought in the harvest."

And that is what he did, choosing to die and leave an honorable name among his people.

Although prison represents a separation of Native people from their land and culture, the fact that the majority of American Indians in prison are there for crimes directly related in one way or another to substance abuse points to the fact that separation from land and culture may be both cause and result. When people are separated from their land and their culture, when they have little or no opportunity for a meaningful life (as is often the case in Native urban and reservation communities), people lose hope. Drugs and alcohol are a way of dulling the pain. And while drunk or stoned, the pain that is still there may be released in acts of violence.

In 1989, I was invited to Alaska by the Institute of Native American Arts. Part of my work was to run workshops in five different state prisons. The majority of people in those prisons were Alaskan Natives—Inupiats, Athabascans, Tlingits. Every single man that I spoke to said that the crime he had committed that placed him in prison was done while he was drunk. Most had little or no memory of their crime, though they did not doubt they had done those terrible things.

"They say I shot and killed my son," one man from King Island said. "I know they would not lie to me about that. I loved my son so much."

Quite a number of them were from King Island, a native community that had been forced to resettle on the mainland and give up their old way of life because their children were required to go to school and the state refused to keep a school going on the island. Soon after they were placed in government housing in Nome, there was a flood that destroyed their new homes and most of their few possessions. King Islanders are known throughout Alaska as being just about the best traditional singers and dancers. Considering their recent history, it is no wonder that they are also known for having problems with alcohol abuse.

"Some day," another man said to me in our little writing workshop, "I will go back to King Island. I will hunt for seals and fish and I will sing our old songs there. I will bring my people back there and our lives will be good again."

The American Indian response to prison is at least as important as the reasons why so many Natives still find themselves behind bars. Many American Indians, like Crazy Horse, would still choose death before prison. But once within those walls, American Indian prisoners may also draw strength from a spirituality that is stronger than steel bars and reinforced concrete. In his autobiography, *Prison Writings: My Life Is My Sundance*, Leonard Peltier writes not just about his political struggle as an Indian inmate but also about the spiritual strength he had continued to draw from tradition. One major issue for American Indian inmates in state and federal prisons has been religious freedom. While Catholics, Protestants, Jews, and Muslims were provided with clergy and allowed to worship in their own way, for decades American Indian religious traditions were ignored or prohibited. Advocacy—often strongly supported by clergy members of other faiths for American Indian religious freedom inside the prisons—eventually resulted in some significant changes during the last two decades of the twentieth century.

Although there are many prisons where American Indian religious practices remain prohibited, some things are now sanctioned. In most state and federal prisons, American Indian men are now allowed to grow their hair as long as they wish—since long hair is viewed in many Native traditions as a sacred right. In terms of ceremony, the *inipi* or sweat lodge is now practiced on a regular basis in a large number of prisons. Secure areas are set aside where a sweat lodge can be erected, stones heated, and the ceremony led by a Native elder who is allowed to enter the prison to conduct the inipi. Even the highly secure federal penitentiary at Leavenworth now allows sweats. It had made a great difference to Indian prisoners. As Leonard Peltier put it in his autobiography, "The inipi makes each Saturday morning holy here in otherwise unholy Leavenworth."

Even though they are in prison, many American Indians still try to see in the old sacred way, knowing that when you look through the heart, a cage cannot imprison the soul. I can think of no time when that was made clearer to me than on a certain warm summer day some years ago when I walked through the front gate of McAlester Prison in Oklahoma. Fourteen Indian inmates were waiting to do a writing workshop with me, a visiting poet from New York. As I entered the room and the guard locked the door behind me, the men looked up from around the big table where they were seated.

My friend Lance Henson, a Cheyenne poet from Oklahoma, was supposed to have joined me there. But after several days of visiting other prisons, including a workshop in the women's facility that morning, Lance had been unable to bear the thought of going through yet another set of barred doors.

"Take this with you, brother," he had said, handing me an eagle feather.

I had placed that perfect eagle feather carefully inside my shirt next to my heart, and I took it out as those men, who'd never seen me before, waited to see what I'd say. I didn't say anything. I just handed that feather to a Cherokee man on my left.

He took it from me reverently, touched it to his forehead, each of his shoulders, and his heart. Then he turned to the man on his left, a Pawnee, and did the same for him. Without a word, that eagle feather went around that table, from one man to the next, each receiving a blessing and then passing it on. Those men were from a dozen different tribes, but every one of them understood the meaning of that feather. The last man in the circle, a Cheyenne, who was seated at my right, stood up. There were tears in both our eyes as he touched me with the eagle feather and then placed it in my hand.

I don't really recall what I said then. I do know that was one of the best writing workshops I've ever experienced. The things that we talked about and the writing that they did were clear, moving, from the heart and the spirit. What I remember most, though, happened just at the end of class. The bell had sounded and people were slowly moving out of the room toward the end of the corridor where they would be counted before going back to their cells. The last man to shake my hand held onto it.

"I want to tell you a story," he said, "because you brought that eagle feather in here. About six months ago, I felt as if I couldn't take it any longer in prison. Even though I was allowed to work on the prison farm outside, I felt as if everything had forgotten me. Then, one day, when I was out there working next to this white guy, I saw a hawk high overhead. So I prayed. I prayed softly to Earth and Sky, asking for a sign that they had not forgotten me, even though I was in prison. Then that hawk started to circle down. 'Look,' I said to the white guy. 'That hawk is coming down to see me.' 'Are you crazy?' he said. 'That hawk isn't coming anywhere near us.' But when it got so close that it was only about ten feet over our heads, just circling there, that guy freaked out and went inside. I stood there with the hawk circling until they called us all in for the count. Next day, when I went out, there was a hawk's tail feather waiting for me on the ground. I figured it was a sign that I had not been forgotten. But then, only a little after that, I got word that my father had died. They wouldn't give me permission to go to the funeral, even in chains. So when my sister came, I handed her that feather. 'Put this in the coffin with Dad,' I told her.

"Then," he said, "I began to wonder if I had done the right thing. I missed that hawk feather and began to feel forgotten again." He squeezed my hand and smiled. "Until you showed up today with that eagle feather. It reminded me that as long as I don't forget the Earth and Sky, they will never forget me."

CHAPTER EIGHT

SINGING THE WORLD: WHY WE'RE HERE TODAY

In the aboriginal world, everything is encoded in the stories, songs, and language. In oral traditions, the stories are what have kept knowledge intact, knowledge about the stars, the times of planting, ways of being. These essays show that the words of singers and speakers define the world for us and, as most say, there is no English equivalent for the words because the meanings and layers are more complex than English. In addition, we can't separate the words from the world. They are the true being of the world. Story, song, and prayer are what give us to know the structure of the cosmos and cosmogony of the people. Here again, we see the aliveness in every element and mineral of the earth. The boy or man speaks with a stone. The stone is alive.

In most traditions, the world is created by story or song. The Marshall Islands were created by humming. Sometimes the world comes into existence because of dreaming. Even in the Bible, God spoke the world into being. We can't separate words out from the world. The enchantment that comes of the Yaqui words and its volumes of prayers and songs attest to this. Words offer hope. They also remind us what happens when we forget to sing praises. Spider Woman knows about the need to have a song in the heart. Everyone has a song. As renowned storyteller and keeper of the Lushootseed language, Vi Hilbert says, "That is why I tell stories."

Parabola
Volume: 2.2
Creation

THE TREES STOOD DEEP ROOTED

Sam Gill

Some time ago, I went to hear Indian elders speak about public education programs for Indians. An old Papago man was among them. When his turn came he rose slowly, and with deliberation began to speak. His style was formal and bore an air of certainty, though for his meaning I had to await the English interpretation. He began with the creation of the Papago world, by telling how Earthmaker had given the Papago land its shape and character. He identified the features of that creation with the land on which he had always lived, as had his father and all his grandfathers before him. Pausing in his story he asked how many of us could locate our heritage so distinctly. Then he went on to tell the stories of Iitoi, a child born in the union of earth and sky, who had acted as protector and teacher of the Papago under the name Elder Brother. He told of the way of life of the Papago people, a way of life they have always enjoyed.

It was perhaps fifteen minutes before he began to speak directly to the subject of education, but the old man had been talking about education all along. He was demonstrating to his audience a basic principle in education: knowledge has meaning and value only when placed within a particular view of the world. He was utilizing the way of his people by consulting the stories of the creation for the proper perspective from which to speak. There was power in his words and his statement was convincing.

As a Papago elder, this old man understood the power of relating the stories of creation. Papago culture abounds in songs and poems ritually uttered in order to provide sustenance and to maintain the Papago way of life. They are the gifts of the gods, not the works of man. Some are attributed to Iitoi who used them to win battles against enemies. The Papago identify the ruins which are found throughout their southern Arizona desert homelands as the villages of these enemy peoples. The Papago people have songs and poems which they recognize as capable of affecting nearly every aspect of life. The feeling of the power the people find in these words is captured in the beautiful lines of one of their sacred poems.

> *With my songs the evening spread*
>   *echoing*
> *And the early dawn emerged with a*
>   *good sound.*
> *The firm mountains stood echoing*
>   *therewith*
> *And the trees stood deep rooted.[1]*

The Papago are not unique among native Americans in recognizing a kind of performative power in the language of their songs, prayers, and poems. In his eloquent address, "Man Made of Words," N. Scott Momaday said, "Whenever the Indian ponders over the mystery of origin he shows a tendency to ascribe to the word a creative power all its own. The word is conceived of as an independent entity, superior even to the gods." According to Momaday, the native American "locates the center of his being within the element of language … It is the dimension in which his existence is most fully accomplished. He does not create language but is himself created within it. In a real sense, his language is both the object and the instrument of his religious experience."[2]

The repetitive nature of native American prayer and song has caused some observers to declare them to be merely the recitation of magical formulae. This is a view to be guarded against. The magic of the word lies mainly in the fact that it is capable, through image and symbol, of placing the speaker in communication with his own being and with the whole world. Native Americans do not restrict language to its capacity to describe the world: they recognize that, from one perspective, it is the world.

There seems to be a remarkable link between the stories of origin and the lifeways of native Americans. It seems to me that this link is the language of ritual that constitutes native American religious traditions. The events of creation are somehow paradigmatic, and the knowledge given in the creation stories permeates the life of the people.

To the Navajo, the world was not created by some powerful earth-making god, but through the creative powers of thought and the ritual language of song and prayer. Indeed, thought and speech were personified prior to the creation of the world. They arose from the sacred bundle out of which all creation was to come and they were said to embody the powers of the bundle. They took the form of a young man and woman of such radiance and beauty that they could scarcely be looked upon. While they were to be present in this form for only a brief time, it was told that they would always be near to the world, for theirs are the powers that sustain life. Their names are often rendered in English as Long Life Boy (thought) and Happiness Girl (speech), reflecting the Navajo view that their names are synonymous with the highest measure of life.

The Navajo ceremonial, Blessingway, demonstrates how the Navajo envision the way thought and speech became manifest in the creation of the world and in the sustenance of life. Of the twenty-five or thirty major ceremonial ways known to the Navajo, Blessingway is generally recognized as fundamental to all others; it is an indivisible body of myth and ritual and a whole religious ideology. The Navajo name for Blessingway, *hozhooji*, reflects the pervasive ideology of creation that supports this ceremonial; a literal translation would be something like, "the way to secure an environment of perfect beauty." The occasion for the first performance of a Blessingway ceremonial was the creation of the Navajo world; consequently, the ways of creation are the model for all versions and all performances of Blessingway. It is because Blessingway is the way of creation that it is called the backbone of Navajo religion and is recognized as the source and pattern of the Navajo way of life and thought.

In Blessingway mythology, the first act in the creation of the world was the building of a ceremonial structure in which the ritual acts of creation could be performed. A version of Blessingway, therefore, is performed on the occasion of the construction of a new Navajo house. But

Blessingway is also incorporated into all other ceremonials as the first-performed rite in order to "bless" the structure in which the rituals are to be carried out—whether the occasion be marriage, the need for rain, or difficult or imminent childbirth. In the mythic prototype, the humanlike beings who were performing the ritual began to construct the ceremonial house. Significantly, these humanlike beings who preceded the creation of the world are known by the Navajo word *yati'ii*, which means "speaker." They readied the support poles and leaned them into position. As the support poles were readied and dropped into place, songs named them and described their placement and significance.

> *Along below the east, Earth's pole I*
> > *first lean into position*
> *As I plan for it, it drops, and as I speak to*
> > *it, it drops, now it listens to me as it*
> > *drops, it yields to my wish as it*
> > *drops.*
> *Long life drops, happiness drops into*
> > *position* ni yo o.[3]

And below the south, Mountain Woman's pole is leaned into position, followed by Water Woman's pole below the west and Corn Woman's pole below the north.

The house described in this ceremony provides the pattern for the common Navajo conical-style hogan. It serves the Navajo both as a place of residence and as a ceremonial structure. But the song identifies this simple four-pole substructure with the pillars that support the Navajo world. The foundations of the poles are located below the horizon in the four cardinal directions. Each pillar is named and given the power to sustain life through its identification with long life (thought) and happiness (speech). The commonplace Navajo home is at the same time the structure of the entire Navajo world.

This linkage between the most commonplace and the most ethereal, made through ritual language, is illustrated even more powerfully in the imagery, found in a Navajo Nightway prayer, of the house whose structure is composed of the life forms of the earth:

House made of dawn,
House made of evening twilight,
House made of dark cloud,
House made of male rain,
House made of dark mist,
House made of female rain,
House made of pollen,
House made of grasshoppers.[4]

Each line focuses the mind on an image of the finite, material, domestic dwelling only to explode that image into fantastic dimensions by identifying its composition with unexpected building materials. A unity is achieved through the lines in their creation of an image of a living universe.

The ideology of Navajo sandpainting also illustrates the way in which creation is fundamental in Navajo life. Paintings made of crushed vegetal materials or ground minerals and rocks are ritually constructed and used as part of several Navajo ceremonials. Hundreds of them have been recorded and their designs and meanings are remarkably complex. Without accounting for all the occasions in which sandpaintings are used, the ritual acts performed upon them, or the various scholarly interpretations made of them, it can be shown that the efficacy of the sandpainting act is derived from the events in the creation of the Navajo world.

In the Blessingway myth it is told that after the "speakers" built the creation hogan, they entered it and proceeded with the creation. From the sacred bundle they took pieces of white shell, abalone, turquoise, and jet. With these materials they constructed representations on the floor of all forms of life that were to be in the Navajo world. These forms of life were personified as holy people having humanlike forms. The ritual construction was like a sandpainting. Each holy being represented was given identity by its dress and placement relative to the others. The resulting design was not a physical model of Navajoland, but rather a map of the Navajo religious conception of the world.

The creation concluded with the intoning of a long prayer to these holy people, who represented the life forms of the earth. The prayer associated and identified them with the physical universe and consequently effected an indivisible unity between the symbolic world of the ceremonial hogan of creation and the non-symbolic world of the Navajo, a unity of the spiritual and the material. A world had been made using only simple materials and the creative powers of thought and speech. Based on this model, Navajos continue to perform acts of creation through the power of symbolic representation in sandpaintings and the ritual language of song and prayer.

Following the creation, the life forms known as Dawn and Evening Twilight went on tour to inspect the new world. Upon ascending mountaintops to gain a vantage point, they found the scene around them to be extremely beautiful. This state of pristine creation is articulated by the Navajo people in many ways and it stands as the inspiration and measure of Navajo life. Life is envisioned as a journey down a road. It is deemed a good life if the traveler is surrounded by an environment of beauty comparable to that of the newly created world. Most Navajo prayers conclude with a passage describing this good life:

> *With beauty before me may I walk*
> *With beauty behind me may I walk*
> *With beauty above me may I walk*
> *With beauty below me may I walk*
> *With beauty all around me may I walk*
> *As one who is long life and happiness*
> *   may I walk*
> *In beauty it is finished.*
> *In beauty it is finished.*

Through the utterance of the prayer one is placed once again on the good road, so that it may be said with confidence and feeling, "In beauty it is finished."

There is yet another way to show how the events of creation are paradigmatic for Navajo lifeways. This centers on the importance in Navajo culture of the possession of a mountain-soil bundle. After the world was created, but before it was made suitable for habitation by Navajo people, a girl-child was created. Her parents are said to be the beautiful youth and maiden, Long Life Boy and Happiness Girl. This child had the remarkable ability to grow older through time, to reach old age and to repeat the cycle of life again and again. Because of this she was called Changing Woman. Changing Woman was given a sacred bundle containing objects and powers that created the world. The bundle was the source of her own existence, since her parents were the personification of the powers it held. Changing Woman was also taught the creation rituals. With the bundle and the Blessingway songs and prayers, Changing Woman at once holds and represents the powers of creation. She personifies the perfect beauty secured in the creation. She is identified with the newly created earth. She is the source and sustenance of all life. She is time. She is the mother of the Navajo people.

After her birth, Changing Woman used her creative powers to make the earth ready and suitable for the Navajo people. She created the plants and animals and cleared the world of the monsters who had come to threaten human life. Having made the earth a suitable place, she created the Navajo people. Her final act before departing from the Navajo world was to pass the knowledge of Blessingway on to the Navajo people. In doing so, she charged them with the responsibility to maintain the world in its state of perfect beauty by the use of Blessingway. She warned them that the Blessingway songs should never be forgotten, for Navajo life depends upon them.

Changing Woman is wholly benevolent and of such beauty that she is rarely represented in any visual form in Navajo ceremonials. But she did show the Navajo how to make a sacred bundle modeled on hers; this was the origin of the mountain-soil bundle. It is made with soil ritually collected from the four sacred mountains which stand in the quarters of the Navajo world. The soil from each mountain is wrapped in buckskin. Maintaining the directional orientations, these four bags are placed around stone representations of Long Life Boy and Happiness Girl. A buckskin is wrapped around all this and the bundle is secured.

The mountain-soil bundle is the nuclear symbol in Blessingway. Many Navajo families keep them as guides to the Navajo way of life and as sources of long life and happiness for the family. The bundle symbolizes the powers of creation, the source of life, and the perfect beauty established by Blessingway.

Navajo people often refer to the relationship of their many ceremonial ways as the branches of a tree which extend over every occasion, bearing and protecting the Navajo way of life. They identify Blessingway as the trunk of this tree which supports all other ceremonial branches. This tree stands deep rooted in the creation of the world.

Certainly the Navajo are not representative of all native American peoples, nor should they be considered typical. Even in the American Southwest, the Navajo are only one among many cultures which contain a wide variety of lifeways and religious practices. While there is tremendous diversity within native American cultures, certain general observations may be drawn from the Navajo example.

We have seen that the Navajo find in the story of their origin a symbolic paradigm for their lifeways and religious practices. The myth of origin serves at once as a prototype for a ceremonial performance and as a wellspring of philosophy and world view. A distinctive characteristic of this symbolic paradigm is the way in which it unifies the mythical and physical geographies, the ethereal and the commonplace, and the spiritual and the material. Frequently the best-known passages from native American literature are ones that illustrate this correlation. Often these passages describe an association of four or six directions with colors, animals, birds, eras, and certain qualities or temperaments. Such well-defined patterns have suggested that native Americans live in simple harmonious integration with the world around them. Black Elk recalled for Joseph Epes Brown the words White Buffalo Cow Woman spoke as she gave the sacred pipe to the Oglala Sioux:

> *With this pipe you will walk upon the Earth; for the Earth is your Grandmother and Mother, and She is sacred. Every step that is taken upon Her should be as a prayer. The bowl of this pipe is of red stone; it is the Earth. Carved in the stone and facing the center of this buffalo calf who represents all the four-leggeds who live on your Mother. The stem of the pipe is of wood, and this represents all that grows upon the Earth. And these twelve feathers which hang here where the stem fits into the bowl are from* Wanbli Galeshka, *the Spotted Eagle, and they represent the eagle and all the wingeds of the air. All these peoples, and all the things of the universe, are joined to you who smoke the pipe—all send their voices to* Wakan-Tanka, *the Great Spirit. When you pray with this pipe, you pray for and with everything.*[5]

In light of the Navajo views of creation and with passages like Black Elk's before us, we should re-examine the common assumption that native Americans are simple children of nature. I believe we will find this view erroneous. Native Americans have shown themselves to be masters of survival in an environment which has often been reluctant to nurture them, but their lifeways can scarcely be called the simple following of natural instincts. It seems almost the opposite. The Navajo, for example, look upon no living thing as simply natural, as a product of some impersonal system of natural law. Life is dependent upon holy people who were created in the beginning and who stand within all living things. Black Elk described a comparable Sioux belief when he attributed the unity of all living things to Wakan-Tanka, the Great Spirit. Native Americans can hold a person-to-person relationship with their environment because in their view of creation the power of life, which is a person, is united with and identical to the physical living world. The nature of these personal relationships is not determined by the aspirations of ego as much as by patterns established in the stories, songs, and prayers which comprise their traditions.

There is also a tendency to assume that the symbolic paradigms which arise from the stories of creation represent the native American view of the permanent status of their world. But these patterns of perfect beauty serve more as an objective and a measure in life than as a description of it. Underlying these global representations of the ideal are infinitely complex principles of relationship which determine and direct the lifeways. In the whole range of human action nothing is exempt. In other words, for native Americans all human action is continually measured against traditional patterns so that the way life is experienced is dependent upon how it is lived.

It is through a tradition of formal ritual acts that native Americans relate to the world, find the significance of life, and uphold the responsibility for maintaining order as it was given to the world in the beginning. From the native American view, their ritual acts are creative acts of the highest order, since the object of their creation is the world itself. This may well be the greatest contrast between native and non-native American views of life. A prevalent non-native attitude is to associate ritual and tradition with lack of innovation and creativity. Twentieth-century art forms illustrate this attitude. It is an age of happenings, chance events, and shapeless forms designed to be independent of the past and tradition. It is an ego-centered culture seeking noble achievements and separate realities. This view is alien to native Americans for they have accepted the charge of responsibility for performing the acts upon which life and reality depend.

The native American view of human creativity is based in religion, not in art. Such a stance is not void of excitement and illumination, for it is the creative genius of the native American way of life to see the uncommon in the common, to find the ethereal in the mundane. Theirs is the way longed for by Artur Sammler, the protagonist in Saul Bellow's novel, *Mr. Sammler's Planet*, who said, "And what is 'common' about 'the common life'? What if some genius were to do with 'common life' what Einstein did with 'matter'? Finding its energetics, uncovering its radiance."[6] Deep rooted in creation, native American traditions energize the common life.

Notes:

1. Ruth Underhill, *Singing for Power: The Song Magic of the Papago Indians of Southern Arizona* (Berkeley and Los Angeles: University of California Press, 1968).

2. Public lecture by N. Scott Momaday, "Man Made of Words," Claremont College.

3. Leland C. Wyman, *Blessingway* (Tucson: The University of Arizona Press, 1970).

4. Washington Matthews, *Night Chant, A Navajo Ceremony*, American Museum of Natural History Memoirs, Vol. 6 (New York: 1902).

5. Joseph Epes Brown, ed., *The Sacred Pipe: Black Elk's Account of the Seven Rites of the Oglala Sioux* (Clinton, Massachusetts: The Colonial Press, Inc., 1971).

6. Saul Bellow, *Mr. Sammler's Planet* (New York: The Viking Press, 1969).

Parabola
Volume: 25.2
Riddle

Singing the World

An Interview with Heather Valencia

Heather Valencia lived for many years on the Pascua Yaqui reservation just outside of Tucson, Arizona, with her husband, Anselmo Valencia, the spiritual leader of the Yaqui people. Of Cherokee and Welsh descent, Heather was a full participant in the "culture"—the spiritual and ritual traditions of the Yaqui people—and has taken on the responsibility of preserving and transmitting the Yaqui culture to younger generations. An accomplished artist, writer and storyteller, she is the author of Queen of Dreams: The Story of a Yaqui Dreaming Woman.*

—Megan Whilden

Parabola: *What is your relationship to the Yaqui?*

Heather Valencia: I am a dreaming woman born with memory of *sewa yo ania*, the enchanted flower world. Anselmo Valencia told me when we married that my spiritual work in this life was entwined with that of his people, and that I would serve as a Mother of the Deer Lodge, where the deer singers, the deer dancers, and all members of the Deer Lodge work together. For many years I had that honor and privilege. He told me further, that it would be my responsibility to help ensure that the memory of these teachings were kept alive for the children who come after us.

Ever since I was a child my soul has remembered this. The humming-bird is the Yaqui symbol for the sweet, sacred essence of joy that lives in the heart of the enchanted flower world. One of my first memories is of a hummingbird coming to me under a bower of jasmine when I was in a bassinet. Throughout my life the hummingbird has tracked me. When I was twenty-four years old, I was on a mountain called Oh Be Joyful in the high Rockies with my young son, and we ate the columbine flower for lunch one day. Shortly after that Anselmo and his best friend Kititu came to our cabin in the form of their *chilkin*. They tracked us through the hummingbird. I then began my journey to the southwest—to these people that were the most intrinsic part of my soul memory.

P: *What is a chilkin?*

HV: Chilkin is the Yaqui word for a dreaming double. If you have a dreaming double, you can be in two places at once. The dreaming double can go through light worlds and gather medicine and power. When Anselmo found me, I lived in the Rocky Mountains, which are a massive ore body. Wherever there is a high concentration of ore, if someone has the capacity to develop a dreaming double, it is enhanced there. That's why I'm sure I was led to the Rocky Mountains.

Arizona, where the Yaqui live, is a massive ore body, and it is the place where there are the most lightning strikes in the world. The earth actually calls the lightning down. The Yaqui word for lightning is *veveoktia*, and it is very important in their culture. They believe they have a special connection with the heart of the creator, and lightning is a vehicle to enhance that connection.

Right before I went to Arizona for the first time, I was in a tremendous lightning storm. After that, I was able to see the violet fire around myself and others. The Yaqui have a word for the violet fire that I cannot say: I have heard it said, but they speak the word only in ceremony because the violet fire is so sacred.

The violet fire is the key to the chilkin. When the violet fire is visible, it is the signal that the seer has returned to a place of perfected memory. When you look at a rainbow, you see that there are seven colors—from red to violet. The violet fire lives in the place between rainbows. It is an eternal place, and it is necessary to be alive in the completed world to reach this place.

P: *So it's a mystery as well, at least from where we are. Can you tell us more about the deer singers and their role in the Deer Lodge?*

HV: There are living worlds and worlds that, though once alive, have been eaten and no longer have life. It is the deer singer's role to keep alive that which is sacred and necessary in the enchanted flower world. He does that through the vibration of his songs. He does that by naming. The Yaqui believe that only through this method can the world be preserved. If the deer singer no longer names everything in the song, the living world will cease to exist. There is no song in the dead world.

The enchanted flower world is the five worlds combined in their original, subtle, shimmering perfection. It is a place of dreaming. From this place of dreaming human beings have named that which is, that which comes into being. Through the deer singer's song, life is maintained. Every single animal, every particle of dust, every rock, every rivulet, every plant, every cloud—all of these things are part of the deer singer's repertoire. There are many deer singers, and each one takes a lineage and a responsibility for keeping a part of the enchanted flower world alive.

P: *Does each deer singer take responsibility for a particular realm—i.e., mineral, vegetable, etc?*

HV: No, it's not like that. Anselmo was a very famous deer singer, and one of his most famous deer songs was about a bay horse. We are told that horses didn't exist in the New World until the Spaniards brought them, but the Yaqui don't remember it that way. They remember that there were horses here a long, long time ago, and then for a while the horses went away. And the bay horse actually is a tricolored horse with red, white, and black coloring—the three sacred colors of the Yaqui. The horse is a blood bay with a white star on its forehead. This was a very famous and ancient song from Anselmo's lineage. He also sang a certain little pig song from his lineage. He sang a very famous water song, a rock song, and a butterfly song. Sometimes he would sing other songs because he had seen a sick animal; he would sing a song for that animal to bring it back to its perfection.

The most beautiful expression I ever saw of that was when a little boy brought us a baby sparrow in the heat of *Sabado Gloria*. The baby sparrow was dying. The bird was given to me by Anselmo's son, and I showed it to Anselmo. He began the song of the sparrow, which he does not normally sing. But as he sang the tiny bird came back to life in my hand, and it trilled, an amazing, beautiful sound. It jumped up onto Anselmo's shoulder and trilled again, filling the deer lodge with song. And the third time the sparrow song was sung, it flew off into the morning, singing. That's how much power the deer songs have. They are sung according to the need of the moment, but people always request that certain songs be sung because they have a liking for them.

P: *I remember you telling me that Anselmo, although he was well known for the many things he had achieved as a political leader of the Yaqui people—establishing them as a legal tribe in the U.S., getting them a homeland—as well as being a powerful medicine man and spiritual leader, the thing that he was most proud of and that was closest to his heart was his deer singing.*

HV: Yes, and on the other side, in the enchanted flower world, that is what he always was and will be. That's the heart of his soul. He was the very finest deer singer. His songs were light and fast. The rhythm that he and his singers had was a quicker rhythm than anyone else's—very beautiful. He could sing for three days and three nights without sleeping because he was alive in the enchanted flower world when he was doing that work.

P: *You mentioned that there were five worlds that combined into the enchanted flower world.*

HV: According to my husband's people, the first world is the physical world. It is called the wilderness world, or *hu ania*. The second world is the mental world, called the enchanted world or *yo ania*. It is called enchanted because a mind is an individual thing. Even though all the human beings may be in one circle and experiencing one ceremony, each individual will have a different perception of it.

The third world is the shadow world, or night world, and this is called *tuka ania*. This is the crucible, the place where all the evolutionary work is done on the human being. This is the world that is the key to our soul memory.

The fourth world is the magical world and is called the sorcerer's world, or *sea ania*. The fifth world is a spiritual world—it is the dreaming place and is called *tenku ania*. Tenku is the word for the dream, the Great Dream.

In order not to be eaten or lost in the third world and to know how to navigate the place of the great mystery, one has to have training, knowledge, and ability. You need help from the beings in the fourth world to make it through the shadow. You can't get through by yourself.

The fifth world you cannot reach without heart, love, and willingness to sacrifice yourself for the tribe and Mother Earth. This world is only accessible through the heart. It is the most refined world, closest to the original dream, to the place of origin, which is the sun, the great central sun.

The Yaqui believe we have lots of lifetimes. We come from the sun to learn and to teach. We have to work to get back there. We try to return every time we die, but the corona of the sun burns us if we have anything left of the shadow or of shadow food in us, and the sun sends us back to try again. Only when you make your way all the way through to the fifth world can you return to the heart of the sun and not come back.

Anselmo said that when he died this time that was what he would do. He had done his work for his people many times, and he was tired and ready to go back to the sun. Everyone believes he did that. He died on May 2, called the Day of the Cross among the Yaqui. If you die on that day, it doesn't matter how much food for the shadow you have within you—the sun will burn it up like cottonwood in a sacred fire and let you go on through. In order to die on that day and get the benefit, you must state your intention beforehand, which is what Anselmo did. He said he would die on that day and he did. He was a fifth-world magician. Yaqui always know when they are going to die. They tell everybody goodbye two or three days before they are going and then they leave.

P: *I have heard that the name Yaqui was given to them by outsiders and that it means "stubborn." What do the Yaqui call themselves?*

HV: The Yaqui name for themselves is very beautiful. It is *Yoeme*. Yoeme means "the hidden ones, the hidden people."

P: *What are they hidden from?*

HV: They are hidden from denser worlds, the dead worlds. The dead cannot see the movement or penetrate the mystery of the Yoeme. The more alive something is, the more likely it is to see the Yoeme. The Yoeme are very pure, and in order to perceive them in their purest form you have to be at least a fourth-world magician. You know how if you're driving in a car and you say, "Do you see those rainbows and sundogs in the sky?" and someone else says, "No," you lend them your sunglasses and say, "Put these on, now do you see them?" Then they can see it, although they couldn't with their naked eye. The hidden ones are hidden in that way.

P: *Do all these different worlds coexist in the same place?*

HV: Yes, all these worlds exist within a human being, but the fourth and fifth worlds only exist in potential and have to be developed. There are many fifth-world dreamers among the Yaqui. The Yaqui came originally as fifth-world dreamers. This is a core teaching. The Yaqui believe first we dream and then the world becomes. They believe that it becomes through the vibration of song.

Knowledge is sought and mystery is revealed where that mystery originates, which is in the shadow. The shadow world is very cherished by the Yaqui, and Yaqui are darkside dreamwalkers because they have shadow mastery. They are very alive in the first two worlds, and the third world is teeming with life from all worlds that feed upon each other. In the third world, there are the hunter and the hunted. In this realm, to be alive and not be eaten one has to have a guide or a teacher to engage with the mystery and make a passage. But this is the fun of it all, this is the place where the Yaqui like to be. The Yaqui have power in the shadow world.

P: This is where the chilkin comes from?

HV: Yes.

P: *Does everyone have a chilkin or the potential of one? Is it something that is developed or tamed?*

HV: When the shadow double comes out like that, some kind of magic has occurred. One way to induce the chilkin to emerge is by eating sacred plants, whether by accident or on purpose. Although not all humans have the chilkin, all Yaqui do, because they drink the milk of their mother, and in their mother's milk is the essence of the sacred plants that cause one to have a dreaming double. This is something that is discussed with the children. Their parents will ask them, "Where did you go last night?" and they will reply, "I went to my aunt's house in Mexico last night and I saw that my cousin Antonia is sick." And then the aunt will call and confirm that she saw their child walking around and that Antonia is ill. The Yaqui get this from the very milk of their mother.

When a Yaqui baby is born, some dirt is put on the baby's tongue, and the baby remembers the shadow. The enchanted flower world is made from the sacrifice of the mother's blood. That is part of the teachings of the shadow world. In the shadow world there is the red, white, and black, but all together it looks black, so the shadow is hungry for red and white—it has to have it to keep existing. White comes from the fifth world and red comes from the first world.

Dreaming is very important to the Yaqui people. Teachings and communications are carried in dreams. Through the dreaming, it is known what's going on, what's coming up, what we need to work with at any given time.

Last month I was at a dreaming circle in Los Angeles, and a beautiful Yaqui woman named Francine, who was not raised in the Yaqui culture, told a dream where she was a mouse. There were many mouse relatives with her, and she recognized each and every one. They were all as individual as humans, all different. She knew that they were all political prisoners. The captors put them in a bathtub, and one mouse knew what do. He was wearing red, white, and black clothing, and he had the other mice form a triangle and thus escape from the bathtub.

As soon as Francine started telling the dream, I was reminded of the story of Baticumsekum (Yaqui for "where the water comes down") in the Sonora desert. During the Mexican-Yaqui war, all the Yaqui women, children, and elders at this place were locked into a church that was boarded up and then set afire by soldiers. The Yaqui turned into mice and escaped. The triangle is the secret battle formation of the Yaqui, given to Anabuluktec at the time of the Talking Tree.

I knew that Francine was truly Yaqui when she told me her dream and I knew she had had family at Baticumsekum. She was very happy to hear that and she's proud of her mouse medicine.

P: *What is the story of the Talking Tree?*

HV: A long time ago, after the time of the great lizards, the people were very, very happy. They only ate creatures of the sea and plants. Something very strange occurred one day. A great tree on Tosalkowee began to shake and vibrate, and the medicine people knew that the tree was talking. The talking of the tree greatly disturbed all the people, but no one could discern exactly what the tree was saying because they did not have any memory upon which to base the information. The wise people knew of a young girl who had come down recently from the stars. Her name was Itzcelli. She did not have a human father. They knew that this girl would understand the talk the tree was making. So the village elders made a journey up to the mountain where this girl lived with her mother. They told the mother that they needed Itzcelli's help, and the girl agreed to go with the village elders to listen to the tree. She sat for nine days beneath the tree, neither eating nor drinking, but receiving the information and crying. At the end of the nine days she came forward and told the elders what the tree had said. The enchanted flower-covered world in which the people were living so joyfully was about to come to an end because there were big people coming from a dense world across the sea. They were going to take the land of the people and kill them, they would want everything and there was no way they would be given enough—they would just want more. The leaders asked the girl what to do, and the girl said the tree had this message: "You can do one of three things. You can choose to stay here in the enchanted flower world, and you will remain as you are and can help the others in the other worlds. You can choose to go into the sea and become one with the enchanted people of the sea and offer help from there. Or you can choose to grow big and to go into the new world to stand up against these ones who are coming and to fight to keep them from taking your land. In order to do so, you will have to eat meat to grow big."

So the people were instructed by Itzcelli to ask Brother Deer, because he was the most beautiful and graceful of all the creatures, if he would make the sacrifice for them. He was the sweetest of all the meats. Brother Deer said he would be glad to make the sacrifice so that the people could grow big and keep their land. Because Brother Deer gave his life for the people, the Deer Dance began. The tree said, "You must say thank you to Brother Deer for allowing your world to continue, for giving you the bridge to the next world with his flesh." So they made the Deer Dance for him, and it is the most sacred and important of all dances to this day. The deer dancer is the most beloved of all the Yaqui people.

When someone dies, when he sheds his mortal flesh, there is a ceremony performed with the death dancers; they are the ones who wear the black, white, and red. They are the navigators of the shadow, and the navigators between worlds. They are called *pascola* dancers. A year later, the ones who died are considered to have been born again in new forms, and to celebrate their rebirth the deer dancers come. The deer dancer celebrates life, rebirth, and life in a new world. This was the gift and teaching of the talking tree.

When Itzcelli finished delivering her talk to the people, they had a final dance around the tree with all the people before they made their choices and separated. A beautiful violet flower bloomed on the tree from the breath of the deer, and at the end of the dance the red roses bloomed. The red rose is a sacred flower to the deer—it is what the deer like to eat best—and it is the flower worn on the horns of the deer dancer. Some of the people went to the sea, some became *surem*, the little enchanted people of the land and forest who watch over us, and the rest became the Yaqui of today.

Deer Song

Tosay Wikit (White Bird)

In the spirit of Anselmo's teachings, I offer these Yaqui words, and only a loose translation:

The spider's web is transporting us, over there,
to the forest of the flower-covered enchanted world.

Tosalwikit tabnaka guitosalipo, yoleia
Junamansu siali juya
Biapa Culiachi guitsalita kalaguikti
Jicaune bokapo jiak ne yoleilia hininan ne machika yolelia
Tosalwikit tabnaka guitosalipo, yoleia

This is repeated three times. Three is the sacred number to the Yaqui, and songs are always performed in sets of three. The "white bird" in this song is the gossamer web of Grandmother Spider moving gracefully on the breeze of the enchanted flower world. The images and feelings these songs convey are subtle and intricate—Anselmo told me there is no direct translation from Yaqui to any other language, and that we cannot dissect the Mystery, only surrender to it. In the presence of the music the being is taken to the *sewa yo ania* and is thrilled by the breath and heartbeat at the center of creation through the deer songs, which are the voice of the enchanted flower world.

Parabola
Volume: 25.3
Teacher

A VOICELESS BLOWING SOUND

An Interview with Vi Hilbert

Vi tagw–sablu Hilbert is a highly respected Native American elder and storyteller of the Upper Skagit tribes of the Salish Nation. She lives in Seattle, overlooking sacred ground of her people. Her native language and culture is Lushootseed, and she has almost singlehandedly kept her language alive while promoting storytelling, particularly among elders who had stopped remembering and repeating the stories they had heard as children. She is revered in her culture and beyond. Vi was named a National Treasure by the Smithsonian and is the recipient of numerous awards. She was a professor at the University of Washington teaching the Lushootseed language and literature. She has made the wisdom of her culture available to many people outside the culture, and has served as an important informant, translator, advisor, and writer for anthropologists and linguists. Vi is an orator, storyteller, editor, and writer, and a grandmother in every sense of the word. Personally, Vi has been my mentor and friend since 1983.

This interview was conducted over the course of several days. In the evenings, I accompanied Vi to different Longhouses for the Winter Dances.

—Laura Simms

Laura Simms: Is there a word for teacher in your language?

Vi Hilbert: There is no actual word for teacher in our Lushootseed language. The closest is *dasu gusage* (*'ugwusaz*), someone who gives you important information. The wise things that he or she gives to you are *Kwadhakk* (*xw dikw*): instruction, important information, and teachings. The word can also be translated as "voiceless blowing sound." So much of the important information is voiceless. It comes to you not in words of instruction but as signals: "This is right. This is not okay."

My parents and our friends and elders were our first teachers. My culture's way of teaching is that you must be there and listen. That's it. Be there and listen. When I was a child, I didn't know that I was being trained to listen and to learn to know how to apply what I heard. My instructions from my parents were: be there, be quiet, listen, and pay attention. I knew it was a discipline. It was never explained to me. I could never ask questions.

LS: *What memories of listening do you recall most?*

VH: Every time I went with my parents to visit friends, there was a feeling of complete joy in the encounter that they shared. It was a reciprocal encounter. My greatest memory is how much they respected and enjoyed one another. They looked forward to listening and sharing, not just for one hour or two hours, but sometimes for a whole day or more.

The purpose of these visits was to reminisce, to remember, and to discuss things that were to be remembered.

If you repeated something, you were more inclined to remember it. It was practical. Aunt Susie Sampson, my relative, used to tell the old stories to herself out loud. It is such a poignant picture to me of her sitting alone, telling stories in an empty room. She was saving them for the future because no one at that time cared to come and listen.

My parents were traditional. They knew they had a responsibility to pass on information, and I was the only one to pass it on to. I was indeed going to listen and remember. They took that for granted. What I heard was implanted inside of me, and I don't doubt that my brain holds a lot that I don't know is there.

LS: *Does it take relationship to release knowledge?*

VH: I think so. You have to realize that I have something in my brain that will come forward if you know enough to ask for it. If someone is skillful in asking, they can get answers out of my head. They and I wait for that to happen. I need someone to press my buttons for me to remember what is implanted in my brain.

LS: *You once told me, in Vancouver, that the Medicine people do not know magic, they know how to listen.*

VH: They truly know how to listen. A voice by itself carries spiritual qualities that are bringing messages. Medicine people listen first to the spiritual quality of the sound of the voice, and then to the information that is carried by that voice. It is a different way of listening, one that is quietly intense and not obvious. I marvel at the way spiritual people listen.

LS: *Does the spiritual leader train the mind to listen so that one can receive knowledge or call upon spirit?*

VH: That is part of the truth. There is a quality that our people have to develop first in order to gain the ability to engage at a deeper level than they ordinarily do when they hear things. When you are hearing, you are not listening with that inner knowing. Your ears hear the sounds, but you are not concentrating with that inner mind. Things can't stay there. They don't get locked into the computer in the brain.

As a child, nothing is ever explained to you. The culture did not and does not allow questions. There are so many things that you can never understand if they have to be explained. You have to be able to listen to the information and know that some day through maturity and realization you will understand it. You have to work on that understanding yourself. If you demand to know the answers and require an explanation, it is like giving you the answers to questions in a book. That is cheating in my culture. You have to listen and think about something long enough to gain insight as to why it was important for you to hear it, and why it was important for that person to say it. Then you come to recognize the wisdom of that kind of teaching.

It requires you to think and use your mind.

LS: *What rituals or structures of ordinary life keep that learning alive?*

VH: Practice, practice. Practice listening intensely, integrating information that you are going to be told many more times than just that once. Each time you will retain another piece of the information. By the time you have done listening many times, if you don't turn off your mind, you will have the whole picture. Then you will know that it is something important to be known.

LS: *Did your parents or elders check on you?*

VH: No one tests you. No one asks you to retell what you have heard. You retell it in your own maturity when you have someone to pass it on to. If you have listened conscientiously enough, then you will have all the pieces to pass on responsibly. Unknowingly, I have been taught to do that, and I am doing it. I am grateful that I have enough information in my brain to be able to do it.

LS: *As a child, were you always patient and able to listen?*

VH: I wanted to ask questions. I was never reprimanded in words. My dad would just look at me, and I knew to go back to listening. I received unconditional love from my parents. My parents believed that because they had instructed me I could never do anything wrong. The people who were part of their circle of spirituality saw me in the same light. Their unconditional love surrounded me with protection so that they could share with me and know it was reciprocal. I knew I could trust them. There is an honor in trusting and respecting one another. It was a beautiful way to grow up.

LS: *In the Longhouse last night [Skokomish House, near Shelton, Washington], the spiritual leader of the House, Subiyeh (Bruce Miller), said there was no need in the past for psychiatric wards, prisons, or courts. There were conflicts, but life itself was the teacher; there was not one person or rule. There was a "constant awakening of responsibility."*

VH: A big part of my growing up was learning to honor and help one another, to share with those who were in need: an unselfish true giving of the heart. There was a family that got burned out. Immediately my mother brought things for the unfortunate family. Not old things, but the best. She took them to the family with a prayer and spent time consoling them for their loss. She brought herself, her spiritual gift of healing. My parents talked about it morning and night. I could hear them discussing the importance of living in this world and sharing with people. I heard the philosophy of it, the soul of it, what should be done, what was strengthening or weakening.

LS: *If there were no white schools, would you have gone to school?*

VH: What my culture had to teach me would have sustained me anyplace because the value systems were so stable. I never got confused about what was right and wrong. I knew what was expected of me, and I tried to rise to it. Their expectations were high. I still live with the teachings of my parents. Even though they are on the other side, I live by what they taught me. I wouldn't ever disappoint them by doing something that would make their spirits sad.

LS: *What happens to our world when that kind of knowing is completely ignored, when there is no cultural or spiritual teacher?*

VH: That is why there is trouble. I have looked at that for many years. So many people are unaware of the importance of the experience of spirit. Knowledge comes to us in many forms, not only in my culture. The knowledge is there for each of us to be aware of: the knowledge that there is a spirit to guide us. It gets lost because people look at words to guide them. The spirit is not God. It is not Jesus. It is not any of these names. The spirit has no name or form. It is there forever for everyone to experience.

Spirit is so abstract that when people can't see it, feel it, or touch it, they cannot believe it. You cannot overcome that kind of doubt. Only those people who are big enough to open their minds to the fact that there is a spirit—that spirit is real—only they have any hope of clearing the path to live with the joy of the gift from the spirit.

Sadness comes to me when, because of greed, the spirit is left outside the door. Giving is a joy. The greedy world doesn't know that this joy exists. They are so busy grabbing that they haven't learned how much more joy there is in the act of giving without any expectations of return. They don't know that the spirit is the receiver when you give anything to anyone. You are not giving to that person or to that thing; you are giving to spirit, and you are rewarded in that.

You learn to be aware that this life is a reward from spirit. The door opens, and you open into something that you have earned. This is the gift. It is so simple.

LS: *Who is the first teacher: spirit, the natural world, one's parents, or the culture?*

VH: The first teacher is the awareness that the world we live in requires discipline. The people who can give you those instructions are parents, grandparents, uncles and aunts—everyone in the world I grew up in. The whole community raised me by watching me, and I knew they were always expecting me to do right. The second teacher is the outside community influence and the way you apply what has been taught by your own people to those situations. So the next teacher is the awareness of how to apply what you have been instructed to do. These are people things.

The spiritual things are another issue. The spiritual world is an every-day practice in my culture because we live in the same room with our elders. We had one room for sleeping and eating. As my parents lived their simple life, they talked about everything and I heard everything: the problem, the discussion and the solution; as well as the dreams that they woke up with every morning. I heard them tell each other their dreams and explain them, as they saw them to be. This was always the most wonderful experience for me.

My father had a lot of respect for my mother's spirituality. She was one of the most brilliant spiritual people. She had a telepathic spirit. She could read situations that were miles away and tell you when something was going to happen. She was clairvoyant. She was also a very expressive, articulate person with lots of fancy and imagination. She was dynamic in her opinions of many things. She acted things out. My dad praised her and encouraged her. Sometimes it was very outrageous, and I could not see how it could all be true.

In later years, the things that she did and said were proven true. A medicine man who became blind came and asked for my mother's help. We sat in our little home, and my mother lit a candle while he confessed to her all the things he had done wrong with the spiritual power he'd been given. He repeated all the things that my mother had talked about to us: lessons about medicine people who were practicing good and bad medicine. It was good for me to hear from that man, because I realized that my mother told the truth.

LS: *The spiritual training in the Longhouse is very rigorous. Did every person in the past go through the rigors of training in the Longhouse? Can anyone become part of the Longhouse culture?*

VH: Many years ago the training was rigorous. Today, there are few leaders who know how to guide someone in that discipline. They prefer to take the easy way and make it superficial. The strict training is hardly there anymore. Subiyeh is nearly the only one that I know that does try to apply it. He lives it completely.

In the best of the Longhouses, discipline is not done angrily, in a way that creates resistance. Discipline is applied so that you realize the responsibility needed to accept the teaching that goes along with the spiritual training. That teaching requires you to conduct yourself in a very straightforward way, applying what you have been taught to your actions in the outside world. The spirit expects you to be obedient and humble. The spirit's needs are not our personal needs. As a result of this training, guided by a spiritual teacher, you learn to treat everyone with respect and kindness. It is a beautiful world.

LS: *What is the spirit world?*

VH: The spirit world is real and a part of us. My parents talked about a world I was not allowed to be part of; but I was to understand that it was a part of me. I was surrounded by all the spiritual help that my family had had from generations back. Unseen spirits are constantly protecting those people who are important.

LS: *What did you see that strengthened this knowing?*

VH: I heard what my parents said. I saw the results of what they were practicing. People who were sick became renewed, and everyone rejoiced in the fact that the spirit was the one who made all these beautiful things happen, and not the person who did the working. But you have to have the spiritual eye to be able to see that spiritual world. I don't, and I never will. But I know one hundred percent in my mind that it is true and it is there.

LS: *Does everyone have spiritual eyes or are certain people chosen?*

VH: I understand that everyone has the capacity to have spiritual eyes. Everyone has a song that they can call on if they choose to, a vehicle in which one can travel to the spirit world and back. I have heard many spiritual leaders say that a person has to know in their life when to have that song come out. All you do is ask for that song to come to you. However, it is not that simple. The way is explained by very respectful spiritual leaders.

You have to be worthy to receive that song. That is where discipline comes in. You have to know how to handle yourself. That song is yours for the rest of your life unless you desecrate it in some way. Then you lose it. I envision it as an invisible path that only you are aware of. You know that you are guided by the spirit to stay on that path, and that you earned the path. The spirit is very powerful. After people sing, you can hear the cry that comes from the very bottom of their souls as the spirit returns.

LS: *Does the spiritual leader simply provide the discipline without interfering in that spiritual path?*

VH: The teacher allows the initiates, if you will, to see and feel. He or she pulls the blinders off their eyes so they can see what was invisible, so they can be a part of their spirit world if they are looking for that. The spiritual leader can feel what help a person needs in order to walk with their spirit.

I once saw a woman in the Longhouse with black paint on her face. [Paint means she was a "Dancer" or trained participant in the Longhouse.] She was formidable. When she sang, it was shocking—so fierce and strong. She danced, slithering onto the floor like a snake and sliding around the Longhouse. Her spirit must have been a snake. Some people have the spirit of a bird and dance holding their arms out. They are not pretending. They receive it from the spirit.

LS: *It seems your ancestors understood that the inner world was the world that provided liberation, like in the story Johnny Moses tells about the shamaness who took her eyes out and turned them around in order to see herself.*

VH: That is why I love to be in the Longhouse. The stories are the teacher; they invite people to think. You listen over and over and all of a sudden you finally get it. It is a joy, a light when one finally understands.

LS: *What is the joy?*

VH: It is comprehending the concept that is being taught, understanding the subtleties embedded in every word and action. It is finally having that understanding surface. Everything you need to know about how the story can be applied to this world arises in your own comprehension.

LS: *What is the essence that is needed to be Skagit, even if all the forms are washed away or forgotten?*

VH: That is a beautiful question. The original ancestor knew all the answers. He taught his son all the important things. Before that son died, he taught *his* son all the places where these things existed. One generation to another the father taught the son all the things he needed to know and showed him where to find all the answers—the place where this sacred information was, the prayer and the words of the prayer, the song and the melody of the song. As time passed, one thing after another left the scope of memory until all that remained was the story. So the story that tells about these things that have been in our world and the knowledge that these things did exist are both important to be remembered. The story lives and reminds the culture about how it lived.

To share teachings from the spirit is a service that is greatly needed for the health, the hearts, and the minds of unfortunate people who have not had the advantage of the teachers that I have had. That is why I tell the stories.

LS: *Can one learn properly without oral instruction?*

VH: Nobody can read a book for this knowledge, no matter what insight they have.

LS: *What is the special bond between the teacher and the student?*

VH: Respect. Mutual respect. There is a respect for the needs of the human being. A spiritual leader realizes the need of people to walk in harmony with the spiritual world. If they are willing to become a part of that, then there is great respect from the spiritual leader. If it is just through curiosity that you want to become a part of the spirits, then the spiritual eyes see that, and you are disgraced.

LS: *Are stories ever forgotten?*

VH: In our culture, a thread of the story will always remain alive, and each person has the capacity to take that thread and reweave that story because it contains all of the information and the truth of what had been important. The memory of that existence remains alive because there are threads in each of us, and we can weave them together through story.

Like the Tibetans, my people say that the most important things of this world are the symbols of the real, not the real itself. They are an echo of what has always been here.

LS: *Is there anything more you want to say about the teacher, or any other stories you would like to add?*

VH: Goodness and wisdom live because people seven generations back took the time to do what you are doing with me: to call on things that come from the past. I never do anything that is original. These things are part of what has been taught to me. So now bits and pieces are in this interview, and centuries of brave things that people have lived by and shared will be remembered.

You are practicing what every teacher honors: that is, making time to listen and call for the information that can be of benefit to somebody—not to everybody, but to somebody. So I am grateful for your presence and your time.

Parabola
Volume: 14.2
Tradition and
Transmission

THE POWER OF NILTSI, THE WIND

Navajo

Springtime came to Tsegi, with its blossoming peach trees, and its floating clouds like flocks of fleecy lambs sporting on the turquoise plains of the sky. Niltsi, the wind, whispered to the opening peach buds, whispered to the green shoots of the cliff rose. "The deer have dropped their antlers," whispered the wind, "and the young eaglets chirp in the shell."

Niltsi whispered to Na Nai and to Bazhnabai, his sister, whispered to Juan and Pedro. A call for friendship sounded in the soft wind, in the hum of the crickets, sounded in the mellowed bleating of distant flocks.

Outside the rock corral where a hundred lambs stood in the sunshine, the children sat watching a newborn lamb which Na Nai held in his lap. The mother sheep remained nearby, obstinately refusing to nourish her offspring.

When the long-legged baby attempted to suckle, mother sheep edged away. This white woolly youngster was her first-born, and she couldn't quite make him out.

"She doesn't know that he's hungry," said Bazhnabai. "Let me take the baby to her."

Gently the little girl stood the lamb on its four wobbly legs and put her arms around the ewe's neck to quiet her. Still she kicked when the baby attempted to get his first breakfast.

"I shall sing for you, little lamb," said Bazhnabai. In all earnestness, the childish voice chanted to the sheep:

I am your son, mother.
Your very own son, mother.
You are the White Shell Woman.
I am the son of the White Shell Woman.

The ewe had no mind for song. She twitched her ears and stared in stubborn stupidity. Bazhnabai patiently repeated her song. Over and over again she sang to the white sheep, addressing her as the White Shell Woman. The lambs in the corral accompanied her song with their bleating.

Finally the baby lamb succeeded in procuring his meal. Bazhnabai removed her arms from the ewe's neck and sat down watching the pair. She continued her song:

I am the son of the White Shell Woman.

The ewe turned her head toward her baby. She bleated gently. She licked his white wool and from that moment nothing could separate her from her child.

In a short time, the woolly novice attempted to climb the rocks which lay warming in the sunshine. Mother sheep, slowly, step by step, and with infinite patience urged her baby, her new-found joy, to use his long wobbly legs. She knew a crevice in the rocks where luscious green weeds grew. She wanted to lead her first-born there.

The children watched the two-hour-old youngster try his legs. They laughed at his awkward attempts to bend his knees.

"Debay yazhi is very wise," said Na Nai. "Debay yazhi knows all. He knows where to find food. He knows how to use his legs. He knows how to talk sheep talk. He knows how to sleep. He is the son of the White Shell Woman. Sho, but he is a wise one!"

"Who is the White Shell Woman?" asked Pedro.

Na Nai looked at his friend in wonder as he answered:

"You ask me who is the White Shell Woman? She is the kind mother who made The Tinneh."

By this time debay yazhi had reached the top of the ledge where his mother stood nibbling the green weed. She gave him a loving lick with her tongue and he knew he was launched into the great adventure of life which is good.

Na Nai laughed. He knew that life was good. In his mind were many wonders. That Which Stood Within him was following the rainbow trail to the holy mountains of the north where Yolkai Estsan had wandered in the beginning. Na Nai knew that he too was a son of the White Shell Woman. He said to Pedro:

"Shall I tell you how Yolkai Estsan made us?"

"Tell us, tell us!" answered Pedro.

"It is a long story. I will tell it as my uncle told me."

The children sat leaning against the stone corral which held the hundred white lambs. They could see a hundred white clouds above the cliffs of Tsegi, and Na Nai could see in his mind the White Shell Woman wandering alone and lonely among the high mountains of the north.

"Yolkai Estsan was all alone. Her sister had left for the wide water of the west to keep the hogan of the Sun Bearer ready for his return at night. Yolkai Estsan was lonely among the mountains. She walked from place to place trying to forget. She looked at the clear water running over stones. She listened to the sound of water falling. She sat down in the shade of quaking aspens.

"Yolkai Estsan, wearing her shining dress of white shells, and with her long black hair hanging about her, sat on the rocks by the mountain stream. Through the green leaves of the quaking aspen, bits of blue sky shone like the flowers that nodded beneath the trees. Yolkai Estsan thought that those flowers hanging like blue stars on slender stems were the loveliest things she had seen in all of her wanderings. She began to cry."

"Why should she cry?" asked Juan.

"Uncle did not tell me why she cried, but I think I know. That Which Stands Within me knows."

Juan looked at Na Nai in awe. He wondered what it was that stood within him and made him so very, very wise.

"Anyway she cried," continued Na Nai. "Uncle said that she cried when she sat under the quaking aspen with blue star flowers on the ground and blue in the sky. And she said out loud as she splashed her toes in the stream:

"'What's the use of blue star flowers on slender stems, if one is all alone?'"

"Ah," said Pedro, "that is why she cried. I know. That is why my mother cries in Cubero. She is all alone."

"How do you know that your mother cries in Cubero?" asked Bazhnabai.

Pedro looked at the girl with a new light shining in his brown eyes as he answered:

"That Which Stands Within me knows."

"So," said Bazhnabai, "you are becoming as wise as Little Chipmunk."

"Anyway, Yolkai Estsan cried," continued Na Nai. "Uncle said that she cried and she stood up under the quaking aspens and walked out of their shade to the top of the mountain. There, where no flowers bloomed among the bare rocks, she felt better. She said to a crooked juniper tree twisting gray limbs above the rocks:

"'I like you better than blue flowers. You do not make me cry. You are twisted and strong. The wind and the storm cannot kill you. I like you because you are strong and have fought.'"

"I know how Yolkai Estsan felt then," said Bazhnabai. "I, too, like strong-growing things, things which fight to live. They make me think of uncle."

"What did the White Shell Woman do when she reached the top of the mountain?" asked Pedro.

"Uncle said that she stood there very tall and very straight, dressed in white shells and with her long hair blowing in the wind. Uncle said that she was quiet as she stood on the mountain top looking at the distant blue peaks streaked with snow, looking at the dark forests of spruce on the hills below her. While she stood there near the twisted juniper, all alone and very quiet, she heard a voice."

Na Nai paused, that his audience might be deeply impressed.

"She heard a voice in the wind."

The children listened intently, waiting for what was to follow.

"It was the voice of Hasyelti, the Dawn God, the shining white one. He was calling, 'Wu hu, wu hu,' like a big owl. At first Yolkai Estsan did not see him. He called again, 'Wu hu, wu hu.' She looked above the twisted juniper tree and there he stood in the air. He wore the twelve eagle feathers in his headdress, and he wore his white buckskin shirt and his kilt outlined with red sunlight. From his wrist his squirrel-skin tobacco pouch hung by a streak of sunlight. Hasyelti always carried his tobacco pouch. He was a great smoker. Even as he looked at the lonely White Shell Woman he smoked his stone pipe. She watched the smoke curl upward in rings above his headdress of eagle feathers, and she thought as she looked at his face that his smile was gentle as the mists which descend on the earth, and rise again to the sky. As she watched his smile, she heard him say softly:

"'You are lonely, sister. Why do you wander alone on the mountain tops?'

"'There is no one who cares to wander with me,' she said sadly. 'My sister has gone to the wide water of the west, and my son is busy elsewhere. Grandfather, from whence do you come? I have been hoping that I might meet someone on the mountain top.'

"'I come from the home of the gods.'

"'I knew it,' said Yolkai Estsan. 'I knew that only gods would come to the mountain top.'

"'You are here,' said Hasyelti, as he puffed more smoke wreaths above his feathers, and looked at the beautiful White Shell Woman. 'You are here and lonely. I wish to help you. Remain here four days, sister. I am going back to bring others with me. In four days I will come.'

"He left and Yolkai Estsan busied herself making a good shelter to sleep in. Already she felt less lonely thinking of Hasyelti and knowing that he would return."

Na Nai stopped his story here and said:

"Are you tired of listening? Shall I go on?"

"Go on," said Pedro. "We want to know what happened. You said you would tell us how the White Shell Woman made The People."

"Yes," said Juan, "go on with the story."

"I have heard the story many times," said Bazhnabai, "and I know that Hasyelti came back and with him were many divine ones. Little Chipmunk will tell you how they came."

"They came two by two," said Na Nai. "They came from north, east, south and west. Two by two, they came from the sacred mountains. And best of all, the sister from the wide water came, and put her arm around the White Shell Woman. She said, 'I told you, little one, that you would be too lonely on the mountain top. See what I have brought from the looms of the sky.'

"She unfolded a dark embroidered blanket and a white embroidered blanket. Hasyelti, the white shining one, took the two blankets and laid them on the ground. All the holy people who had come stood in a circle around the blankets. Then Hasyelti spread a sacred buckskin on top of the blankets. He laid it down with its head pointing to the west. All the divine ones stood very still. They knew that a most important ceremony was to take place. They had met to make companions for Yolkai Estsan, the beautiful lonely White Shell Woman.

"There was one holy girl who had come to the mountain top walking arm in arm with a holy boy. She carried a turquoise bowl in her hands. In it were two ears of corn, a white ear and a yellow ear. Hasyelti took the corn and gave the yellow ear to the Yellow Corn Girl. He gave the white ear of corn to the Rock Crystal Boy.

"The divine ones waited and watched while Rock Crystal Boy and Yellow Corn Girl laid the ears of corn on the buckskin. They placed the yellow ear with its tip toward the west, and the white one with its tip towards the east. They did everything right. Uncle says they did not make one mistake."

"Gods never make mistakes," said Bazhnabai. "Tell Juan and Pedro what happened next."

"What happened next was very, very important. While everyone was silent and thinking, Hasyelti picked up both ears of corn and cried, 'Wu hu, wu, hu.' He nearly laid the ears down again with both tips to the east."

"He nearly laid them down," interrupted Bazhnabai, "but he did not quite touch the buckskin."

"No, he did not quite touch the buckskin," continued Na Nai. "After he had nearly laid them down in the south, west and north, he decided to put them on the buckskin with both tips to the east.

"The divine ones watched very closely. They had never seen this done before. They watched Hasyelti cover the corn with another buckskin with its head to the east. All was ready now."

"Ready for what?" asked Juan.

"Ready for Niltsi, the wind, to breathe upon. The yellow and white ears of corn waited under the buckskin for Niltsi the Breath to make them into man and woman. Yolkai Estsan hardly breathed as she watched. She knew that something beautiful would happen because the Dawn God with twelve eagle feathers on his head was smoking his pipe and blowing smoke rings to the sky. She knew something would happen. Four times Hasyelti peeped under the buckskin to see if anything had changed, if the corn had quickened. The fourth time he looked he saw with joy that the white ear of corn had turned into a man, and the yellow into a woman. 'It is done,' he said to all. 'Niltsi has entered at their heads and come out through their toes and fingers.'"

"Look at the ends of your fingers," said Bazhnabai, "and you can see the mark of the wind where it whirled through."

Juan looked at his finger tips. It was hard to see the little ridges of skin running round and round to end in a tiny circle. He held his hand in the sunshine and looked again.

"I see the marks," he cried, "like the marks the wind makes on sand. I see. It must be true."

"What happened next?" asked Pedro.

"The most important of all happened next," said Na Nai. "While all the divine ones stood around in a circle, Niltsi the wind gave to the new forms the breath of life. The Rock Crystal Boy gave them mind, That Which Stands Within us, clear as crystal. The Grasshopper Girl gave them voices."

"It is a very good story," said Pedro, "but I thought you said that the White Shell Woman made The People."

"Didn't she make us?" said Na Nai. "Would anything have happened if she hadn't wandered lonely on the mountain? Would anything have happened if the Dawn God had not found her on the mountain? Would anything have happened if he had not blown smoke wreaths to the sky to please the White Shell Woman?"

"I don't know," said Pedro. "Something might have happened anyway."

"No, it would not," said Bazhnabai with conviction. "A woman must be lonely and a man must smoke to make anything happen. My mother knows that."

"I do not know anything about such matters," said Pedro, "but I'm glad something happened."

"And so am I," "and so am I," "and so am I," said three voices in chorus.

The lambs still bleated in the corral. A few fresh drops of rain fell from the clouds onto the rocks where the children sat. Na Nai knew that it was the soft rain sent by Yolkai Estsan, the beautiful White Shell Woman. He sang the song that his sister had sung to the mother sheep:

> *I am the son of the White Shell Woman.*
> *I am the son of the White Shell Woman.*
> *Yolkai Estsan bi yazhi i nish lin.*

Parabola
Volume: 20.3
Language

THE STORY OF THE ARROWMAKER

N. Scott Momaday

When I was a child, my father told me the story of the arrowmaker, and he told it to me many times, for I fell in love with it. I have no memory that is older than that of hearing it. This is the way it goes:

If an arrow is well made, it will have tooth marks upon it. That is how you know. The Kiowas made fine arrows and straightened them in their teeth. Then they drew them to the bow to see that they were straight. Once there was a man and his wife. They were alone at night in their tipi. By the light of the fire the man was making arrows. After a while he caught sight of something. There was a small opening in the tipi where two hides had been sewn together. Someone was there on the outside, looking in. The man went on with his work, but he said to his wife, "Someone is standing outside. Do not be afraid. Let us talk easily, as of ordinary things." He took up an arrow and straightened it in his teeth: then, as it was right for him to do, he drew it to the bow and took aim, first in this direction and then in that. And all the while he was talking, as if to his wife. But this is how he spoke: "I know that you are there on the outside, for I can feel your eyes upon me. If you are a Kiowa, you will understand what I am saying, and you will speak your name." But there was no answer, and the man went on in the same way, pointing the arrow all around. At last his aim fell upon the place where his enemy stood, and he let go of the string. The arrow went straight to the enemy's heart.

Heretofore the story of the arrowmaker has been the private possession of a very few, a tenuous link in that most ancient chain of language which we call the oral tradition: tenuous because the tradition itself is so; for as many times as the story has been told, it was always but one generation removed from extinction. But it was held dear, too, on that same account. That is to say, it has been neither more nor less durable than the human voice, and neither more nor less concerned to express the meaning of the human condition. And this brings us to the heart of the matter at hand: The story of the arrowmaker is also a link between language and literature. It is a remarkable act of the mind, a realization of words and the world that is altogether simple and direct, yet nonetheless rare and profound, and it illustrates more clearly than anything else in my own experience, at least, something of the essential character of the imagination—and in particular of that personification which in this instance emerges from it: the man made of words.

It is a fine story, whole, intricately beautiful, precisely realized. It is worth thinking about, for it yields something of value; indeed, it is full of provocation, rich with suggestion and consequent meaning. There is often an inherent danger that we might impose too much of ourselves upon it. It is informed by an integrity that bears examination easily and well, and in the process it seems to appropriate our own reality and experience.

It is significant that the story of the arrowmaker returns in a special way upon itself. It is about language, after all, and it is therefore part and parcel of its own subject; virtually, there is no difference between the telling and that which is told. The point of the story lies, not so much in what the arrowmaker does, but in what he says—and indeed that he says it. The principal fact is that he speaks, and in so doing he places his very life in the balance. It is this aspect of the story which interests me most, for it is here that the language becomes most conscious of itself; we are close to the origin and object of literature, I believe: our sense of the verbal dimension is very keen, and we are aware of something in the nature of language that is at once perilous and compelling. "If you are a Kiowa, you will understand what I am saying, and you will speak your name." Everything is ventured in this simple declaration, which is also a question and a plea. The conditional element with which it begins is remarkably tentative and pathetic; precisely at this moment is the arrowmaker realized completely, and his reality consists in language, and it is poor and precarious. And all of this occurs to him as surely as it does to us. Implicit in that simple occurrence is all of his definition and his destiny, and all of ours. He ventures to speak because he must; language is the repository of his whole knowledge and experience, and it represents the only chance he has for survival. Instinctively, and with great care, he deals in the most honest and basic way with words. "Let us talk easily, as of ordinary things," he says. And of the ominous unknown he asks only the utterance of a name, only the most nominal sign that he is understood, that his words are returned to him on the sheer edge of meaning. But there is no answer, and the arrowmaker knows at once what he has not known before; that his enemy is, and that he has gained an advantage over him. This he knows certainly, and the certainty itself is his advantage, and it is crucial; he makes the most of it. The venture is complete and irrevocable, and it ends in success. The story is meaningful. It is so primarily because it is composed of language, and it is in the nature of language in turn that it proceeds to the formulation of meaning. Moreover, the story of the arrowmaker, as opposed to other stories in general, centers upon his procession of words toward meaning. It seems in fact to turn upon the very idea that language involves the elements of risk and responsibility; and in this it seeks to confirm itself. In a word, it seems to say, everything is a risk. That may be true, and it may also be that the whole of literature rests upon that truth.

The arrowmaker is preeminently the man made of words. He has consummate being in language; it is the world of his origin and of his posterity, and there is no other. But it is a world of definite reality and of infinite possibility. I have come to believe that there is a sense in which the arrowmaker has more nearly perfect being than have other men, by and large, as he imagines himself, whole and vital, going on into the unknown darkness and beyond. And this last aspect of his being is primordial and profound.

And yet the story has it that he is cautious and alone, and we are given to understand that his peril is great and immediate, and that he confronts it in the only way he can. I have no doubt that this is true, and

I believe that there are implications which point directly to the determination of our literary experience and which must not be lost upon us. A final word, then, on an essential irony which marks this story and gives peculiar substance to the man made of words. The storyteller is nameless and unlettered. From one point of view we know very little about him, except that he is somehow translated for us in the person of an arrowmaker. But, from another, that is all we need to know. He tells us of his life in language, and of the awful risk involved. It must occur to us that he is one with the arrowmaker and that he has survived, by word of mouth, beyond other men. We said a moment ago that, for the arrowmaker, language represented the only chance of survival. It is worth considering that he survives in our own time, and that he has survived over a period of untold generations.

Excerpted from N. Scott Momaday, "The Man Made of Words," in *Indian Voices: The First Convocation of American Indian Scholars* (San Francisco: The Indian Historian Press, 1970), 49–62. Reprinted by permission of The Indian Historian Press.

Parabola
Volume: 24.2
Prayer

Why We're Here Today

An Interview with Chief Tom Porter

Tom Porter is a highly respected Mohawk traditionalist whose lifelong commitment to the preservation and sharing of Mohawk language and culture led him to found a new community named Kanatsiohareke (The Place of the Clean Pot) on the site of an ancient Mohawk village near Fonda, New York. This interview took place at Kanatsiohareke very early on a cold morning. We sat near the kitchen stove and talked, interrupted now and then by members of the community coming in to say hello, to give us the good morning greeting, to discuss that day's work projects, and then to serve us breakfast.

—Joseph Bruchac

Joseph Bruchac: *Tom, for many people you're respected as one who cares about the spiritual side of life and the way that we're connected to all things and creation. I wanted to ask you, with that in mind, what is the purpose that prayer serves?*

Tom Porter: Well, I wasn't trained to read books. But one time I picked up a book by a Lakota man, *Fool's Crow.* He's talking about healers. When you heal, you have to make a prayer first. Some people thought that he was a good healer, but he said he was not the healer; it was God, the Creator. All he was is an air pipe. The Creator's spirit goes through this pipe and into whoever needs healing.

Our job is to use prayer to keep the air pipe open and clean so the spirit can pass at will to do the job of healing and make a spiritual good life.

I liked that, and I thought it was a really good description; in fact, I immediately felt good about it. So that's what I call prayer. That's what prayer is for: to keep communication going in a spiritual world. I taught my kids since they were little babies how to pray. If you do that you're always aware—you can see good, and you can hear good too. You can see its beauty, and you can see everything there. That's what prayer does.

JB: *Is prayer a way of making that connection that we have all around us, if not visible then tangible? We sense and connect to it through prayer. By giving breath to prayer we connect to the world.*

TP: Yeah. If you don't, you become numb, callused. You don't really see and hear what you're supposed to: the birds singing, how beautiful it is. You don't enjoy the winter and the spring, the rain and the fog, and the days of sunshine.

JB: *In some cultures, prayer is a way of asking for things. Do you see prayer that way?*

TP: No. No, to the contrary. We rarely ever ask anything, because we don't have to. Everything's already here. The world is right here with us. All we have to do is say thank you. The Iroquois people's prayer is mostly "Thank you, thank you, thank you. ..." If you say "Thank you," once in a while, then those things that gave you your gifts, be it the earth, be it the sun, or thunder ... well, then probably tomorrow they'll be happy to come back.

JB: *So even something like, say, a lacrosse game could be a prayer. Anything we do can be a prayer, taking the Creator into creation.*

TP: Thanking the Creator for the enjoyment of lacrosse, and its power to heal people.

JB: *One thing you mentioned is the number of times traditional people would pray in the old days. What were you saying about that?*

TP: Let me see if I can run through it the way it was told to us in our longhouse. As soon as you get up in the morning, even before you get out of bed, you see the light from the sun coming in the window. The first thing I say is, "You who are my Creator, I give you thankfulness and my greetings, my hello, and also my love." That's a prayer. As soon as you see the light, before you even get out of bed, that's how it begins.

Then, after greeting the Creator, you say, "My older brother, who is the sun, I who am the younger brother, give you greetings, too, and hello." That's already two. Then you get up and dress yourself, and you come down, and you see your mother or your father and you say to them, "Greetings and hello," and you give your love to your mother and father. Whenever you say "Hi," to someone, we consider that prayer, too. Everybody is a part of the Creator. That's why you're supposed to be nice to the animals, and to other human beings—and you're supposed to be nice to yourself, too, because the Creator is in your body as well. Every time you see somebody, say "hello" to them. Never forget this, because you are in fact saying hello to the Creator.

After you greet your family, you eat. When you finish your food, you say, "*Niawen*," and that is a prayer; it means "thank you," first to Creator—you said it only once, but the Creator hears it first—and then whoever fixed the food hears it second. The spirit of the food is the third one—or they hear it simultaneously, however it works. When you're in a real traditional longhouse people's house, or if you go to a big meeting, you hear that all the time: Niawen. That's prayer for the food. It's not like Europeans; they have blessings for the food, but we Iroquois think the food is already blessed by the Creator in the beginning of the world. That's why it makes seeds. Every time we eat, that's a prayer.

You finish your food, you drink water. The minute you drink water, you say, "Niawen *Shonkwaiàtíson*." That means, "Thank you, my Creator," and "I give my hello, my greetings, my love, to the spirit of water." You can do it before, you can do it after; usually it's after. However many times you drink water in one day, you pray that many times. When you go swimming in a river, you never jump in that river before you first talk to it, and that's another prayer. So you say, "I give you my love, my hello, and my greetings," to the water spirit. That way, when you jump into the water it doesn't get scared, startled, or cause you to drown. That shows your respect for the river and the power that it stands for. You also have to acknowledge the spirit of that river or creek if you're passing over a bridge. As you're going over you say, "I'm crossing, I give you my greetings," so the water spirits don't bother you.

If you go by without acknowledging them, they can make you depressed and lonesome. Even kids—if they cry and nobody knows why, well, maybe it's because they crossed that river and didn't pay respects by prayer.

When you go outside, the fresh morning air touches your face. Again you say, "Four sacred winds, my love to you, my thankfulness and my hello to you this morning as I felt you touch me, the fresh air touches my body. So I give you my greetings." That's to the four winds and to the Creator. I usually walk in the morning, a couple of miles, and when I see the grass I say "hello." That's prayer. I see the woods, trees, I say "hello." I see the birds, I say "hello."

When you see the actual sun, too, you stop and say again: "My Creator, thank you. Brother Sun, I thank you." Even though you said it earlier, you hadn't seen him directly, only his light. When you see his face, acknowledge again. Whatever you're doing that morning—even if you go to the barn to see the horses, you say "hello," to them, too. That's prayer, too. You're supposed to talk to the animals: "How are you doing? You doing okay?" If you have a dog or a cat, you say "hello," to them, too; and that's a prayer.

Say you're working in a garden. You're never supposed to go in a garden when you're angry or frustrated. You have to be happy and have a good mind in a garden. You talk to the corn and the beans, the potatoes or watermelon or strawberries, and you say "hello" to them. You say, "I come to clean your bed, where you live, to take the grass out so you can grow," and that's a prayer again. As you work, the sun is walking— that's what they call the sun's movements in the sky. When it reaches the middle of the sky, you stop what you're doing right there and you say to the sun, "My Creator, thank you again for sending my love. Real high in the sky, right in the middle of the universe, where you are, I thank you again, my older brother. Thank you for shining light. Thank you for bringing the energies and power I need to live." The sun goes by, and just before he goes over the horizon in the west, you stop again and you give greetings again for the day, all the day. You say, "Thank you for this day, all the miracles you've made. I hope I see you tomorrow." That's prayer.

These are examples of the way the Iroquois pray. If you go to a big mountain, you pray, too. If you see a big tree, you pray. And then when the sun has gone down and you're ready to go to bed, you say, "Creator, I give you my love again, and my greetings. I had a wonderful day today— I was working, I was healthy, everything was good, I got lots of things done. I didn't finish everything; maybe tomorrow I can finish, or the next day. So, Creator, I sleep tonight now, I give you my gratefulness for this past day. Hopefully, I will go peacefully through this night, and I will have the good fortune, with your power, to open my eyes to another miraculous day tomorrow." That's the way I was told by my elders.

Then there's the prayer of opening. That takes about an hour, or an hour and a half, the old way. I can still do it like that, but today everybody's in a hurry, so as soon as you start, everyone's looking at their clocks. (laugh) The old people didn't do that.

JB: *The traditional opening prayer, which begins ... how does it begin? With the earth itself?*

TP: No, it begins with the Creator. Then the people, then the Mother Earth, and it goes up. ...

JB: *It works all the way through creation. How did the form of that prayer come to be?*

TP: When the world, the creation, was made, that's where it came from. In the story of creation that prayer is built. It's the first thing we were given, to live on this earth, this thanksgiving.

JB: *How does laughter relate to the sacred and to prayer?*

TP: It's medicine. It can also be a diversion, but mostly it's a healing agent, a healing mechanism. You can make fun of somebody and that can hurt, if you laugh at the wrong time, but most laughter comes because of joy. That's why in Indian country they're always laughing. They should be crying, actually, but they're laughing. It's a form of protecting them-selves.

JB: *Is prayer needed by the natural world?*

TP: I'm not sure what "prayer" means in English. If it's my definition of prayer, yes. And my definition is: When you take a moment to communicate with the spiritual life that surrounds you. If you do this enough, then you communicate with spiritual lives around you. They become important to you, and you find your place in peace and good mind. But if you don't, then you are imbalanced, unhappy, and ungrateful. You are just a greed-monster, like a bulldozer, without regard to life. Without prayer that's what you become; that's what society becomes, too, if it doesn't know how to pray.

Because, see, if the sun goes out, if the wind stops blowing, we all go out. If the Mother Earth stops growing the corn and the fruit, we're all going to go out. These are the things we need to ally with, the things we need to talk to and harmonize with. That harmony that we've had since the beginning of time is why we're here today.

CHAPTER NINE

Wholeness

Within these essays, it is possible for a person to dance themselves back to the human that dwells inside. Wholeness is knowing one's place in the world and the cosmos, as well as opening to the other parts of self. We keep the heart and the spirit together, yet allow for the entrance to other realms and sacred geographies, remembering "the dreaming" and, for a time perhaps, living it.

Harmony and balance are necessities for wholeness. *Hozho*, the Navajo word that signifies this balance, is the place where we want to remain. Among tribal nations, some children are born and recognized as having special qualities, a natural wholeness, the ability to offer prayer, song, or healing to the community. They often become the keepers of tradition or the ones who know wholeness, or a ceremony may bring us to the center. Stomp dances that begin at midnight. But in all, it is a reminder that we are rooted in the land and the sacred values reside here and in this relationship, in the power of our words and our constant presence.

Parabola
Volume: 24.2
Prayer

HOLY AND ALONE

Stalking Wolf, Apache Elder

Grandfather, Great Spirit,
Master of all things, you who are called by so
    many names,
and worshipped in so many ways;
allow me to become the Earth,
teach me to surrender to the tracks,
so that I may become that which I follow,
and if I am worthy,
allow these tracks to lead me closer to You.

Parabola
Volume: 3.1
Sacred Space

SONG OF THE SKY LOOM

Tewa Pueblo

> O our Mother the Earth, O our Father the Sky,
> Your children are we, and with tired backs
> We bring you the gifts that you love.
> Then weave for us a garment of brightness;
> May the warp be the white light of morning,
> May the weft be the red light of evening,
> May the fringes be the falling rain,
> May the border be the standing rainbow.
> Thus weave for us a garment of brightness
> That we may walk fittingly where grass is green,
> O our Mother the Earth, O our Father the Sky!

Susan Harnly Peterson, *The Living Tradition of Maria Martinez* (Tokyo and New York: Kodansha International, 1977, 2006). Reprinted by permission of author.

Parabola
Volume: 7.2
Dreaming and
Seeing

Our Other Selves: The Lakota Dream Experience

Arthur Amiotte

Black Elk told us:

I was four years old then, and I think it must have been the next summer that I first heard the voices. It was a happy summer and nothing was afraid, because in the Moon When the Ponies Shed [May] word came from the Wasichus that there would be peace and that they would not use the road any more and that all the soldiers would go away. The soldiers did go away and their towns were torn down; and in the Moon of Falling Leaves [November], they made a treaty with Red Cloud that said our country would be ours as long as grass should grow and water flow. You can see that it is not the grass and the water that have forgotten.

Maybe it was not this summer when I first heard the voices, but I think it was, because I know it was before I played with bows and arrows or rode a horse, and I was out playing alone when I heard them. It was like somebody calling me, and I thought it was my mother, but there was nobody there. This happened more than once, and always made me afraid, so I ran home.

It was when I was five years old that my Grandfather made me a bow and some arrows. The grass was young and I was horseback. A thunder storm was coming from where the sun goes down, and just as I was riding into the woods along a creek, there was a kingbird sitting on a limb. This was not a dream, it happened. And I was going to shoot at the kingbird with the bow my Grandfather made, when the bird spoke and said: "The clouds all over are one-sided." Perhaps it meant that all the clouds were looking at me. And then it said: "Listen! A voice is calling you!" Then I looked up at the clouds, and two men were coming from there, headfirst like arrows slanting down; and as they came, they sang a sacred song and the thunder was like drumming. I will sing it for you. The song and the drumming were like this:

> Behold, a sacred voice is calling you;
> All over the sky a sacred voice is calling.

I sat there gazing at them, and they were coming from the place where the giant lives [north]. But when they were very close to me, they wheeled about toward where the sun goes down, and suddenly they were geese. Then they were gone, and the rain came with a big wind and a roaring.

I did not tell this vision to any one. I like to think about it, but I was afraid to tell it."[1]

Time and time again, in the literature and in the oral tradition of the Lakota, references are made to visions, ghosts, and dreams. Specific differences are also made between the common dream—what modern research calls REM dreams—and what the Lakota believe to be the capacity to pierce a barrier and participate in another realm which is considered sacred.

To grasp the significance to Native people of the dream experience, one must take into account the unique stance from which they describe the metaphysical underpinnings of person and personality, not only of the human being but of all creatures, plants, the world, and the universe.

Central to a host of beliefs connected with dreams and dreaming is the conviction of the transparency and mutability of all *things*. The mythologies of the tribes affirm for the Native the synchronous existence of various planes of reality in which both linear time and physical geography are only one level—one that consistently needs one's attention, for it appears to be incomplete and mutable, still in a process of ongoing creation. The other planes are the sacred counterparts of what we know to exist in the temporal world, but which are imbued with their own sacred power—often under the control of, or operative because of, the intervention of the gods.

Often, through the powerful language of metaphor, the sacred world is delineated and anthropomorphized, a process by which the various dimensions of the personality of the Wakan (Great Mystery or gods) are made comprehensible and visible to the mind of the Native. This capacity of the Native mind to sustain the mythological presence of the transparent world, to integrate sacred time and geography with ordinary time and space, gives rise to a unique view of self in relation to all things and to others, including those who dwell in the sacred or "spirit" world, or as the Australian Natives call it, the "dreaming."

Attempts to delve deeper into the nature of the spirit world give one the idea that perhaps it is not for everyone to know, and that many people—Native Americans as well as others—who have been touched too deeply by technological and scientific modes of living and thinking cannot again recapture the capacity to operate in it. "Wondering about it" and listening to the tribal wise men sometimes gives us clues about the potential that is inherent in this capacity to live in both worlds; and yet only through the unique experience of witnessing the transforma-tion of the contemporary practicing shamans do we get a glimpse of its awesome reality. It seems like the shamans are now still the vital link between the contemporary student of the phenomenon on one hand and the spiritual efficacy for the Native worshipper on the other.

Within the context of a specific tribal group, the Lakota wise men tell that "All things in the world are sacred. All things in the world in their order of creation were given four spiritual counterparts besides the gross," or physical form which is the most obvious. All things were cre-ated first in the spirit world, and there they first learn and know that plane of existence, its language, and the gods who dwell there. Through a miraculous process of transubstantiation, often depending upon the cooperation of living, earthly people through the fulfillment of ritual acts, entrance into earthly life is given to the four spiritual counterparts of all things, or as they will be referred to from now on, the four souls.

The first one to be considered is the *Niya*, which is described as the *life-breath* of a being. The word itself is derived from the Lakota *woniya*, which means the capacity of a being to breathe or possess living breath.

This soul is very much a part of the body, for it is this that gives life to the organism, that causes it to live and to have its limited movement in the life process; it cannot *move fully* unless the other souls are also in harmony, in "working order." This is the basis of the importance of ritual preparation of foods; proper care and nourishment of the body is "to strengthen and keep strong the Niya"; physical activity is to keep the body attuned as an instrument by which life tasks can be accomplished. Ritual cleansing in the sweat lodge is thought not only good for expelling toxic matter, the *miniwatutkala*, through the pores, but also for strengthening and purifying the Niya through ritualized union with the spirit world. This is accomplished within the lodge through song and communion utilizing the sacred pipe. The final act of the sweat lodge is the emergence from within to the outside—a ritual act of rebirth and rejuvenation witnessed by sighs of "How refreshing it was" or "Ah ... I feel so light and good now." All rejoice and give thanks while sharing a ritual meal and feeling blessed to be able to breathe anew.

The ritual "doctoring" and healing processes, then, treat not only the body but also the Niya, a relation the modern world has begun to realize with the holistic approach to medicine. In this sense we see one dimension of the Lakota belief that dreams are explanations of medical realities. For if a person's Niya leaves his body, probably accompanied by the second soul or *Nagi*, and re-enters the spirit world, the body is quite without motion and the Niya must be retrieved and reintegrated with the body. While away, the Niya may once again dwell in the sacred world, dreamland, consorting with all kinds of other Niya and spirit-like beings. Following the regaining of this-world consciousness, a person who has been reintegrated has been known to report fantastic experiences to others who have kept a vigil near what to all appearances was a corpse, devoid of life-breath. It is this possibility of return and revival that gave rise to the Lakota tradition of above-ground burial and of keeping a vigil with ritual feedings for a minimum of four days and nights. There are many old stories of a moving camp of Lakota passing a scaffold burial and being surprised by the moving and thrashing about of the supposed dead body, returned to life and trying to release itself from the tightly bound burial wrappings. When freed by the passing party, such "born again" people were said to have reported many things about the spirit world, or about "being away as in a dream," including having seen spirits of people long passed away.

A similar situation in recorded history is the phenomenon of the Ghost Dance of the Lakota in the 1890s. Numerous accounts, written and oral, tell of dancers, after long and exhausting periods of dancing, falling into a trance-like state, "like being dead." Upon their regaining consciousness, without the aid of a shaman (for "no one was to touch them") they reported having seen their relatives and others who had died and a world full of peace and beauty, a restored world of primordial completeness.

The second soul, known as the Nagi, is closely akin to the stereotyped definition of ghosts as described in books, films, and oral tradition. Much more personal and individualistic than the Niya, the Nagi is much like a mirror image of the person's form, at once ephemeral when seen, transparent, and capable of easy transition to and from the spirit world. With its adeptness at mobility, the Nagi is thought to be capricious and a cause for concern when it is out of harmony with the form that it reflects. This can result in a type of soul loss or disequilibrium when it is absent from the body, but which is different from the loss of the Niya. If by chance the Nagi should leave and the Niya remain, the body would continue to function, but in a state of coma or in semiconsciousness. In such a state the person may appear to others as strange in his or her actions and attitudes.

In many cases the temporary absence of the Nagi is cause for illness or insanity. It is believed that the Nagi retains the idiosyncrasies of the this-worldly nature of the personality, and hence can be capricious and unpredictable, reliable or benevolent, depending on the nature of the person or the being. So it is that it may linger near the temporal world and be seen on occasion by those with the capacity to see it. Or it may migrate deeper into the spirit realm, where it may have to be retrieved through the shaman's art and his ability to make contact with it and attempt to lure it back or to rejoin it with the body.

Among the Lakota there are those who at a very young age exhibit a pre-knowledge of the world and of customs or persons long passed away. Such a person is said to be the explicit and individual Nagi of one who has lived before, returning in another body to participate again in the earthly life. This is frequently believed of twins and of certain shamans with their sacred and often mysterious ability to comprehend what ordinarily appears illusive to others. Such people, when meeting for the first time, will often have feelings of inordinate familiarity with each other, as if recognizing their strange commonality.

A case of which I was a witness took place several years ago at a Lakota Sundance in northern South Dakota. A middle-aged couple appeared in the camp of the head intercessor, who was exhausted and suffering from the rigors of the ceremony, asking him to come and see their daughter. I went with him and the parents to their camp. The daughter, who appeared to be ten or twelve years old, was dressed in conservative old-fashioned clothes more suitable to a grandmother than to a young girl of the present time. She talked to the shaman alone, with downcast eyes, in a polite and almost inaudible voice. Then she opened a small bundle and handed him water and food including a piece of melon, which is a preferred food after long periods of fasting and dancing in the heat of the Dakota sun.

Later the shaman explained that this girl was believed by her family to have lived before. On this day she had identified him with all his birthmarks, scars, and other physical characteristics as someone she recognized from her previous life. A year before, the shaman had had extensive surgery and bore a great scar on his abdomen. The girl explained to him that in her previous life, she and her husband had been through a terrible battle with enemies resulting in her husband's suffering similar if not identical scars and wounds from which he eventually died.

She had insisted that her parents bring her by car many miles to this Sundance because she had dreamed the night before that she saw her husband from her previous life dancing and suffering and in need of refreshment.

The shaman himself took all this matter-of-factly and had treated her with all the respect Lakota etiquette demands of the younger meeting the elderly, although at this point in time he himself was the elder and could indeed have been her grandfather.

Arising from these beliefs are the rituals for putting the Nagi in contact with the spirit world to gain insight, vision, and strength. The Lakota still believe firmly in the efficacy of the vision quest, a ritual fasting and sacrifice through which contact is made with the dream world and the spirit-selves of the other realm.

Since all creatures possess Nagi, they are able to commune with the *Wica-nagi* or spirits of men and women in the one language all Nagi learned in the spirit world. It is, therefore, not uncommon that the spirit visitor to the man seeking a vision on his isolated hilltop is that of any of the Nagi of people, animals, or birds believed to possess special god-like powers originating in the other world.

The term *Hanbleceya* is usually translated as "crying for a dream." A deeper meaning hidden in the word's root suggests a standing and enduring. The *ceya*—crying or suffering—indicates the need for sacrifice, which appears in the ritual of the vision quest as the giving up of water, food, and protection from the elements. In the process of sacrifice, *sacer facere*, to make sacred, one is ritually denying the physical existence of the mundane world in order to reach into or experience the sacred world by numbing the senses required for ordinary life. For the Lakota, to sacrifice is to ritually transform physical substance into spiritual substance, and in doing so, to transcend the gross in order to reach the greater reality of non-pain and the non-suffering, non-physical parameters of being. In the spirit world—dream time—all becomes possible. There, if the quester has a good heart and a pure mind, the dream beings may reward him or her with special powers which can be activated and translated into means of attaining harmony and balance between the spiritual and the mundane.

This brings us to the third aspect of soul or manifestation of spirit-like principle. The wise men tell us again, "All things possess a special power of their own which can be added to, expanded, and utilized to help others and themselves." The *Sicun* is that mysterious spirit-like power which all things possess. For the plant it may be its life-giving fruits, seeds, leaves, or roots or their chemical results as medicines. For animals it may be their unique traits, or the knowledge they have of plants or of celestial and earthly phenomena or behavior, that man desires for himself to help to survive. In some animals, it is their possession of the eternal and unfettered wisdom of the gods which man desires to know. This can only be communicated while in the state of the Nagi, transported and placed over the ritually prepared sacred area where the suppliant stands, or in a magical flight from that place where the Nagi of the seeker enters upon a mystical journey to that outer world and returns, as in a waking dream, to reinhabit his original body, now weak with hunger, thirst, and weariness.

While in the other realm, the encounter might have been a most dramatic affair endowed with all the trappings of a pageant, or as a solitary meeting with an old friend. Emerging none the less, whatever the form, the Nagi of the seeker is offered a portion of the Sicun of his spirit visitor, and instructed about its use and about the ritual songs, dances, or prayers to be utilized in activating it once he returns to the ordinary world.

It is just such Sicun that is contained in sacred bundles, stones, or animal parts worn or used by the shaman, warrior, or Native doctor in the ceremonies and rituals designed to make life efficacious.

As such, it can be said that some people possess more Sicun than others, or that some have fostered their Sicun well and have thus continued to insure its potency. While all things possess Sicun, those who have received more of it by crying for a dream are supposed to be particularly blessed, and hence responsible that it will always be used for the benefit it can bring to the people so that the proper relationship of all life will be maintained.

Relationship and harmony form the foundation upon which the fourth soul lives in all things. The Lakota conceive of *Taku Skan Skan*, or that which moves and causes all of life to move or to live, as though the entire universe were injected or infused with a common source and type of cosmic energy. This which causes all movement was the original source of all things at the beginning, says our mythology. From it came all of the energy of life, ranging from that of the stars, sun, and earth to that which causes the tiniest insect to move about and know its rhythm and part in the scheme of things. This Taku Skan Skan in all things is referred to as the *Nagila*, or *little ghost* that dwells in everything. Less personal and more magnanimous than other souls, the Nagila is responsible for wholeness—much like the web or sacred cord that binds and holds together all components. It is a bit of the divine essence—the mysterious force that makes all things and beings relatives to each other and to their common ancestor.

The profundity of this realization is expressed in the shortest and most commonly expressed Lakota prayer as a total response in ritual situations or as an ending to a longer narrative prayer. That prayer is *mitakuye oyasin*, "all my relatives," or "I am related to all that is."

Realizing, then, that one is more than mere physical being, the possibility for interaction, transaction, and intercourse within other dimensions of time, place, and being is what the dream experience is to the Lakota: an alternative avenue to knowing.

When Black Elk and others tell us of their great visions and subsequent excursions into the sacred realms, we are compelled to believe that something greater happened than a "train of thoughts or images passing through the mind in sleep," as the dictionary tells us,[2] or "... expression during sleep of various aspects of the ego and super-ego typically withdrawn from consciousness but, when recorded and analyzed, having some value in the diagnosis, interpretation and treatment of certain maladjustments of the personality."

The importance of the Lakota belief about dreams is not just a memory contained in accounts by such men as Black Elk. Today and perhaps at this very moment, traditional activities are taking place on contemporary reservations. Legitimate shamans and healers regularly maintain a schedule of clients whose requests range from dream interpretation to the rectifying of personal disequilibrium to the ritual preparation and strengthening of soul for future participation in the spring and summer high ceremonies. These include the contemporary Sundance and Hanbleceya with all their attendant rites for encountering the sacred world, from which will come that "stuff" of ethnicity that causes the Lakota to persist as tribal people in a twentieth century society.

It is not uncommon for professionally educated and employed Lakota living in urban centers to travel great distances, leaving behind the ways of contemporary life to participate in the mysterious, in the tribally prescribed mode. Often this is because they are still beckoned by the dream encounter that moves them to do as the messenger instructs them.

This should give us insight into and respect for the diversity and uniqueness of humankind's ability to participate in and explore the inner and outer landscapes of mind and myth, where truth abideth in many guises.

Notes:

1. Black Elk from John G. Neihardt, *Black Elk Speaks* (New York: Simon & Schuster, 1972) 15–16.

2. Britannica World Language edition of *Funk & Wagnall's Standard Dictionary.*

Parabola
Volume: 12.1
Knight and Hermit

Seeking the Spirit Path

Lewis P. Johnson

The ceremony of the vision quest is an active symbol of humanity dreaming God and God dreaming humanity. For the Nishnawbe ("original people") on this continent, it is a necessary part of the conviction that you cannot live fully in relationship to yourself or your community unless you are also aware of Spirit.

The idea is to seek a vision that gives you purpose in life and then to implement that vision. The vision by itself is one half, one part, of a process. It implies the necessity of living that vision, otherwise the vision will sink back into itself. It isn't any one person's vision that is unfolding but the vision of Gitche Manitou, and we all have the opportunity to participate in that. Humanity and Gitche Manitou are in process together.

Human beings are the only creatures with the ability to understand Gitche Manitou's vision; the other creatures and elements know it instinctively, or their role in it; but a human being, with his tool for understanding, can reach up into Spirit and touch Spirit.

Gitche Manitou wants very much for humanity to reach up; then humanity becomes an opening, a pole, to help Gitche Manitou's vision become manifest. Through human beings, Gitche Manitou can touch and understand himself. We are part of the spirit of Gitche Manitou.

That's why we feel such longing to touch Spirit, and one way we have of doing this is to go on a vision quest.

As we begin to reach up and touch Spirit, we begin to understand what our real work is. Gitche Manitou is not self-aware. He needs us to help him understand his own nature. Pure Spirit is not conscious of itself, so when we talk about the process of the vision quest, we are really talking about the relationship between consciousness and unconsciousness and the going in and out between the two. When Gitche Manitou's vision is one day fully manifest on this earth and humanity is working consciously and harmoniously to implement that vision, then we will have become that vision.

The existence of Gitche Manitou is not something you need to take on faith but something you can learn through direct perception. On my vision quest, I perceived a little facet of Gitche Manitou. I could not perceive the whole and remain myself, but I perceived a part. Through the vision, I caught a glimpse of the "warrior" both within and without; and now, as I was told then I must do, my effort is to realize that warrior in my life.

The vision quest is usually a four-day fast conducted in a consecrated place. It puts the individual in touch with the spirit world through deprivation of food, sleep, water, and physical comfort. (Some in the medical community might say this process is simply one whereby you are stressing the nerves and body chemistry in such a way that you perceive things differently. They would be partially right. The process *is* one of stressing the body, stressing the senses to a point where non-sensory material can come through; if they care to call this *nonsense*, it is a play on words.)

The conscious mind is a good and necessary guardian for us, but it also keeps us from experiencing some things that we can only experience once that barrier is removed. The primary function of the vision quest is to get beyond consciousness and find the voice of the soul. It is not so much self-knowledge that is gained (although that is gained) as awareness of the whole of life and one's relationship to it. Not only do we all exist as a whole, but we can bring that spiritual wholeness into manifestation only through real participation in physical life.

Usually there's a reason why someone chooses to go on a vision quest. Sometimes it's simply a matter of coming of age and wanting to find one's direction. In my case, although my grown sons had had vision quests as part of their initiation into manhood, I hadn't had one as a young man, because there had been no one to guide me. The Indian religion was illegal until 1978 when President Carter signed the Freedom of Religion Act.

I had had visions and meaningful dreams thoughout my life (fortunately there is no way to outlaw those), but at the point I undertook my vision quest and four-day fast, I felt I needed this process in order to understand my relationship with my family and my wife. My wife had had our baby, which was her version of a vision quest, and I felt I needed a new kind of understanding in order to give fully to my family and also in order to grow in self-knowledge. I was not without doubts about my physical ability to sustain four days without food or water. I was forty-eight and diabetic, as nervous, well-meaning friends pointed out to me. But my life up to that point had been one of trust in the truth, the sincere seeking of the spirit path. Now I had a strong emotional need to define that search. I took the first steps by making a public announcement and seeking approval from tribal elders. In this way, I set up the conditions through which Spirit could give its approval or disapproval. I awaited a sign.

One day while meditating and walking in the woods I stumbled over a football-sized gray rock. On the rock in whitish-gray was the clear outline of a man "dancing" over a snake. At first I thought the outline was organic, perhaps bird droppings. On closer examination, I saw it was clearly part of the rock itself. When I brought the rock home, a reddish line began to expand outward around the man. The form of the man has remained clear in the rock, but the reddish line has become faint again. The rock gave me the assurance I needed.

Visions are usually viewed as part of the individual and not to be talked about. In my case, part of my vision was to share the process of the vision quest, which is in the account that follows. I have changed the names of the Medewin people who prayed for me and the medicine man who helped me out of respect for their privacy, and I have also disguised the name and description of the "Place of Visions" in order to protect its sacredness.

Wednesday, 3 October 1984

Temperature hovering around 45 degrees today, intermittent showers with dramatic clouds, winds, and sunlight mixed; saw flying bear shape with well-developed head and paws in clouds outside Sault Sainte Marie heading north on Canadian side. Woods very colorful now. Met young pipe carrier Dale and his uncle, Frank Little Hawk, a Medewin priest from Manitoba. Frank is very familiar with the Place of Sacred Visions. Says it is hollow and sounds like drum when you are on it alone, walking around. Says it is spot where Nanabozo had Muskrat bring up mud to make world from ocean floor. Hollow spot on top of rock where Nanabozo's wolf rested after going around entire earth island to make it dry. Started out as pup, came back as old wolf after doing his job. Hole in top of rock where wolf rested.

Also this spot where Nanabozo cut ribbon into forty-eight pieces, being the beginning of multiple languages. Also spot where Nanabozo wrote on cliff with old Indian pictographs. These pictographs are hidden and are waiting to be interpreted yet by right person.

These two, Dale and Frank, with others, will be taking sweat with me tomorrow. I am staying with Tony and his wife.

10:35 pm

Tony left earlier to go out and make some special arrangements. He is not back yet. I am to wait up and have pipe ceremony yet tonight. Says we will both need strength of pipe for work at hand.

Thursday, 4 October 1984

At noon I must be at Tony's for last meal of fish before fast begins. Tony says Sunday night he will personally come up to take me off the hill and to listen to what I have to say, but he must be in Ottawa tomorrow for meeting with new Canadian government (he has just been re-elected as chief by write-in-ballot, as he was not actually running). He will leave at noon after fish dinner, and come back immediately. He asks me to pray for him while in sweat on hill.

5:00 pm

At Tony's house. We are supposed to meet here at five and start sweat. Had plenty of time to go up to rock, so I carried up the tarp at the same time, as it is quite heavy. Don't believe I will have much trouble carrying everything downhill on Sunday night. I miss my family and hope everything is all right. Prayed for sun to come out while on rock. It did. Otherwise spitting rain all day.

Later

Sweat was deep in woods of very large pines by Loon Lake on Wakami Reserve and is their special (spiritual) place. Four guys are waiting for us, and I find out that this is to be a Medewin sweat. I am very courteously questioned with real deference but with some depth as to my beliefs, background, experiences, and opinions of Medewin. While my little inquisition is going on, the water drum is being tied and made ready, tobacco offerings being made, and cautions and instructions being given for time at Place of Visions. I must have a small fire going constantly while on hill to guide in all spirits to this spot and to advertise the fact that it is in use again in old way.

At this point, rocks are ready, drummers ready, all offerings are made and Dale and his uncle Frank auspiciously appear out of the night. Frank begins immediately to tell story of water-drum (Little Boy) and how drum was first acquired, creation story, how voice of Little Boy (water-drum) grew so weak it almost died, and how Little Boy's voice is growing strong again. No pipe is used, but rattles and water-drum are used in sweat. When it is my turn to talk and I sound water-drum four times, there is drum answering outside lodge. Frank says it is little people, as we are in middle of their special area. After sweat is over, everyone has feast of moose steak (except me, as I began my fast at noon).

I go to the Place of Sacred Visions with newly presented eagle feather in hand. I spend a good part of night awake, very cold, as it is too dark to gather wood or make a shelter. At one point I hear what sounds like a bunch of giggly laughing girls on trail. They have got to be spirits as it is about 2:00 am, but they never actually appear to me.

Friday, 5 October 1984

Very cold but clear morning. I greet sun, gather wood, make fire and offerings. I put up tobacco ties and make tent of Larry's canvas. I am now settled in. It is a lovely clear cool day. I pray, make offerings, keep fire going all day. Mid-to late afternoon, I hear young man talking on other side of rock, go to look to see who has come up. Look all over, no one here. I was never able to make out words, but was clearly a voice, really sure someone physical was there. Guess next time I'll just make offering and wait. I have several times today mistaken my feather for a person as it hangs there in the tree.

4:30 pm

Soon I must go and look for more wood to last through the night. This dry pine burns so fast. So far I am neither hungry or thirsty. I do have a mild headache. I am going to smoke my pipe before I go for wood. Kind of tired. Wonder how everyone is at home. When gathering firewood found very soft grassy spot, unusual up here; lay down for a moment, and as I was apparently falling asleep, four miniature thunderbirds flew up and stayed. I think I slept for only five minutes.

7:00 pm

Sun slides over horizon. It is getting a little colder now in the twilight. I dream and am awakened being told to repeat out loud what I have just seen. It works and I do not forget:

I was in a white well-lighted room with two beds directly across from each other. I was in one bed, and this other person was in the other one. Both of us were lying on top of white sheets. I was startled to see that the other person was me also. First, I was amused to see that I had lost a little more weight; then I noticed that it was only the torso with arms and head but no legs. Also, it was only the outer shell, and although alive, it (me) apparently had no consciousness of its self or condition. I was told to look at its lower right abdomen near the groin area. I saw a hole about the size of a quarter; very old looking, puncture-type wound that the skin had grown around. I thought to myself that, yes, there is a hole there, but it does not look too big and it must have been there a long time. A voice said, "You do

not think it is too big?" I watched as a man's fist stretched the hole and
came right through. Another voice said that they will fix the hole, but
that I walk on the only legs I have, my spirit legs, and I must think
about what that means or else my physical legs will no longer support
me—dream ends.

Saturday, 6 October 1984

Sleep well, plenty warm; wake up early, stars are out, a good wind
blowing, and I notice fire is out. I rebuild fire and make tobacco offerings
to spirits for good dream. Straighten things out and sit down to pray and
try to understand dream. Dawn is coming, and I get out pipe to have
sunrise ceremony. My little area seems very friendly with tobacco ties flying and feathers moving in the wind. I go to top of rock with special shirt
and blanket and pipe bag. I sing and pack pipe awaiting actual moment
of sunrise on horizon. I pray to sun as it peeks above horizon. When it is
about one-half visible, large blue-gray figure emerges from top of sun to
maybe seven to eight times size of sun. Another blue sun emerges from
sun and takes up position to upper right of sun. Then maybe four to seven
transparent blue suns start to come straight at me and merge with me and
surrounding rocks. A figure detaches from blue sun.

Anyway, during first part of this, rocks glowed blue; in second part,
rocks glowed lavender. It is early morning on Saturday; the wind continues to blow steadily.

My mood seems to be changing. Yesterday I moved around a great
deal, exploring, gathering wood, looking, thinking, praying out loud.
Today, all I'm doing is contemplating, little to no desire for activity or
encounters. I feel really good, but desire or need for movement just about
zero. Today, I will burn some of the tobacco ties and pray for the people
who sent them along to the top of the rock here. Early afternoon three
young teenage girls come up and stand around on rocks for ten to fifteen
minutes and leave as quietly as they came. Midafternoon, an older man,
a young woman, and a young man briefly and noisily climb around rocks
and then leave.

Late afternoon, I pray that this is the time of my spiritual maturity, that finally now I come of age. I am tired of selfishness and killing
self-interest. I wish to do only that for which I was put on this place

to do: "Grandfather, I seek no self-defining graduation, but only a real beginning of my real and true work as you define and lead me to it. I accept that my life is completely in your hands, to do with as you see fit, to come, to go, to stop, to start, but above this, to live the life you have sent me here for, to do everything I possibly can for my family and my people. Grandfather, I would be reborn to your truth, not as I would define it, but as you show me in the work for you, for which I am here. Grandfather, help me now; send your spirits to this man who seeks you, his family, his people, and his real self."

Just after sunset beautiful Indian flute music answers my rattle's call for help.

Sunday, 7 October 1984

Almost dawn

Voice says: "You have heard 'the meek shall inherit the earth,' but those who are willing to die shall inherit this earth. Wake up, Lewis, repeat this, many times." I woke up repeating the phrase, put what remaining wood I had on the fire, made offering of more tobacco and ties, worrying about what that hard saying meant.

A voice weak and far away said, "Think about what you were saying as you came up the trail." As I sit here now and remember, I was saying with all the yearning heart within me, asking the spirits to take me and return me only if I was worthy to go on with a real life for my family and people; but not my decision, rather that of Spirit. I was ready to die if that was asked of me or if it somehow happened that I did not return from this place. Does this mean that people must again seek visions or dreams, or does it mean we must all seek God in our own way? But, what was said was we must be willing to die. I think that must mean that by some act we must demonstrate we are willing to give up self.

After renewing fire, dawn truly did come, even though cloudy. Had real good sunrise, and I had sunrise ceremony; and while pipe was still out, felt it was correct time to burn remaining ties. Very bright night up here and not very cold. Wood is finally gone now, and I must get some more.

This early afternoon, Indian man about thirty-five with an approximately twelve-year-old boy and seven-year-old girl come up to rock. They do not see me, but he makes tobacco offerings to directions, and as he is about to leave, he notices me and comes over. Boy is rather sullen, but curious. I give him four small rocks with colors of directions. I give father tobacco pouch and little girl small brass container of dry flowers with minijewel in flower. I tell her it is a spirit-flower given to me by a little girl about her age with special prayers for a good fast. She seems pleased with gift, but eyes open real big when I mention name of Spirit Flower. Her father says that is her name. They all make tobacco offerings to my little fire.

He now says in almost shy, hushed voice, "The woman who sits beside me, she is a spirit traveler. She sits now down below in our van. Would you like me to call on her to help give you strength? Hey, why don't you just come with us to the ceremonies? Will someone be coming after you? We didn't see any car. ..."

I give him a little red bag with jewel attached to it for his wife, and tell him I know about ceremonies but cannot come because I have to fast on hill. When he sees the little jewel bag, he says, "That's my wife's name also! Her name is Sparkling Stone!"

We are both startled by the accuracy of the gifts, but he seems flabbergasted. He then leaves in a big hurry, saying he does not know if he should even be talking to me while I am fasting. All three, with their little dog, leave then in the rain.

About 4:00 pm

Feeling very strong, and am conscious of drawing great strength from the rocks. Am drawn to a pinnacle of rock I am leaning against; feel great gray circles of power coming up from rocks into me. I know then that I have joined with rocks and island hill and that even though a part of me will now always stay on this hill, the Place of Sacred Visions will always be with me to give me strength to carry it to the people. I feel as if I could fly, but instead my mouth opens and I begin to sing in Indian to the directions. The words I hear, but do not understand. Yet, I do know what I am saying.

> *Awaken, you lands.*
> *All you people out there, live.*
> *Live strong.*
> *The Power is still here.*

Live strongly and true, you birds,
    animals, creeping and swimming ones.
Awaken, my people.
Return to the old ways;
    it is not too late.
Remember, and live again.
Live strongly.

I am conscious of great power moving in all directions from Place of Sacred Visions. I think I must have sung this over and over for about half an hour. It is as if I cannot stop. At about 5:00 pm I see two figures approaching the rock. One turns and heads back. About 5:30, more or less, Tony appears. He stands and sits by the fire as I recount the days and what has occurred in a more or less chronological manner. The dream he interprets to mean that I must take the spiritual way to the people and bring it fully into my own everyday life; that my outer physical life is nothing without giving a full expression of my spirit, which is whole and healthy, but which until now has been disjointed and separated.

He says I must now walk with my spiritual legs as a whole man. I must bring the rock back to the people—that they will eventually listen, perhaps sooner than I think. He is most interested in vision of figures I had during sunrise ceremonies. He says figure to left is not an animal standing on its tail but a spiritual warrior of Geiss (Sun) doing spirit dance of life. He says I must strive to realize that warrior within me, because the spirit is always there, and if I strive to know it—and he means I can only do that by my life dance for the people—then it will come through.

He lapses into Ottawa and prays with sweet grass for about fifteen minutes or so. Coming out of it he says, "Very powerful, very powerful. Let's go down now. You have been successful on your first trial. Usually it takes three or four trials before an answer is given." He says as we are leaving, "Jeez, this place is sure loaded with spirits up here. Boy, did you have lots of help!" He asks, "You weren't afraid up here, were you?" I say, "No, it was very friendly, but mostly very strong." He says, "Good."

On the way down, I tell him about flute music I heard. Halfway down, we stop and listen to long beautiful bird song. It sings twice for about three minutes each time. Sounds like it is saying good-bye. He listens very carefully and says, "You will leave a part of yourself here, but you will carry the rock with you now." We saw a partridge right alongside the trail at the bottom of the rock. It just looked at us, then walked away. He asks if I was singing just before they arrived. I am startled to say, "Yes." He says he and his wife both heard me separately on the highway and together at the gate with many other voices, all singing in Ottawa with a very powerful drum. Gate is about one mile from the Place of Sacred Visions.

At gate I am given fish soup, orange, and tomato juice. It is now dark, and Tony says good-bye, telling me to eat a hearty meal along the way after some hours have passed.

I head on to Sault Sainte Marie, crossing border about midnight. I am now exhausted and sleep for a few hours in American Soo (nickname for Sault Sainte Marie).

Monday, 8 October 1984

6:40 am

Have been awake now for about an hour writing in this journal. I feel fairly well rested and will leave as soon as gas stations open up. Rain continues, but it is not cold. Town is getting busy now, and people are going to work.

Parabola
Volume: 7.3
Ceremonies

Becoming Part of It

Joseph Epes Brown

In talking about sacred dimensions in Native American life, I must proceed not just as a descriptive ethnographer but also as a historian of religion, and with what I hope is a basic humanistic concern; that is, I believe it important to ask about the relevance of these primal values to a dominant contemporary world with life-ways which are oriented towards very different directions and with contrasting priorities. One notices very clearly today our increasing malaise and sometimes even fear, which—at least in certain segments of our society—is leading to a growing mood for re-evaluation and reassessment, a wish even to take a backward look, so to say, at "progress," that concept which for so long has been an unquestioned quasi-religious dogma in our lives. Many of those early studies of Native American peoples and cultures suffered from the kinds of prejudices that came out of this prevailing concept of progress.

An expression of this new and growing mood is found in an increasing concern to seek out our ancient origins, with a view to rediscovering and perhaps even identifying with what is our own proper heritage. I put the question in this manner because very often when I speak about the relevance and the reality of American Indian values, I am misunderstood, especially by students who like to believe that what I am trying to say is that they should go out and live and be American Indians; this is not my point at all, because for those of us who are non-Indians it is an impossibility. One has to be brought up in these cultures and traditions, one has to live the languages, in order truly to identify with the ethos of an American Indian people. What I *am* trying to say is that these traditions could be taken as models which might provide us with answers to some of the dilemmas with which we are currently struggling in our own society.

In the '60s, in our restlessness with where we found ourselves, we began to turn to the religions and methods of the Orient, with all the attractions and mystique which distance provides. By the '70s, however, with our rapidly growing ecological concerns, there developed an increasing awareness that certain answers could be found in the spiritual traditions of the Native Americans; for here the sacred values which so many of us were seeking out were actually rooted in this land, where they have survived through some sixty to eighty thousand years. Out of this mood there has come a vast array of new literature, both genuine and spurious, relating to Native American life-ways and world view; and even if the approach has often been overly romantic, there is here a change from earlier attitudes and prejudices, which is a positive sign even if it is only a beginning.

Although greatly oversimplified and generalized, let me give at least a brief sampling of what I think are some of the core Native American values and perspectives, through which we can perhaps come to relearn a little bit about ourselves and about our own proper spiritual heritage, the hope being that what has been lost can still be rediscovered. Certainly the Native American people themselves, especially the younger ones today, are trying to regain and revitalize their own traditions which may have been lost, or taken from them through a variety of pressures and prejudices. We have, I suggest, in this struggle a model for our own proper quest. What are some of its contours?

Tribal cultures, it seems to me, present a model of what a religious tradition *is*; and this is a basic reality which we have lost sight of. That is, what really is a true religious tradition? What does it encompass, what are its dimensions? These cultures demonstrate how all components of a culture can be interconnected: how the presence of the sacred can permeate all life-ways to such a degree that what we call religion is here integrated into the totality of life and into all of life's activities. Religion here is so pervasive in life that there is probably no Native American language in which there is a term which could be translated as "religion" in the way we understand it. As Peter Nabokov tells us in his book, *Indian Running*, when you track down a seemingly isolated or minimal feature of Indian life, such as running, the whole system opens before your eyes; and this is true because of the interrelatedness of all the components of a genuine tradition. Obviously in such a system life cannot be fragmented, due to that binding and interconnecting thread of the presence of the sacred.

In terms of interconnections, a dominant theme in all Native American cultures is that of relationship, or a series of relationships that are always reaching further and further out; relationships within the immediate family reaching out to the extended family, to the band, outward again to the clan, to the tribal group; and relationships do not stop there but extend out to embrace and relate to the environment: to the land, to the animals, to the plants, and to the clouds, the elements, the heavens, the stars; and ultimately those relationships that people express and live, extend to embrace the entire universe.

In the Plains area, to give an example, one of the most profound rites is that of the smoking of the pipe. In this ritual smoking of the pipe, all who participate are joined in a communal ritual act, and when it is finished, everybody who has shared in the smoking of the pipe recites the phrase, in Lakota in this case, "*mitakuye oyasin*"—"we are all relatives." We *are* all related, because in this rite we have all become one within a mystery that is greater than any of its parts. I shall talk more about the general importance of rituals and ceremonies later.

Associated with relationship there should be mentioned the theme of reciprocity which permeates so many aspects of North American cultures. Put very simply, reciprocity here refers again to that process wherein if you receive or take away you must also give back. This is a living statement of the importance of the cycle permeating all of life: the cycle of life and death, of life leading to old age and then coming back to life. Everything in their world of experience is conceived in terms of such cycles or of the circle; everything comes back upon itself. Black Elk so often said that all the forces of the world work in cycles or circles: the birds build their nests in circular form, the foxes have their dens in circles, the wind in its greatest power moves in a circle, and life is as a circle. I recall once how this reality was beautifully expressed in a living manner, when I noticed how this dignified old man would relate to little children. He would get down on his hands and knees and pretend he was a horse, and the children would squeal with joy on the old man's back. Here there obviously was no generation gap; he was one with the child. I once asked him how it was that he could so relate to the child, and he replied: "I who am an old man am about to return *to* the Great Mysterious" (*Wakan-Tanka*, in Lakota) "and a young child is a being who has just come *from* the Great Mysterious; so it is that we are very close together." Because of such cyclical understanding, both are very nearly at the same point.

Such attitudes could be spelled out in terms of any number of cultural expressions, but the point I want to draw from this is that we have here an example which contrasts with our own dominant concept of process which is in terms of linearity—the straight line which moves from here to there and onward indefinitely. Indeed, this theme of linearity permeates all aspects of our life. The way we read, for instance, is in lines; we have sayings in our vocabulary that tell us to "Line up!" "Let's get this straight!" Or if we refer to somebody who is a little bit crazy, we make a circular motion alongside our head, by which we indicate the reason is going in circles. There is something here from which we can learn, something about ourselves and our concept of progress, with all the loaded meanings which this term bears.

One must mention also the special nature of Native American languages, which contrasts with our understanding of language and our use of words. In Native languages the understanding is that the meaning *is* in the sound, it *is* in the word; the word is not a symbol for a meaning which has been abstracted out, word and meaning are together in one experience. Thus, to name a being, for example an animal, is actually to conjure up the powers latent in that animal. Added to this is the fact that when we create words we use our breath, and for these people and these traditions breath is associated with the principle of life; breath is life itself. And so if a word is born from this sacred principle of breath, this lends an added sacred dimension to the spoken word. It is because of this special feeling about words that people avoid using sacred personal names, because they contain the power of the beings named, and if you use them too much the power becomes dissipated. So usually one has to refer to a person in a very circuitous manner, or use a term which expresses relationship.

In this context one must also emphasize the positive values that could be attached to non-literacy. I use that term rather than illiteracy, which connotes the *inability* to read and write, which is negative and derogatory. Too often we have branded people as being backward and uncivilized if they are illiterate, whereas one can make a strong case for the advantages of growing up and living in a society which is non-literate. For in such a society all the lore which is central and sacred to the culture is borne *within* the individual in a living manner; you do not have to go outside of yourself, for all that is essential to life is carried with you, is ever-present. It seems that where you have people who are *non-literate* in this positive sense, you tend to have a special quality of person, a quality of being that cannot be described—a very different quality from that of the literate person. It has been my experience when among primal peoples in many parts of the world that there is something here that is very special.

Paralleling this primal concept of language, and of the word not as "symbol" but as an immediate event, is the quality of experiencing the visual arts and crafts. I should stress first of all that for primal peoples generally there is no dichotomy between the arts and crafts, in the manner that our art historians insist on, where art is one kind of thing that can be placed on a mantelpiece or hung on the wall, and the craft item is inferior because it is made for utilitarian ends. This seems to me a most artificial distinction and I think it is time that we outgrew it; indeed there is today evidence that we *are* reevaluating such prejudiced dichotomies. For why cannot a utilitarian object also be beautiful? All necessary implements, utensils, and tools in Native American life-ways are of technical excellence and are also beautiful. They must be made in special sacred ways, and the materials of the tools and objects made have to be gathered with prayer and offerings. Beauty and truth are here one! When a Pomo basketmaker, for example, goes out to collect the grasses for her basket, she prays to the grasses, she enters into a relationship with them as she gathers, and makes offerings in return for having taken their life. When a woman weaves a basket she will pass the grass between her lips to moisten it, but also to breathe upon it, to give her life breath into the grass and thus give to the basket a special sacred quality that is always present in its use and tangible presence.

Through these few selected examples which have been given, I am suggesting that, where such traditions are still alive and spiritually viable, there tend to be present, within all of life's necessary activities, dimensions and expressions of the sacred. Actions of such quality could therefore be considered to manifest a ritual element in the sense that they tend to *order* life around and toward a Center. In this context, however, one must also speak of those special great rites and ceremonies, many often related to the seasonal cycles, which serve not just to support continuing orientations toward the sacred in everyday activities, but work for the *intensification* of such Presence and experience; such rites may also be the source and origin of new rites, ceremonies, and other sacred expressions through the visual arts, songs, or special dance forms.

One example of a ritual complex which is central to the lives of Plains people is the well known "vision" or "guardian spirit quest." This ritualized retreat is for the benefit of the individual man and woman, and yet means are present for the eventual sharing of received vision powers or messages with the larger community. After rigorous preparations, which always include the rites of the purifying sweat lodge and instructions by a qualified elder, the candidate goes to a high and remote place with the resolve to fast and pray continually and to suffer through acts of sacrifice and exposure to the elements for a specified number of days. The ordeal is highly ritualized and may involve the establishing of an altar, or the setting out of poles at the center and to the four directions of space. The person may also be instructed to remain within this established space and not to move about casually but to walk only out from the center to each of the poles in turn, always returning to the center. Prayers may be addressed to the powers of the four directions, and one may also use repetitive prayers such as the one the Lakota Black Elk has given us: "Grandfather, Great Mysterious, have pity on me." One may also remain silent, for it has been said that "silence *is* the voice of *Wakan-Tanka*, the *Great Mysterious*." If tired, one may sleep, for dreams of power may come to the candidate in this manner; yet it is understood that the true vision is of greater power than the dream. Often the sacred experience comes in the mysterious appearance of an animal or a winged being, or perhaps in one of the powers of nature. A special message is often communicated to the seeker, and this will serve as a guide and reminder throughout the person's life. After three or four days one returns to camp where a sweat lodge has again been prepared; within this lodge the candidate will explain the vision or dream which will be interpreted by the guiding elder, who will then give instructions as to what should now be accomplished in order to insure the continuity of the participation of the spiritual throughout the person's life. From such experiences have come the "medicine bundles" with rich and complex rites specific to each bundle and their ceremonial opening of special occasions. They have also been the origin of sacred types of art forms, such as the painted shields, or special songs of power, or even the great ritual dances, such as the horse dance, involving four groups of eight horses not representing, but *being* the powers of the four directions of space. It is in this manner that something of the sacred experience which had come to a particular individual is shared by all members of the larger community.

What is remarkable about the rites of the vision quest among the Plains peoples is that it is accomplished not just by special people as is the case in the Arctic, but that every man or woman after the age of puberty is expected to participate either once or even continually throughout his or her life.

What concerns us in this example is not just the detailed pattern of the ritual elements of the quest as such, which can encompass a multitude of very diverse possibilities, but that here we have one sample as a model of traditional ritual structures and acts which must involve initial purification, choice of appropriate site, the defining and delimiting of a special sacred place, and the fixing of a center. Further, ritualized *actions* are prescribed for the participant, which means that participation is not just with the mind, or a part of one's being, but with the totality of who one is. Also provided are means for continuity and development of the sacred experiences received, and the eventual responsibility for sharing something of them with the larger community.

As complement to the individually oriented "vision quest," one could mention the great communal "Sun Dance," referred to by different terms across the Plains groups. For this great complex of solemn rites, ceremonies, fasting, sacred song and dance fulfills not just the particular spiritual needs of the actively participating individuals, but also those of the entire tribal group gathered in circular camp for the occasion. The event is indeed for the welfare of the entire world. These are ceremonies, interspersed with special sacred rites, which celebrate world and life renewal at the time of spring. The ritualized dance forms again involve orientation around and towards a center which is either the sun itself or the cottonwood tree as axis of the world, standing at the center of a circular frame lodge carefully constructed in imitation of the cosmos. The ritual and ceremonial language of the total celebration speaks to and encompasses a plurality of spiritual possibilities at the levels of microcosm, macrocosm, and metacosm. It is believed by many that should the sacrificial rites of this "thirst lodge" be neglected or forgotten, the energy of the world will run out and the cycle in which we are living will close. It is an example to the world that these rites and ceremonies are far from being neglected, for today in ever increasing numbers the people are participating and are finding renewed strength and spiritual resolve.

All spiritually effective rites must accomplish three cumulative possibilities which may be termed purification, expansion—wholeness or virtue—and identity. A ritual means which embodies these possibilities may be found in the sacred nature and use of the Plains Indian tobacco pipe, the smoking of which constitutes a communion. The shape of the pipe with its stem, bowl or "heart," and foot, is identified with the human person. In purifying the pipe before a ritual smoking there is an analogy to man's own purification; for in concentrating on the hollow of the straight stem leading to the bowl comes the understanding that one's mind should be this straight and pure. In filling the bowl of the pipe a prayer is said for each grain of tobacco in such a manner that everything in the world is mentioned. The filled bowl or the heart of man, in thus containing all possibilities, is then the universe. Finally the fire which is put into the tobacco is the Presence of the ultimate all-inclusive Principle, Wakan Tanka, the "Great Mysterious." In smoking the pipe through the aid of breath the totality of all creation is absorbed within this ultimate Principle. And since in the pipe there is a grain of tobacco identified with the one who smokes, there is here enacted a sacrificial communion of identity. With this understanding, the phrase "we are all related," recited by the individual or group after the smoking, takes on the deepest possible meaning.

I will sum up by simply saying that in all that I have tried to speak of in such brief fashion, we have expressions through different means of a special quality among traditional peoples that could be called oneness of experience: a lack of dichotomizing or fragmenting, a unity in the word and in visual image. In the painted image, for example, the understanding is that in that being that is represented, or even in a depicted part of that being—the paw of a bear, let us say—all the power of the animal is present. One can draw from all Native American cultures examples to reinforce such interpretation. One final example I will use is that of the Navajo dry painting or "sandpainting" as it is sometimes called. These are made in a rich ceremonial context for the curing of individuals who have gotten out of balance with their world. They are long ceremonies which can go on for four or five or up to ten days, during which time sacred chants are used with all the meaning of the *word* as I have tried to explain it. At a certain moment during the ceremony the ill person is placed at the center of one of the dry paintings; the understanding is that the person thus becomes identified with the power that is in the image painted on the earth with colored sand and pollen. And the singer takes some of the painted image and presses it to the body of the ill person, again to emphasize this element of identity: the painting is not a symbol of some meaning or power, the power *is* there present in it, and as the person identifies with it the appropriate cure is accomplished.

I conclude with this portion of a Navajo chant:

> *The mountains, I become part of it...*
> *The herbs, the fir tree, I become part of it.*
> *The morning mists, the clouds, the gathering*
> *   waters,*
> *I become part of it.*
> *The wilderness, the dew drops, the pollen...*
> *I become part of it.*

And in the context of the other chants there is always the conclusion that indeed, I *am* the universe. We are not separate, but are one.

Parabola
Volume: 7.3
Ceremonies

First Sweat for the Sundancers

Joseph Bruchac

Rain which falls
through thin leaves of late summer
cold on our skins
stones from a wall
my great-grandfather piled
have turned white with heat
from the fire of logs
stacked chest-high

within the sweat lodge
Crow Dog's voice
speaks to the grandfathers
hiss of water
whispering against the red of stones
glowing inside the fire pit
is the voice of earth
at the time when Creation
first turned to life

my sons on each side,
bent sapling against my back
we go into the darkness together
six stones added to the sixteen
cedar needles fall and rise again

in smoke which burns eyes into vision

then we sing, together we sing
words we did not know we knew
heat driving foreheads down
to touch the mats of woven grass

breaths go shallow in moist heat
which burns our backs, the touch of a flaming wing
until the blanket lifts
and we realize we have been seeing
each other with only our ears and our skins,
that the prayers we heard each other offer
were not spoken by our lips

and when Sitting Bull's pipe
circles the lodge, glowing like the rising sun,
given me by my son's hand, passed on to my other son
I realize in many ways what it means to sing
We shall live again
We shall live again

Parabola
Volume: 16.3
Crafts

The Basket and World Renewal

Julian Lang

By today's standards the task of weaving a basket must seem silly to some, compared to deep space exploration or the transmittal of data concerning the origin of the universe. After all, a basket consists of woven sticks, plaited together into containers. Some of us put our dirty clothes into a basket, but for the most part, basketry has fallen into disuse if not obsolescence. It seems the time has passed when basketry was marveled at for its utility and perfected design. In northwestern California, however, a uniquely shaped, non-utilitarian basket is still essential to three local Indian tribes for conducting their ceremonies to "fix the world." Without the baskets the Hupa, Karuk, and Yurok would not be able to perform the highly important Jump Dance without solving extremely difficult problems and taking drastic measures.

I am a Karuk Indian and have held these dance baskets in my hands many times. Each possesses its own weight, shape, and danceability. Some of these baskets display the innovative mark of the artist, while others suggest strict adherence to traditional proportion and construction. Whatever the sensibility of the weaver, the baskets are known to the Karuk people as *vikapuhich*; the Yurok call them *e'gor*; the Hupa say *na'wech*. Their curious cylindrical shape suggest the feminine; their decoration, the sublime.

These little baskets are found nowhere else in the world. Within our traditional culture and psyche, the baskets are like jewels.

In order for us to fully appreciate the role that baskets play in our ceremonies and life, it is necessary to look to our *pikva*, our stories, and also to the voices of our oldest generations. The stories give us a glimpse of the foundation of our cultural identity. When we saw the high regard in which the white man held the Bible, we translated it into our language as *apxantinihichpikva*, or "white man's myths."

One of many stories about basket weaving takes place during the *pikvahahirak* ("myth-time-and-place"), when an Ikxaréeyav family (the Ikxaréeyav are the Spirit-beings of the *pivka* stories) lived in a good way until the father abandoned them in favor of a new wife, and their family life was disrupted. The jilted mother told the children they were going "a different way." They were going to be transformed. The father knew this was about to happen and returned to the house of his first wife, but it had already been abandoned. He caught up with his family on the hillside above the ranch and killed them in a fit of blind rage. Before dying, the wife cursed him, "You will be nothing once Human has arrived! Human will have nothing to do with you! We will be sitting in front of Human (at the annual World Renewal ceremonies). We will be beauty!" The slain family then metamorphosed into the materials used to weave a basket: hazel, willow, bull pine, maidenhair fern, and woodwardia fern. Thus, basketry materials are to us not just natural fibers, but gifts of divine origin.

The three local tribes perform the Jump Dance as part of the ceremony to fix the world. This dance is a ten-day ceremony that is held to rid the earth of sickness and other potential natural catastrophes. It is solemn, ecstatic, and beautiful in its simplicity. The songs are slow and sonorous. Each song begins quietly but is repeated at a higher pitch and intensity as it continues. In steady cadence a line of male dancers stamps the earth to rid it of sickness and all bad thoughts, to set the world back on its axis. Each stamp is followed by the swift lifting heavenward of a smallish, cylindrical basket that we call a vikapuhich. The body of the basket is decorated with bold, shiny black designs on a creamy ground. It has been split lengthwise and attached to a hazel stick handle that is wrapped in finely tanned buckskin. A small bunch of yellowhammer feathers is attached at one end.

A popular symbolic interpretation of this basket is that of family, home, and village. The vikapuhich contains a prayer for the world to be in balance. The basket is lifted to heaven and then retracted, bringing with it the spirit world's acknowledgment and luck. In unison the line of dancers then stamp out all that is bad. Over and over the basket is raised, then retracted, followed by the stamping out of sickness. Accompanied by songs originally inspired by the wind, the dance soon brings on a collective illumination: the elders cry, the young yearn.

Last fall I attended the Yurok Jump Dance at Pekwon, an ancient village about fifteen miles from the mouth of the Klamath River. After ten days, the time of the culmination dance had arrived. I had the distinct honor of choreographing the Pekwon camp's display of wealth, when all the regalia that has been contributed is brought out "to dance," in accordance with Indian law. So, the dance skirts of deerhide were laid out on the earthen floor. Then I brought armload after armload of Jump Dance baskets into the open air ceremonial house. They were stacked into a pile to hip level and four feet long. I carried into the house the fifty necklaces of shell and glass beads which were then laid across the baskets. I brought in the four remaining broad buckskin headbands, each decorated with the brilliant crimson-scarlet of at least forty pileated woodpeckers. Finally, the fifty eagle feather plumes were sent in, making a magnificent sight.

I ran back to the regalia-camp to make sure that nothing had been left behind. As I was returning to the dance, I heard someone running up behind me. I turned and saw a Yurok man named Pordie Blake. He said, "Here. Put this in. I just finished it up this morning," and handed me a small, twelve-inch-long Jump Dance basket. It was pure white except for the dark orange-shafted yellowhammer feathers bunched at its end, and the shiny black design that ran along its side. I immediately perceived it as a newborn. It was light, perfect in proportion, and wonderful to behold. The spectators were already visibly transfixed by the sheer volume of regalia and the frenzy for which the culmination dance is noted. Nevertheless, as I carried the new little basket into the dance house, there was an audible sigh, a look-at-the-beautiful-baby sigh. The world renewal was now complete with the entrance of the basket.

Ada Charles, the white-haired Yurok woman who had woven the little basket cylinder, sat with Pordie, the regalia maker in his mid-forties who had assembled its parts (the hazel stick, yellowhammer feathers, and buckskin) into its finished state. Earlier in the week the Pekwon dancemakers had choreographed a tribute dance to Ada. Each of nine dancers had held a basket she had made. The central dancer had lifted to heaven the first Jump Dance basket she had ever made, back when she was sixteen years old. Included in the line had been a brand new basket, the companion to the little basket I was about to carry into the dance house. The world was being made with the old and the new.

Twenty-two men and four women dance in the culmination dance. Each man raises a basket into the air, and then stamps out all sickness and bad thoughts. In the end the dancers separate into two lines, one side going west and one side going east. They dance and sing pointing the baskets north and south, and then into the sunrise and sunset. They spread their prayers all around this world and the sky-world and bring back the luck. They fix the world for us all.

I am a singer and dancer, and oddly, this was the first dance at which I participated as a spectator. For the first time I saw the weavers and regalia makers "look on" at the dance. Guests to the ceremony are invariably moved by the experience. It is truly a wonderful spectacle, and it is repeated every two years. The basket-makers and owners bring out the baskets, and prepare them, telling their families and friends where each basket came from, who wove it, and how their family came to own it. All along the Klamath River the baskets come out. We believe the baskets are alive and want to dance. That is why they were created, to help us fix the world.

Parabola
Volume: 24.2
Prayer

THE THANKSGIVING PRAYER

Haudenosaunee

These words of thanksgiving come to us from the Native people known as the Haudenosaunee (also Iroquois or Six Nations—Mohawk, Oneida, Cayuga, Onondaga, Seneca and Tuscarora) of upstate New York and Canada. The Thanksgiving Address has ancient roots, dating back over a thousand years to the formation of the Great Law of Peace by a man called the Peacemaker, and perhaps before that. Today these words are still spoken at the opening and closing of all ceremonial and governmental gatherings held by the Six Nations. A speaker is chosen to give the Thanksgiving Greetings on behalf of the people. They choose their own words, for we are all unique and have our own style, but the general form is traditional. It follows an order in which we can relate to all of the Creation. The Address is based on the belief that the world cannot be taken for granted, that a spiritual communication of thankfulness and acknowledgement of all living things must be given to align the minds and hearts of the people with Nature. This forms a guiding principle of culture. We believe that all people at one time in their history had similar words to acknowledge the works of the Creator. With this in mind, we offer these words in a written form as a way to re-acquaint ourselves with this shared vision. Our version of the Thanksgiving Address has been modified for a young, general audience—it has been shortened and many specific references to the culture of the Six Nations have been generalized. We hope this will enhance the accessibility of the words for readers around the world. It was Jake Swamp's original vision that this Address would go out to the children of the world, "so that later in life, when they go out and meet one another, they will find that they are all coming from the same place." This booklet is printed in the Mohawk and English languages. Other editions are available in Mohawk/German, Japanese, Portuguese, Spanish, Swedish, Bisayan and French; and future editions are planned in Hawaiian, Chinese.... . You are invited—encouraged—to share in these words, that our concentrated attention might help us rediscover our balance, respect, and oneness with Nature. Now our minds are one.

> *John Stokes*
> *The Tracking Project*

The People

Today we have gathered and we see that the cycles of life continue. We have been given the duty to live in balance and harmony with each other and all living things. So now, we bring our minds together as one as we give greetings and thanks to each other as People.

Now our minds are one.

The Earth Mother

We are thankful to our Mother, the Earth, for she gives us all that we need for life. She supports our feet as we walk about upon her. It gives us joy that she continues to care for us as she has from the beginning of time. To our Mother, we send greetings and thanks.

Now our minds are one.

The Waters

We give thanks to all the Waters of the world for quenching our thirst and providing us with strength. Water is life. We know its power in many forms—waterfalls and rain, mists and streams, rivers and oceans. With one mind, we send greetings and thanks to the spirit of Water.

Now our minds are one.

The Fish

We turn our minds to all the Fish life in the water. They were instructed to cleanse and purify the water. They also give themselves to us as food. We are grateful that we can still find pure water. So, we turn now to the Fish and send our greetings and thanks.

Now our minds are one.

The Plants

Now we turn toward the vast fields of Plant life. As far as the eye can see, the Plants grow, working many wonders. They sustain many life forms. With our minds gathered together, we give thanks and look forward to seeing Plant life for many generations to come.

Now our minds are one.

The Food Plants

With one mind, we turn to honor and thank all the Food Plants we harvest from the garden. Since the beginning of time, the grains, vegetables, beans, and berries have helped the people survive. Many other living things draw strength from them too. We gather all the Food Plants together as one and send them a greeting and thanks.

Now our minds are one.

The Medicine Herbs

Now we turn to all the Medicine Herbs of the world. From the beginning, they were instructed to take away sickness. They are always waiting and ready to heal us. We are happy there are still among us those special few who remember how to use these plants for healing. With one mind, we send greetings and thanks to the Medicines and to the keepers of the Medicines.

Now our minds are one.

The Animals

We gather our minds together to send greetings and thanks to all the Animal life in the world. They have many things to teach us as people.

We see them near our homes and in the deep forests. We are glad they are still here and we hope that it will always be so.

Now our minds are one.

The Trees

We now turn our thoughts to the Trees. The Earth has many families of Trees who have their own instructions and uses. Some provide us with shelter and shade, others with fruit, beauty, and other useful things. Many peoples of the world use a Tree as a symbol of peace and strength. With one mind, we greet and thank the Tree life.

Now our minds are one.

The Birds

We put our minds together as one and thank all the Birds who move and fly about over our heads. The Creator gave them beautiful songs. Each day they remind us to enjoy and appreciate life. The Eagle was chosen to be their leader. To all the Birds—from the smallest to the largest—we send our joyful greetings and thanks.

Now our minds are one.

The Four Winds

We are all thankful to the powers we know as the Four Winds. We hear their voices in the moving air as they refresh us and purify the air we breathe. They help to bring the change of seasons. From the four directions they come, bringing us messages and giving us strength. With one mind, we send our greetings and thanks to the Four Winds.

Now our minds are one.

The Thunderers

Now we turn to the west where our Grandfathers, the Thunder Beings, live. With lightning and thundering voices, they bring with them the water that renews life. We bring our minds together as one to send greetings and thanks to our Grandfathers, the Thunderers.

Now our minds are one.

The Sun

We now send greetings and thanks to our eldest Brother, the Sun. Each day without fail he travels the sky from east to west, bringing the light of a new day. He is the source of all the fires of life. With one mind, we send greetings and thanks to our Brother, the Sun.

Now our minds are one.

Grandmother Moon

We put our minds together and give thanks to our oldest Grandmother, the Moon, who lights the nighttime sky. She is the leader of women all over the world, and she governs the movement of the ocean tides. By her changing face we measure time, and it is the Moon who watches over the arrival of children here on earth. With one mind, we send greetings and thanks to our Grandmother, the Moon.

Now our minds are one.

The Stars

We give thanks to the Stars who are spread across the sky like jewelry. We see them in the night, helping the Moon to light the darkness and bringing dew to the gardens and growing things. When we travel at night, they guide us home. With our minds gathered together as one, we send greetings and thanks to all the Stars.

Now our minds are one.

The Enlightened Teachers

We gather our minds to greet and thank the enlightened Teachers who have come to help throughout the ages. When we forget how to live in harmony, they remind us of the way we were instructed to live as people. With one mind, we send greetings and thanks to these caring Teachers.

Now our minds are one.

The Creator

Now we turn our thoughts to the Creator, or Great Spirit, and send greetings and thanks for all the gifts of Creation. Everything we need to live a good life is here on this Mother Earth. For all the love that is still around us, we gather our minds together as one and send our choicest words of greetings and thanks to the Creator.

Now our minds are one.

Closing Words

We have now arrived at the place where we end our words. Of all the things we have named, it was not our intention to leave anything out. If something was forgotten, we leave it to each individual to send such greetings and thanks in their own way.

And now our minds are one.

Originally published as *Thanksgiving Address: Greetings to the Natural World* by The Tracking Project, P.O. Box 266, Corrales, NM 87048. Copyright © 1993 Six Nations Indian Museum and The Tracking Project. Reprinted by permission.

Contributor Profiles

Arthur Amiotte is a Lakota artist and educator who was born on the Pine Ridge reservation in South Dakota. He is a founding member of the Plains Indian Museum Advisory Board.

Ramon Gil Barros is a spiritual and political leader of the indigenous people of the Sierra Nevada de Santa Maria in Colombia.

Benjamin Baynham OCSO was a monk of the Abbey of Gethsemani in Trappist, Kentucky, in 1991. He had lived for a year among the Naskapi of Labrador.

Black Elk (1863-1950) was a well-known medicine man and distinguished elder of the Oglala Lakota. He was a warrior in the Battle of Little Bighorn and, years later, observed the Massacre at Wounded Knee. Black Elk shared his most intimate visions and views with John Neihardt, who wrote *Black Elk Speaks*. Many of Black Elk's descriptions of spiritual life and religion can also be found in Joseph Epes Brown's *The Sacred Pipe*.

Joseph Epes Brown (1920–2000) is an American scholar who was on the faculty of the University of Montana for many years. He was the recorder and editor of *The Sacred Pipe: Black Elk's Account of the Seven Rites of the Oglala Sioux*, and author of *Animals of the Soul: Sacred Animals of the Oglala Sioux*.

Joseph Bruchac is a storyteller, educator and poet of Abenaki descent who lives in Greenfield Center, New York, in the Adirondack Mountain foothills. Among his many books are *The Faithful Hunter: Abenaki Stories* and *Return of the Sun: Native American Stories of the Northeastern Woodlands*.

Thomas Buckley, anthropologist, professor, and author, worked with the Yurok tribe of northern California. His written accounts of the Yurok tribe include *Blood Magic: The Anthropology of Menstruation* and *Standing Ground: Yurok Indian Spirituality, 1850–1990*.

Vine Deloria, Jr. (1933-2005) was a Sioux from South Dakota who promoted Native American cultural nationalism and a greater understanding of Native American history and philosophy. His works include *Red Earth, White Lies: Native Americans and the Myth of Scientific Fact, Custer Died for Your Sins: An Indian Manifesto,* and *Indians of the Pacific Northwest.*

Sam Gill teaches in the Religious Studies Department at the University of Colorado at Boulder. He is involved in the research and teaching of dance history and also teaches salsa. Among his books are *Songs of Life: An Introduction to Navajo Religious Culture* and *Sacred Words: A Study of Navaho Religion and Prayer.*

Tom Harmer lived for many years with the Salish people of the Okanogan region of the Pacific Northwest. He has written of his experiences in *What I've Always Known: Living in Full Awareness of the Earth* and *Going Native.*

Bernard Hoehner (1924–1995), a Hunkpapa/Blackfoot Sioux, was born and raised on the Standing Rock Reservation in South Dakota. He taught in the Department of American Indian Studies at San Francisco State University, practiced veterinary medicine, and was active in the Bay Area Indian community for many years.

Linda Hogan, a Chickasaw writer and environmentalist, is the editor of the eighth volume of the Parabola Anthology Series. She has written many short stories, poems, novels, and plays, which include *Mean Spirit, Calling Myself Home,* and her most recent works, *People of the Whale* and *Rounding the Human Corners: Poems.*

Elaine Jahner (1942-2003) was a professor of English and Native American Studies at Dartmouth College. She coedited James Walker's *Lakota Myth* and *Lakota Belief and Ritual,* with Raymond DeMaillie.

Lewis Johnson, a Native American from Michigan went on a vision quest in 1984.

Trebbe Johnson writes about myth, nature, and spirit. She is the author of *The World Is a Waiting Lover*.

Linda Johnston of the Leech Lake Band of the Ojibwe tribe writes of spirit, peace, and tradition.

Sister Maria José Hobday, a Seneca elder, is a Sister of St. Francis of Assisi. She has degrees in Native American English, Theology, Architecture and Engineering. She is engaged in teaching, writing, and storytelling and leads workshops in prayer and spirituality.

Julian Lang, storyteller, poet, writer, artist, and native speaker is a member of the Karuk Tribe in northwestern California.

Kent Lebsock, Lakota Sioux, is executive director of American Indian Law Alliance.

Oren Lyons is a traditional Faithkeeper and a member of the Seneca Nation. He is a principal figure in the Traditional Circle of Indian Elders, a council of traditional grassroots leadership of North American Indian nations. In 1992 he was invited to address the General Assembly of the United Nations and to open the International Year of the World's Indigenous People.

Peter Matthiessen is an American novelist and nonfiction writer and environmental activist. He was named to the American Academy of Arts and Letters in 1974. Among his books are *In the Spirit of Crazy Horse, The Snow Leopard,* and *At Play in the Fields of the Lord.*

Scott Momaday is a Kiowa writer, storyteller and poet from Oklahoma. He has been awarded the Pulitzer Prize, for Fiction and the Academy of American Poets Prize and has taught at Berkeley, Stanford, and the University of Arizona.

Joel Monture is a Mohawk from the Six Nations of the Grand River Territory, Ohsweken, Ontario. He has been a professor at the Institute of American Indian Arts in Santa Fe, New Mexico, and currently lives in Wisconsin.

Leslie Marmon Silko grew up on the Laguna Pueblo Reservation. She is a professor of English, a novelist, poet, and short story writer.

Don C. Talayesva (1890–?) was born in Oraibi, Arizona, where he lived in the traditional Hopi way, except for the years he was sent to English schools. He wrote *Sun Chief: Autobiography of a Hopi Indian* with Leo Simmons.

Barre Toelken is a professor of English and History as well as Director of the Folklore Program at Utah State University. His most recent book is *Morning Dew and Roses: Nuance, Metaphor and Meaning in Folksongs*.

For Further Reading

Allen, Paula. *The Sacred Hoop: Recovering the Feminine in American Indian Traditions.* Boston: Beacon Press, 1986, 1992.

"Akwesasne Notes" (in the Mohawk Nation, Rooseveltown, NY, ed.). *Basic Call to Consciousness,* Summertown, TN: Book Publishing, 1978, 1981, 2005.

Basso, Keith. *Wisdom Sits in Places: Landscape and Language Among the Western Apache.* Albuquerque: University of New Mexico Press, 1996.

Columbus, Christopher. *The Journal of Christopher Columbus.* Ed. Cecil Jane. Modesto: Bonanza Books, 1960.

Cordova, Viola. *How It Is: The Native American Philosophy Of V. F. Cordova.* Ed. Kathleen Dean Moore, Ken Peters, Ted Jojola and Amber Lacy. Tucson: University of Arizona Press, 2007.

Deloria, Vine. *The World We Used to Live In: Remembering the Power of Medicine Men.* Golden, CO: Fulcrum, 2006.

———. *For This Land: Writings on Religion in America.* New York: Routledge, 1999.

———. *God Is Red: A Native View of Religion.* Golden, CO: Fulcrum, 1994.

Dooling, D.M. and Paul Jordan-Smith, eds. *I Become Part of It: Sacred Dimensions in Native American Life.* New York: Parabola, 2002.

Evers, Larry and Felipe S. Molina. *Yaqui Deer Songs/Maso Bwikam: A Native American Poetry.* Tucson: Sun Tracks and the University of Arizona Press, 1987.

Galeano, Eduardo. *Genesis: Memory of Fire Trilogy,* Part 1. New York: Norton, 1998.

———. *Faces and Masks: Memory of Fire Trilogy,* Part 2. New York: Norton, 1998.

———. *Century of the Wind: Memory of Fire Trilogy,* Part 3. New York: Norton, 1998.

Hultkrantz, Ake. *Shamanic Healing and Ritual Drama: Health and Medicine in Native North American Religious Traditions.* New York: Crossroad Publishing Company, 1992.

Irwin, Lee. *The Dream Seekers: Native American Visionary Traditions of the Great Plains.* Norman, OK: University of Oklahoma Press, 1994.

Keeling, Richard. *Cry for Luck: Sacred Song and Speech Among the Yurok, Hupa and Karok Indians of Northwestern California.* Berkeley: University of California Press, 1992.

Lewis, Thomas H. *The Medicine Men: Oglala Sioux Ceremony and Healing.* Lincoln, NE: University of Nebraska Press, 1992.

Lomatuway'ma, Michael. *Stories of Maasaw: A Hopi God.* Lincoln, NE: University of Nebraska Press, 1987.

Martin, Calvin Luther. *The Way of the Human Being.* New Haven: Yale University Press, 1999.

Matthews, Washington. *The Night Chant: A Navaho Ceremony.* Salt Lake City: University of Utah Press, 2002. (originally published in 1902).

———. *Navajo Myths, Songs, Prayers.* Berkeley: University of California Press, 2007. (originally published in 1907).

Merton, Thomas. *Ishi Means Man: Essays on Native Americans.* Greensboro, NC: Unicorn Press, 1976.

Ortiz, Alfonso. *The Tewa World: Space, Time, Being, and Becoming in a Pueblo Society.* Chicago: University of Chicago Press, 1969.

Reichard, Gladys. *Navajo Religion: A Study of Symbolism.* Princeton: Princeton University Press, 1990.

Smith, Huston. *A Seat at the Table: Huston Smith in Conversation with Native Americans on Religious Freedom.* Ed. Phil Cousineau. Berkeley: University of California Press, 2005.

Sarris, Greg. *Keeping Slug Woman Alive: A Holistic Approach to American Indian Texts.* Berkeley: University of California Press, 1993.

Underhill, Ruth. *Papago Woman.* Long Grove, IL: Waveland Press, 1985.

Walker, James R. *Lakota Belief and Ritual.* Ed. Elaine Jahner and Raymond DeMallie. Lincoln, NE: University of Nebraska Press, 1991.

Walters, Anna, Peggy Beck, and Francisco Nia. *The Sacred: Ways of Knowledge, Sources of Life.* Tsaile, AZ: Dine College Press, 1977.